THE CALL . . .

"Where've you been?" I asked.

"I've been everywhere. After I got out, I was in the wild for a while; I lived on insects, berries, moss off the trees, anything I could find . . . they got pretty close a few times . . ."

"Chris, I'm going to have to tell them you called."

"I'm leaving here in a few minutes. I'll be gone." The impression he left was that he was at an airport, ready to jump onto a plane.

"Chris, I really will have to tell 'em about you calling."

"Do what you have to do." . . .

Books by Robert Lindsey

The Falcon and the Snowman
The Flight of the Falcon

Published by POCKET BOOKS

THE FLIGHT OF THE FALCON

ROBERT LINDSEY

PUBLISHED BY POCKET BOOKS NEW YORK

Distributed in Canada by PaperJacks Ltd., a Licensee
of the trademarks of Simon & Schuster, Inc.

POCKET BOOKS, a division of Simon & Schuster, Inc.
1230 Avenue of the Americas, New York, N.Y. 10020
In Canada distributed by PaperJacks Ltd.,
330 Steelcase Road, Markham, Ontario

Published by arrangement with Simon & Schuster, Inc.
Library of Congress Catalog Card Number: 83-14885

ISBN: 0-671-45160-X

First Pocket Books printing February, 1985

10 9 8 7 6 5 4 3 2 1

Printed in Canada

TO SUSAN AND STEVEN,
WITH LOVE

Contents

What follows is a true story.
The names of some of the
participants have been changed
to protect their privacy.

Prologue

TWO HANDS REACHED UP, AS IF FROM A GRAVE, and pushed aside the grate. It fell softly onto damp grass, and a head rose from out of the earth. In the distance he could hear the voices of unhappy men echoing against the hard walls of the cellblock and muffled strains of the music they played in their sorrowful effort to forget the hell in which they lived.

A thin veil of fog shrouded the Lompoc Valley of Central California on the evening of January 21, 1980. But the mists were too frail that night to hide the young man who lifted himself out of the ground just after dusk. He looked up and saw a face lighted behind the glass panes of a rifle tower. For a moment, their eyes met, or so he thought, and the young man stood transfixed. But the guard, preoccupied, turned away.

He lifted out the broomstick and the ladder, bent low to the ground and started to run. But as he did, his legs, numb from being confined for so long in the tiny hole, crumpled beneath him, and on his first steps to freedom, he stumbled.

The ladder was crudely made of pine, about three feet long, with a block at one end wide enough for one foot. He reached the fence and placed it against the pillar and climbed up on it so that he stood high enough to reach the first strand of barbed wire. The hard wire snapped in the jaws of the rose-pruning shears, and he reached out to cut the next-lower strand. But his knees were trembling so violently from fright that he lost his footing, and he slipped and tumbled backward.

The ten-foot-high chain-link fence trembled with an eerie wail as he slammed into the ground. Then there was silence, except for the pounding of his heart. He lay on the ground rolled into a ball and stared up at the luminescent glow of the rifle tower, waiting for its searchlight to swivel around and flash a beam across his body. Nothing happened. The guard had not heard him fall. He jumped up and threw the ladder against the pillar again, stepped on it, squeezed the pruning shears hard until he heard the second strand of wire break and then studied the third and lowest strand of barbed wire. It was less than four inches from the snitch wire. The slightest movement of the snitch wire, even a jiggle, would instantly flash an alarm to the rifle tower.

As gently as if he were about to touch a bomb, he reached out and started to cut the final strand of barbed wire. As he did a searchlight lunged out of the darkness, panning in his direction. He jerked back instinctively. It wasn't a searchlight. It was a pair of headlights from a mobile patrol perhaps three hundred yards away and advancing swiftly along the perimeter of the fence. He listened to its engine get louder until it was less than fifty yards away. He dropped to the ground, grabbed the ladder and sat down behind the pillar, facing the prison. Before he did, he looked up and saw the severed wire dangling in the air, and he wished that he were someplace else.

The van stopped, its engine idling, no more than twenty yards from the pillar. A door opened and he heard a murmur of male voices. Minutes passed—or was it seconds?—before the door closed. He peered around the pillar and watched the red taillights of the van and the twin shafts of its headlights moving away from him, slicing through the misty darkness farther along the fence.

Except for the distant voices in the cellblock and his heart, the night was silent again. He left his refuge behind the pillar and for a third time climbed the ladder. Looking down on him, above the snitch wire and the limp ends of severed barbed wire, were shiny coils of steel ribbon whose edges were bristling with teeth honed to the sharpness of razors. He cut the last strand of barbed wire, pulled himself to the top and, avoiding the snitch wire, stood up straight, his feet ten feet above the ground. Below him in the Kill Zone, the no-man's-land beyond the fence where guards are allowed to shoot to kill, there was more razor wire. Steel thorns glistened in the dim starlight, as lethal if he fell onto them as a den of rattlesnakes. Ahead of him, on the ledge that he had to tightrope-walk until it was safe to jump, there was more razor wire.

Using the scepter he had improvised for the task—a stubby broomstick with a toothbrush taped at one end—he reached out and pushed it out of the way, remembering that someone had once told him that razor wire had been banned for warfare by the Geneva Convention. Finally there was an opening in the razor wire as wide as his body.

He bent his knees, stiffened and jumped.

As he left the top of the fence, one foot slipped out from under him, and then the other, and he plunged head first. Sailing toward the ground, he heard the razor wire rip into the side of one of his new running shoes, and for a moment he had a vision of being found the next morning hanging from the fence by one foot.

He hit the dirt, rolled into a crouch and remembered the Flashing Light.

He had watched them shoot Mark and Daoud when they tried to climb over the fence; he had heard the bullets rip into their flesh; for months, he had imagined what it would be like if a rifle bullet from the tower smashed into his head, and he had decided that he would see a Flashing Light, arriving silently and quickly turning into darkness even before he heard the shot.

He got up and ran.

He sprinted to the darkness past the power plant and toward the tall row of eucalyptus trees that rose like sentries a quarter-mile behind the institution. And then he disappeared into the hills beyond the prison. He knew these hills as well as he knew the hills around his home in Palos Verdes; he had hiked and camped and flown his falcons here during some of the happiest moments of his life. Now they would be his sanctuary.

He ran all night beneath a canopy of moonlight diffused by soft winter mists, accompanied by the sound of his steps and the

3

throbbing of his lungs. As he ran, he tried to log the distance he traveled from the prison—one mile, three miles . . . five miles, ten . . . twenty-five . . . thirty miles.

At dawn, he felt the welcome warmth of the morning sun rising over the California coastal range, and exhausted, he decided to rest a moment at the crest of a hill near a large chaparral.

But his solitude was disturbed by a loud, familiar sound.

He pushed back a stand of brush and tried to discover where the sound was coming from. Then he saw the prison, less than half a mile away.

It was the prison work whistle.

He had run in a circle all night.

He heard voices in the distance, and then he saw a helicopter flying toward him very low. He spun around and looked for a place to hide.

I

Could anyone in this
Chamber tell me
what has become of
Mr. Boyce?

1

LARRY HOMENICK WENT INTO THE LIVING ROOM, pulled back the curtains and checked the street again. It was dark and quiet outside, and he returned to the kitchen, passing the mug shots on the kitchen table. The faces looked up at him of the hit men hired to kill the man who sat in the other room watching a re-run of *Ironsides*.

Homenick was getting tired of pork chops. But the man he was guarding—the former insurance man who had gotten rich by bribing union bosses with money and clothes and hookers and then, when he was caught, become one of the Justice Department's best snitches ever against organized crime—always asked for a din-ner of pork chops and applesauce to go with his buttermilk. Home-nick wondered how he could eat all that fatty meat when he had an ulcer.

Homenick was three days short of his thirty-first birthday. He was a wiry, compact man with a boyish face, modishly styled long hair, a mustache and enough nervous energy to make it hard for him to relax in the confining safe house. As he flipped over the chops, a .357 magnum revolver drooped from his shoulder holster and almost scraped the frying pan. Homenick had no doubt that he would use the gun if necessary to save the man in the other room. But unlike some cops, he didn't have a fondness for guns. Some cops liked to take out their guns and fondle them. Homenick carried one because it was part of his job, but it made him feel uncomfortable having one at home around Erik, his year-old son.

Some of the Mafia killers and fallen White House officials whom he had guarded during the Watergate era had liked to cook and show off what they could do in the kitchens of the safe houses where they awaited trial. But this arrogant man wanted to be treated like the Beverly Hills millionaire he had once been, and Homenick not only had to protect his life but had to cook his meals and wash his dishes.

He heard something outside and walked back to the living-room window and pulled back the curtains again. It was a passing car. As he glanced out, he saw a familiar image, a reflection from the television set, smeared across the rain-spattered glass. It was the evening news, but he couldn't hear the sound because water was running in the sink. He tried to bring the image into focus—and when it began to take shape, he saw something he couldn't believe. It was a face that he knew as well as his own.

"Turn it up," he told the star witness.

. . . *the twenty-six-year-old spy who, along with a childhood friend, was convicted in 1977 of selling American satellite secrets to the Soviet Union apparently scaled a fence at the maximum-security prison before disappearing into the night. Officials at Lompoc said they have no clues to his whereabouts or whether he had had any help in pulling off the daring escape. . . .*

That night the face of Christopher John Boyce remained in Homenick's mind long after the picture was gone from the screen.

"Who's Christopher Boyce?" asked Howard Safir.

Safir, a fanatical Los Angeles Rams booster, had just arrived back in his office from Los Angeles, and his mood was mixed: the Rams had lost to the Pittsburgh Steelers in the Super Bowl, but the game had been close, and most Rams fans, including Safir, had been at least moderately proud of their performance.

Considering his job, Safir's office was in a curious location. It was on the second floor of a shopping mall in suburban Washington, hidden among department stores, lingerie shops and motion-picture theaters. His office was the nerve center for an agency of the U.S. Government that had a proud history but had fallen on hard times. The shopping center, at Tysons Corner, Virginia, was headquarters for the U.S. Marshals Service. Created by the Judiciary Act of 1789, the Marshals Service was America's oldest federal law-enforcement agency. For most of a century, the deputy U.S. marshal, a star on his chest, had been a legendary figure in the American West, a manhunter on horseback who tracked down mail robbers, thieves and murderers and helped tame the frontier. But after the frontier was tamed, he suddenly became an anachronism. In the twentieth century, the Marshals Service had deteriorated into a refuge for aging political hacks appointed by senators and congressmen to pay off political debts. They served subpoenas, transported prisoners to jails and drowsily stood guard in federal courtrooms. Mostly, the descendants of the legendary lawmen of the Old West did little but enjoy the fruits of political patronage, while aggressive new agencies, especially the Federal Bureau of Investigation, had moved in and taken over much of the Service's old turf. It was largely manhunts for famous gangsters like John Dillinger and Pretty Boy Floyd that had given J. Edgar Hoover the publicity he needed to transform a minor federal department into perhaps the best-known law-enforcement agency in the world.

About the only thing that had saved the Marshals Service from terminal atrophy was the civil rights movement. When Southern communities began to defy orders from the federal courts to integrate their schools in the 1960s, President Johnson had discovered that short of sending in the troops, the United States of America didn't have any means to enforce the mandate of federal courts. The Justice Department turned to the Marshals Service to enforce the courts' demands. The drive to integrate Southern schools touched off a period of expansion and rebuilding that began to bring the Marshals Service into the twentieth century. A few years after the civil rights movement peaked, when an epidemic of aircraft hijackings plagued American airlines, additional deputy marshals were hired and trained to combat skyjacking. Until the early 1970s, little attention had been given to establishing high standards for new recruits or special training for deputies; each of the ninety-four appointed marshals around the country hired his own deputies, a practice rooted deep in the history of the Service which perpetuated patronage and defied efforts to make the Service more professional. But in 1973, recruiting of deputies was centralized, standards were raised and recruiters began bringing in higher-caliber, better-educated deputies. Many of the younger deputies, wanting more excitement, gravitated to the Warrants squads in each Federal Court district, which were responsible for arresting parole and probation violators.

Despite the expansion and new blood, the agency was still hounded by its reputation as an inept, past-its-prime refuge for tired old ward heelers. Many of the people who joined the agency in the '70s, however, had ambitious ideas for the Marshals Service, and Howard Safir was one of them.

It did not take Safir long to find out who Christopher Boyce was.

Nor was it long before he realized that Christopher John Boyce was exactly the fugitive whom he was looking for.

In fact, he was just the fugitive whom Howard Safir *wanted* to be looking for.

He told his secretary that he wanted a seat on the next plane back to Los Angeles.

2

TONY PEREZ PEERED INTO THE HOLE AND WON-
dered how anyone could have hidden in such a small space. It was
a hollowed-out drainage sump about forty yards from the rear
fence. Lying beside it was a steel grate that apparently was meant
to cover the hole.

An improvised ladder was still resting against a pillar beside the
fence. A pair of shears and part of a broom handle with a toothbrush taped to it at a 90-degree angle was lying near the fence.

Once they had discovered the severed strands of barbed wire the
night before, it hadn't taken guards long to pinpoint where Boyce
had gone over the fence. But how he had done it was a mystery.
The prisoners had been locked up in their cellblocks after the 4
P.M. head count the day before, and the guards said that he had
been in his bunk when the count was made.

Perez saw a shallow imprint in the dirt at the bottom of the drainage hole, probably made by the ladder. Boyce must have had it in
the hole with him. Somehow he had managed to get to the fence
after lock-down the night before, avoided being seen by the
guards, concealed himself in the sump with the ladder and a pair of
rose-pruning shears from the prison garden shop, then scaled the
fence and made his way through an obstacle course of barbed wire
and razor wire.

The prison staff had given him only a few details about the missing prisoner: Christopher John Boyce was twenty-six years old,

11

unmarried, five feet, nine inches tall and weighing 160 pounds, with brown hair and blue eyes. He had had no criminal record until he was arrested in January 1977. The following spring, he had been convicted of being a Soviet spy and sentenced to forty years in prison.

Perez, supervising inspector of the U.S. Marshals Service Warrants squad in Los Angeles, 170 miles south of the Lompoc Federal Correctional Institution, had been awakened in his apartment at 2 A.M. and informed about the escape. Already, he was told, the search had gotten off to a bad start. Guards at Lompoc had waited almost an hour before telling law-enforcement agencies about Boyce's escape because they were hunting for him in the woods behind the prison. When they couldn't find him, they had blundered again and called the FBI instead of the Marshals Service. And when the Marshals Service duty officer was finally notified, he requested a copy of the file on Boyce from the FBI and was told it was locked in a special vault because it contained classified information, and the vault couldn't be opened without special authority.

Before dawn, Perez made sure the obvious things were done: an all-points bulletin was issued; the Federal Aviation Administration, Coast Guard, Border Patrol, local airports and marinas, the Santa Barbara County Sheriff's Department, which patrolled rural areas around the prison, and security officers at Vandenberg Air Force Base, a large missile- and satellite-launching center near the prison, were all notified. Two deputy marshals who were based nearby, Al Villegas and Lou Stefanelli, were sent out to begin looking for Boyce in the wilderness near the prison.

Now that he was at Lompoc, the people at the prison offered Perez little to go on:

—As far as they could tell, the only things Boyce had taken when he escaped were standard prison-issue jeans and jacket and, possibly, a green-and-white jogging shirt and jogging shoes he had been seen wearing at the institution.

—The guard on duty in the tower closest to the spot where Boyce scaled the fence said that he had not seen or heard anything unusual the night before, and no alarm had been sounded by the snitch-wire system. As part of a new program to tighten security, a high-level tower had been built to monitor the rear fence; but the older, unoc-cupied tower it replaced had not yet been razed, and it had partially blocked the guard's view from the new tower, creating a "blind spot" which Boyce had apparently exploited.

—Two guards on a mobile-patrol detail said they had checked the rear fence about seven o'clock but seen no sign of Boyce or any cuts in the barbed wire.

—The supervisor of the prison grounds crew said that Boyce had asked him two weeks earlier to be placed on the crew, saying he thought the assignment, a menial job unpopular with most inmates, would help him get in shape physically. The supervisor had thought Boyce already looked in pretty good shape, but he was lik-able, and he had given him the job. The supervisor remembered that Boyce had been friendly with another man on the crew, a con-victed bank robber from Seattle named Freddy Gray, a straw boss on the grounds crew, who had recommended him for the job; on the day of the escape, he said, they had checked out shovels and a wheel barrow. Guards said they had watched them wheel loads of dirt across the prison yard and dump it against a building, but no one had thought to inquire about the *source* of the dirt. It was only later that they discovered that the dirt had been shoveled out of the drainage sump, which had been only a few inches deep before Christopher Boyce vanished.

As Perez looked down into the hole on the afternoon of January 22, he estimated that at most, it was eighteen inches wide and about four feet deep. Perez had once rowed a small boat eight days and seven nights over a rough ocean to reach political freedom. What kind of man, he wondered, could discipline himself so much that he could fold his body into such a small cavity, possibly for hours, and then climb a fence covered with lethal razor wire where he could be picked off by a man with a .30-caliber rifle a few yards away? It was a man, Perez thought, like himself, to whom freedom meant a lot.

Who, he wondered, was Christopher John Boyce?

To Joel Levine, one of the federal attorneys who had prosecuted him in 1977, Christopher Boyce was a traitor whose espionage had constituted "perhaps the greatest breach of security in the United States since the Rosenbergs," the Americans who had provided details of the Manhattan Project to the Soviet Union during World War II. But beyond this damning indictment, government officials had been vague. They had refused to discuss the nature of most of the documents that he and his friend had sold to the Soviet Union; the National Security Council had ordered that the full extent of the loss be concealed at their trial, and a mystery had remained over the full extent to which they had damaged their country.

To Monsignor Thomas J. McCarthy, Boyce's parish priest, he was "one of the finest boys I'd ever met or taught . . . bright, curious, devout, idealistic, interested in everything." To Monsignor McCarthy, to his family and to the adults he knew, he was the quintessential All-American Boy.

Christopher John Boyce was born February 16, 1953, in Santa Monica, California, the first of nine children of Charles and Noreen Boyce. His father had recently resigned as an FBI agent in Connecticut and moved west to become an industrial-security executive for a large aircraft manufacturer in Southern California; his mother had been a postulant of the Ursuline order of Roman Catholic nuns until she decided, after spending more than a year in a convent, that she did not have a religious vocation.

In the early 1960s, the Boyces moved to Palos Verdes, a hilly peninsula that juts into the Pacific about thirty miles from downtown Los Angeles. The Palos Verdes Peninsula had its origins, like most Southern California communities, as a real estate promotion. In the 1920s, a large part of the undeveloped peninsula was purchased by a syndicate of wealthy Easterners who wanted to exploit its pleasant climate and Mediterranean-like ambiance and develop it into an exclusive residential community for the rich. But the Great Depression and World War II intervened, and it wasn't until after the war that large numbers of people began to colonize "The Hill," as local residents called the Peninsula, and then it became a prestigious address. Most residents were upwardly mobile arrivals from the East and the Middle West who had found success in business, in the professions or, for many, in the region's booming aerospace industry down on the "flatlands," as the rest of Southern California was referred to by people on The Hill.

As a child, Christopher plunged enthusiastically into the Roman Catholic faith of his mother, served as an altar boy at the new parish of St. John Fisher and got straight A's at the parish school, where he scored 142 on an I.Q. test. Some of his teachers noticed that he had several distinctive traits: he had a passionate interest in history, especially political and military history; he was very conservative in his religious views and whether in sports, in climbing a tree or in hiking into a wilderness where he had never been before, he seemed to enjoy taking risks far more than his classmates; indeed, they said he thrived on it.

After serving as student-body president in his last year of grade school, Christopher Boyce entered Palos Verdes High School at about the same time that widespread dissent was surfacing in America over the Vietnam War and a tide of illicit drugs was flooding Palos Verdes and many other middle-class communities around the country. In high school he renewed his acquaintanceship with Andrew Daulton Lee, the adopted son of a well-to-do physician with whom he had served Mass as a child at St. John Fisher and with whom he shared an interest in falconry, the centuries-old sport of training hawks and other birds of prey to hunt.

Following high school, Daulton, a born entrepreneur, became a drug dealer and, eventually, a heroin addict. Drug dealing was lucrative for him, but he had the misfortune of being busted regularly after selling dope to an undercover officer. Chris drifted from college to college, trying to adjust, he said later, to a disillusionment that was sweeping over him on two levels. His faith in Roman Catholicism had been badly shaken when, at about sixteen, he decided he doubted the divinity of Jesus, which was the cornerstone of Church dogma; he had also become disillusioned because he felt the America that he had read about in his history books was not the America that he experienced as a young man. He said he was troubled by what he saw as a betrayal of American values in Vietnam and in Latin America where the United States propped up exploitive dictatorships out of self-interest.

After Chris dropped out of his third college, his father called a friend, an executive for another aerospace company, TRW Systems Group in the town of Redondo Beach near Palos Verdes, and asked him if he could give his eldest son a job. The friend hired Chris, and within a few months he was given Top Security clearances from the Defense Department and the Central Intelligence Agency and a cryptographic clearance from the National Security Agency and was assigned to a communications vault processing classified messages between TRW, CIA Headquarters in Langley, Virginia, and two secret CIA bases near Alice Springs, Australia, which process data sent back from space by American satellites that maintain surveillance over the Soviet Union, the People's Republic of China and other countries.

TRW manufactured several kinds of satellites that were used by the intelligence agency to spy on the Soviet Union from space, including one called Rhyolite, which collected information about new Soviet ICBMs and data about other Soviet military capabilities. At the time he took the job in the communications room—it was called the "Black Vault" because of its secret operation—nothing had a higher priority in the CIA than determining the capabilities of new Soviet missiles, because, in a very literal sense, the stakes were the survival of the United States in the nuclear age. Through his hands and mind passed plans and operational details of how America was secretly monitoring the evolution of Soviet weapons from space and what it was learning, as well as information about new American satellite systems and other CIA secret projects.

One night in April 1975, after a night of smoking marijuana, Christopher Boyce blurted out the secret details of his work to his friend Daulton Lee and proposed that they go into the business of selling secrets to the Soviet Union.

And they did, for more than a year and a half, until Daulton was arrested by a policeman in front of the Soviet Embassy in Mexico City in January 1977 with a pocket stuffed with microfilm detailing plans for a proposed espionage satellite system called Pyramider.

When Chris was arrested a few days later, he confessed that he had sold thousands of documents about secret intelligence projects to the Russians.

In the years that followed, many questions would be asked about how such a thing could have taken place, including this one: how was it possible for an inexperienced twenty-one-year-old college drop-out to get a job at the heart of one of America's most secret espionage operations? In a way, the answer was simple: no one expected a place like Palos Verdes, where young people seemed to have all the riches and opportunity that a democracy can bestow on its youth, to produce a Soviet spy.

Tony Perez sifted through the few things Boyce had left in his cell. The jackals of the prison had already been there to claim whatever clothing he had left behind; there were a few letters, a couple of magazines about flying, several books about birds and aviation, not much else. The trail was already cold, he told Tysons Corner. Headquarters told him to report his progress on the manhunt hourly.

It wasn't only Christopher Boyce and his bosses in Tysons Corner that Perez had to worry about.

He also had to worry about the FBI.

3

FBI AGENTS WERE SWARMING ALL OVER THE
place, wearing matching dark blue jump suits and issuing state-
ments to the press. "We have no reason to believe anybody
scooped him up with a helicopter," one agent from Los Angeles
told reporters when asked if he thought the KGB had broken Boyce
out of prison.

They weren't even supposed to *be* there.

Three months earlier, the Marshals Service had won a battle to
reclaim some of the agency's heritage from the days of the Old
West. Oddly, it came as a result of an attempt to put the Mafia out
of business. In October 1979, the Carter Administration ordered
the FBI to apply more of its resources to halting the spread of organized crime and to do a better job of putting white-collar swindlers
behind bars. So that the Bureau could free some of its manpower
for these jobs, the Administration transferred some of its responsibilities to the Marshals Service, including primary jurisdiction for
apprehending prisoners who escaped from federal penitentiaries.
Suddenly, the Marshals Service was elevated again to the status of
a major federal law-enforcement agency. William E. Hall, its director, jumped at the chance to expand its jurisdiction. But in en-
larging the responsibilities of the Marshals Service, the Justice
Department did not increase its manpower or budget proportion-
ately. Nationally, there were fewer than 1,500 deputy marshals, a
small fraction of the number of FBI agents. Many senior officials

of the FBI, who had been content to have the Marshals Service go after minor-league probation and parole violators, objected to the transfer and said it wasn't up to handling the new responsibilities. In Congress, the Justice Department and the U.S. Bureau of Prisons, others predicted that the rusty old Marshals Service, no matter how effective it might have been in the nineteenth century, would be a flop at manhunting during the twentieth. Without the training and experience of FBI agents and the FBI's computers, crime laboratory and underworld informants, they said, it would fall on its face if it ever had to go after a sophisticated fugitive smart enough, and desperate enough, to break out of a major federal penitentiary.

When Tony Perez told Service Headquarters that FBI agents were flooding Lompoc and telling reporters that *they* were in charge of the investigation, an explosion went off in Tysons Corner. Not only did top officials of the agency object to the Bureau's grandstanding, there was a danger that tipsters, thinking that the Bureau was in charge, would go to the FBI with information about Boyce's whereabouts; then the Bureau could claim credit for finding him without doing any work. Perez was ordered to let the men from the Bureau know that *he* was in charge.

He did as he was told, but it didn't make any difference. The FBI agents said they were staying. They said that they were only following orders from *their* bosses, and their orders were to find Boyce. Since Christopher John Boyce was a Soviet spy, he fell within the Bureau's jurisdiction for counterespionage.

Until things could be sorted out by their bosses in Washington, the rival factions decided to work together. Dozens of armed men from the two agencies, along with tracking dogs, set out to comb the mountains behind the prison for Boyce.

"It's common knowledge that there was a dummy in his bed at the four-o'clock count and it was taken out of his cell after the count," one inmate told a guard with whom he was friendly on the afternoon of January 22. It was the first break in solving the puzzle of how Boyce had gotten out of his locked-down cell after 4 P.M. The scuttlebutt around the yard, the informant said, was that he had left a dummy in his bed so that he wouldn't be missed at four

19

o'clock, had hidden somewhere until after dark and then had gone over the fence.

Boyce must have had help, Perez decided, but who was it?

The newspapers were speculating that the KGB had sprung him, or that the CIA had done it to retrieve a double agent who had been sent to prison as part of a ruse to convince the Russians he was a bona fide spy. There were rumors among the inmates that a guard had seen him go over the fence but had been paid off by the CIA not to stop him.

Tony Perez, born José Antonio Pérez in Havana, Cuba, was a handsome man with a small mustache and a dark Latin complexion. He did not have a conspiratorial mind, and ordinarily he would not have paid much attention to conspiracy theories. But he hated Russians almost as much as he hated Fidel Castro; the ease with which the prisoner who had betrayed his country had escaped was puzzling, and he was prepared to believe anything about the Russians.

As for the CIA, he only wondered.

Perez had come to America in 1965 when he was fifteen, rowing a fourteen-foot boat ninety miles to Florida with an uncle. When they reached Miami he had all but kissed the American soil, and he felt a reverence for the country that almost matched his love for Cuba. He had three ambitions then: the first was to learn English; the second was to own a pair of American cowboy boots; the third was to become a sergeant in the Marine Corps and return to Cuba and drive Castro and the Russians out of his country.

He was speaking English within a few months. He sold fruit on the streets of Miami to help support his family, and he saved enough money to buy a pair of cowboy boots; and he became a sergeant in the Marines. But instead of liberating Cuba, he went to Vietnam, where he won a Bronze Star for saving the lives of several comrades by fighting off a force of Viet Cong riflemen who overran their unit.

By the time he returned from Vietnam in 1972, he had a fourth ambition: he wanted to be a cop. He learned the basics of police work in a small town near the Marine Corps's big base at Camp Pendleton and then heard a pitch from a recruiter for the Marshals

Service who showed him pictures of Wyatt Earp and dangled old leg irons from the frontier in front of him. The immigrant from Cuba who had loved to watch old American Western movies in Havana and dreamed of owning cowboy boots decided quickly that he wanted to be a deputy U.S. marshal.

After he got his star, he discovered that his work consisted largely of transporting prisoners and protecting witnesses and judges from the underworld. Now that the Service had a more challenging new assignment, he wished Washington had given it more money to carry it out. He was impressed by the equipment brought to Lompoc by the Bureau agents; they had walkie-talkies on which they could talk directly to Los Angeles or Washington and an expensive motor home for their command post. He looked at their jump suits with the FBI insignia and then the Levi's and old work shirts worn by the contingent of marshals. When they had piled into their cars that morning to hurry to the prison, the old clothes had seemed appropriate for beating the bushes for an escaped prisoner. Now even the FBI's jump suits were intimidating.

But as the day wore on, something occurred to Perez: the FBI agents, despite their airplanes and walkie-talkies and all their modern equipment, hadn't been able to find Boyce either.

"Look," the pilot of the FBI plane said as he banked the craft low over the rolling hills north of Lompoc.

"It looks like some guy in a yoga position," his spotter replied as they stared at a motionless male figure dressed in shorts and an athletic shirt who was crouched close to the ground on his knees, oblivious to the low-flying plane.

Speaking into his microphone, the pilot alerted a team of marshals and FBI agents on the ground: "There's some guy about a quarter of a mile from your location. He appears to be in some kind of yoga position. Maybe you ought to check him out."

"Roger. What's he wearing?"

"It appears to be some kind of a jogging outfit," the pilot said as he continued to circle over the figure on the ground. "Jogging shorts and a sweater.

"He's up now and starting to run," the pilot said.

"Which way is he heading?"

"It looks like he's running toward the institution; it looks like he's just a jogger."

"Okay, let's forget him," the spokesman for the ground team radioed back, and they continued tracking the path of a set of running shoes that, according to a tracker who had been rushed to the prison, began at the prison fence and led into the woods.

Several hours later, as the sun was beginning to set on the California coastal range, Deputy Marshals Lou Stefanelli and Al Villegas were following the footprints as they led farther and farther from the prison.

Almost at the same moment, they discovered something crazy: Their fugitive had become a centipede. His tracks had suddenly become the tracks of forty or fifty people, all with the same kind of shoes.

Only later did they discover that the Lompoc High School cross-country team practiced in the hills behind the prison, and that they had wasted most of a day following the tracks of the high school runners.

At day's end, Perez reviewed what the investigators had learned about the escape and drew up a list of suspects who might have helped Boyce. There were three names on the list: Freddy Gray, the young bank robber who worked with him on the yard crew; Cameron Johnson, a six-foot, six-inch counterfeiter with whom several guards said Boyce had jogged in the days before his escape; and Mike Adams, a boyhood friend of Boyce's from Palos Verdes who, according to a letter found in his cell, lived near Santa Barbara, about seventy miles south of the prison.

Gray turned out to be a fair-skinned inmate in his early twenties with curly blond hair and a nervous twitch in one cheek. He admitted helping Boyce get a job on the grounds crew. But when Tony Perez asked him what else he knew about the escape, Gray shut up. He said he wanted to talk to a lawyer.

Cameron Johnson, Perez learned, had been released from Lompoc two weeks earlier and was living in a halfway house in Oakland, about three hundred miles north of the prison, and working full time at a civilian job while completing his sentence. The following morning, at Perez' request, Marshals Inspector Jim Ledgewood inquired about Johnson at the halfway house and was told he had just left for work.

"By the way," the counselor said, "an FBI agent was just here and he talked to Johnson about something."

It was typical of the first few days of the investigation: marshals and FBI agents tripped over each other from coast to coast, competing to be first to interview a possible source of information about the escaped spy, sometimes arriving at the same doorstep at the same time. The agent who had interviewed Johnson later told Ledgewood that he was convinced the convict had been genuinely surprised by news of the escape; he said Johnson had admitted knowing Boyce, but that it was a superficial "jailhouse acquaintance," and he promised he wouldn't have anything to do with him on the outside.

In the next few days, dozens of inmates and ex-cons would say much the same thing that Johnson did: Christopher John Boyce was a likable convict to spend time with in the yard, but he was a loner who kept to himself and didn't make many friends. They all said they had no idea where he was.

. . . *Federal agents said today they still have no clues to the whereabouts of convicted spy Christopher John Boyce, who escaped this week from the Federal Correctional Institution at Lompoc, California.* . . .

Freddy Gray was lounging on a bunk in his cell when the news broadcast came on, and he shouted to other inmates to quiet down: "Shut up; there's something on about the Falcon."

. . . *Investigators said they have no evidence that the CIA or the KGB arranged his escape or that he had any other assistance in pulling off the daring escape.* . . .

"God damn it, that's bullshit!" Gray shouted. "That's bullshit! *I* did it! *I* did it!"

He picked up the radio, yanked it from the outlet and smashed it against a wall.

An hour later, another inmate who lived in the same unit whispered to a guard that he wanted to pass on some information about Freddy Gray.

4

WHEN MIKE ADAMS HEARD A NEWS BULLETIN about the escape, he recalled later, a single thought bolted into his mind: "Fly, Falcon, fly!" As children, Adams and Chris Boyce had played together on the rocky headlands and beaches of Palos Verdes, and later, as teenagers, they had flown their falcons in the hills overlooking the sea. There had been five of them then—Chris Boyce, Daulton Lee, Fred Lyle, George Brent and himself, in a friendship knitted together by a mutual interest in falconry. It was a curious sport for American children of affluence in the final third of the twentieth century. But many curious things were happening to this generation, whose parents had endured the Depression and were determined to give their children a more comfortable life. It was a time when old values were being questioned, when young people were challenging established institutions and rising up against the Vietnam War, and many were vanishing into a psychic netherworld induced by drugs.

For most of the well-to-do teenagers who dabbled in falconry during those years it was a fad, soon to be replaced by others. But for Christopher Boyce falconry became an obsession that would preoccupy most of his waking hours and many of his dreams. When he became a spy for the Soviet Union, his code name became, appropriately, the Falcon.

Adams eventually drifted away from the group, after Daulton Lee became a drug dealer and got the nickname "Snowman" because of the snowy-white granules of cocaine he sold. As the years passed, Mike tried to keep in touch with his friends, but in time he began to wonder if perhaps there might be what he called a "dark star" over the group: George and Fred both died in automobile accidents before they were twenty-five, and Chris and Daulton both went to prison.

Adams closed the door of his apartment in San Luis Obispo, a college town nestled in a green valley about seventy miles northeast of Lompoc, on the morning of January 26, 1980, planning to go for a workout at a local gym. A van was parked outside the apartment with two men in it, and he noticed that they stared at him as he passed. Then he remembered that they had been there the day before, too. He returned home an hour or two later and the van was still there, and he noticed something strange about it: there was a vent on the roof with a periscope sticking out of it, and as he walked along the street, the periscope was turning and following him. He walked back and forth to confirm that he was right, and the periscope moved too. Adams went inside and called the local police department to report that a strange vehicle was parked in his neighborhood, and he left again to run some errands downtown.

A few minutes later, two police cars with red and blue flashing lights skidded to a stop beside the van and four policemen jumped out. They ordered the occupants of the van to come out with hands raised. The two men complied and, as quietly as they could, said, "U.S. marshals. This is a stakeout."

It took a few minutes to straighten things out, but when they produced their badges, the policemen left—and after a while, so did most of the people who had rushed out of their apartments to discover what the excitement was about.

Some of the neighbors, however, were still outside talking about the mysterious van when Howard Safir arrived.

The Assistant Director for Operations of the U.S. Marshals Service had come from Tysons Corner to supervise the search for Christopher Boyce, and he wasn't very happy.

Studying the scene from his unmarked car, he couldn't figure out what was happening. On this sunlit day, he saw three deputy marshals standing in the street outside the apartment where they were supposed to be waiting for a fugitive Soviet spy to arrive.

When the deputies saw their boss, they ran up to his car to explain what had happened, but that didn't make Safir any happier. He waved them back into the van and shouted that if they had anything to say, they should do it over their two-way radio.

"What the hell's going on?" Safir's voice boomed over the radio circuit. "Don't you know how to conduct a surveillance? What are you doing out there?"

"We've been burned," one of the chagrined deputies answered. After he recited the details of the visit by the local police department, Safir decided that it was a good idea that he had come to California.

In New York City, where Safir had grown up, it used to be said, not always accurately, that the sons of Irish immigrants went into the Police Department, the children of Italian immigrants went to work for the Sanitation Department and the children of Jewish immigrants became teachers. Safir, a descendant of Russian Jews who at the turn of the century had helped unionize the sweatshops of the Lower East Side of Manhattan, earned the kind of marks in school that give parents hope for their children's success in an intellectual career. But after one of his uncles, a New York Police Department detective, came to his home and spun tales about chasing bank robbers and other crooks, Safir decided that he wanted to be a cop. He left New York to attend a small college in Iowa, later returned to attend Hofstra University on Long Island and then joined the New York State Police. After only a few months, he passed a qualification test for a job as a federal treasury agent, and before long he was a member of the Federal Bureau of Narcotics, which later became the U.S. Drug Enforcement Administration. He grew a beard, acquired an Austin Healy sports car and then a toga and became an itinerant "narc," traveling the country to places like the East Village of New York and San Francisco's Haight-Ashbury, where he set up drug buys that became drug busts. There were assignments to Southeast Asia, Mexico, France and Turkey, then a series of administrative jobs in Washington as he rose through the ranks of the DEA. In 1978, Peter Bensinger, the head of the agency, asked Safir, "How'd you like to go to the Marshals Service for a year?" and Safir responded, "What'd I do wrong, Chief?"

Several years earlier, the Justice Department had decided that one of the main reasons it was so unsuccessful at putting major organized-crime leaders behind bars was fear: witnesses whose testimony was essential to obtain convictions were too frightened to talk. The department persuaded Congress to offer a deal to selected crooks and others: in exchange for their testimony, Uncle Sam would create a new life for them in another place—a new name, new identification papers, a completely new persona for themselves and their family in a distant town. The U.S. Marshals Service was given the job of administering the program, which meant finding new homes and jobs for the witnesses and baby-sitting them until their new lives were under way.

In many ways the plan was successful. During the 1970s, the sense of security that it gave witnesses helped send hundreds of front-rank criminals to prison. But as with many programs bred in Washington, theory and good intentions were soon overtaken by practical realities. Although government prosecutors soon began sending hundreds of witnesses into the program, little planning had gone into solving even such mundane problems as obtaining department-store credit for families whose entire past was a lie. And nobody had anticipated that when some of the crooks-turned-witnesses were relocated, they would resume the work they knew best. In 1978, the witness-relocation program was under heavy attack in Congress and the press. Howard Safir was lent to the Marshals Service by the DEA with orders to shape it up. Within two years, he had completely reorganized the witness-relocation program and quieted most of the criticism; after the job was done, he decided not to return to the DEA.

Along with Hall, Safir believed the Marshals Service had the potential to evolve from the enforcement and protective arm of federal courts into a front-rank federal law-enforcement agency, despite admitted obstacles. It was underfunded; it was burdened with aging deputies from an earlier era who were content to serve subpoenas and guard prisoners as they waited for retirement; it was

27

hampered by an ambiguous, almost impossible chain of command. Deputies in each federal court district reported not only to bosses in Washington but to the local U.S. marshal in each city, who was usually a political appointee with no background in police work but who often claimed control of investigations in his city.

Much of the optimism for revitalizing the old frontier police force was rooted in the new generation of deputies who were then entering the service. They were mostly young veterans of the Vietnam War, many of them college-educated, who gravitated to the fugitive squads in each city and were eager for bigger challenges. The Carter Administration had responded to the agency's boasts that it could handle bigger things. The FBI retained primary jurisdiction over several kinds of major-league fugitives, including bank robbers, kidnappers and criminals who crossed state borders in so-called "unlawful flight to avoid prosecution"; but the Marshals Service was assigned the principal responsibility for finding about ten thousand other federal fugitives a year, including escapees from federal prisons and those wanted for committing a variety of other federal crimes.

To many people at Tysons Corner, the new jurisdiction given the agency in October 1979 was viewed as only the first step in reclaiming the turf it had lost to the FBI. First, though, it had to prove itself capable of handling these new responsibilities. Three months after it received its new jurisdiction over escaped federal prisoners, Christopher John Boyce became the Marshals Service's first celebrity fugitive—the kind of fugitive newspapers write about. Howard Safir, the kind of boss who inspires fear as well as respect in the people who work for him, sent word to deputies around the country that it was *essential* for the future of the Service that they catch him.

5

AFTER THE POLICE RAIDED THE VAN, THE PERI-
scope surveillance was abandoned at the apartment of Mike
Adams and the deputies knocked at his door and introduced themselves. He greeted them cheerfully and said he had been expecting
them.

"Yes, he was a friend of mine in school," he admitted, "but I
haven't seen him in over a year."

That afternoon, he guided Howard Safir on a long helicopter
tour of the hills near the prison where, in happier years, he and
Chris and Daulton and their friends had camped and hiked and
trapped birds.

"He knows this area extremely well," Adams said. "I think he
could hide out here for months if he wanted to." Adams' own
theory was that Boyce had gone to Mexico, where he had also
spent a lot of time in the wilderness.

Adams said that he hadn't seen Chris since he had gone away to
prison, and although he had written him a letter, Chris hadn't answered it and, as far as he knew, didn't know that Adams had
moved from Santa Barbara, from where he'd sent the letter, to San
Luis Obispo.

"Do you know any friends he would be likely to go to for
help?" Safir asked.

Adams mentioned some of their old friends in Palos Verdes and

29

a girl named Alana. "I'd heard they were going to get married just before Chris was arrested."

The next day, John Pascucci, a deputy marshal based in the Federal Courthouse in San Diego, found the home of Alana MacDonald in a San Diego suburb. She wasn't there. A friend who answered the door said that she was on her honeymoon. For a while after Chris went to prison, Alana had told friends that she continued to love him; but with forty years' confinement facing him, he had encouraged her to find another boyfriend, and she had.

The same day that Howard Safir and Mike Adams made their long flight over the coastal mountain range of Central California, Freddy Gray, the third man on Tony Perez' list of suspects, called a newspaper reporter and asked him to visit him in prison.

Gray, like most people in any prison, claimed that he didn't really belong there; indeed, he said that he *wouldn't* have been there if he hadn't made a single business miscalculation. He had been working successfully as a drug dealer near Seattle when he made the mistake of ordering 650 pounds of marijuana at a time when he didn't have the money on hand to pay for it; in order to cope with his cash-flow problem, he had decided to rob a bank.

To build up his courage for the mission, Gray had smoked a marijuana joint before entering the bank. But his debut as a bank robber was brief: in a marijuana haze, he dropped his gun; he was arrested, convicted and sent to Lompoc.

"It was me that got Boyce out of here," he whispered to the reporter as they sat in a visiting room at the prison, with a guard sitting outside the door.

Boyce, he declared, had not masterminded the escape, as they were saying on the radio.

"*I did*," he said. Whispering, Gray said he had arranged for Boyce to be transferred to the grounds-maintenance crew; he had helped him make a papier-mâché dummy and painted its face to look like Boyce and even glued some of Boyce's own hair on it; they had dug out the drainage sump as a hiding place, made a ladder and stolen pruning shears from the grounds shop. And he said it was he who had placed the dummy in Boyce's bunk for the four-o'clock count and then removed it.

He had masterminded the whole thing, Gray declared, and Hollywood, which was already going to make a movie about Boyce's life, would probably be willing to pay him a million dollars for the story of how the Falcon got out of prison.

"What was Chris going to do when he got out?"

"Go to Arizona."

When Boyce had been spying for the Russians, Gray explained, he had not sold all of the documents he had; he had buried some in the Arizona desert, and he planned to make his way to the hiding place, sell the documents to the Russians for traveling money and then head for Ireland, via Nicaragua.

As Gray was speaking to a reporter, a bulletin was being sent to law-enforcement agencies around the country:

> BOYCE IS WELL DISCIPLINED AND CAN ENDURE LONG PERIODS OF TIME IN THE MOUNTAINS. SEARCH OF THE SURROUNDING MOUNTAINS IS STILL BEING CONTINUED. INFORMATION HAS BEEN RECEIVED THAT BOYCE WILL STAY IN THE MOUNTAINS BEFORE WORKING HIS WAY SOUTH TO MEXICO, PROBABLY THROUGH SOUTHERN CALIFORNIA, ARIZONA, NEW MEXICO OR TEXAS. THIS INFORMATION HAS NOT BEEN SUBSTANTIATED AND BOYCE COULD BE TRAVELING IN ANY DIRECTION FROM LOMPOC.

After an article based on his interview was published, Freddy Gray told Deputy Marshal Al Villegas that he didn't know anything about buried documents.

"There aren't any documents that I know about," he said.

Gray admitted talking to a reporter, but he hadn't said anything to anybody about Arizona, Nicaragua, Ireland or buried documents. Beyond that, Gray said, he wasn't going to say anything until the government promised him he wouldn't be prosecuted for helping Boyce escape.

* * *

A week had passed since Christopher Boyce had gone over the fence. With each hour that passed, Safir knew that his trail was growing colder.

"I need a good man to work full time on this case," he told Tony Perez, who had to return to Los Angeles to catch up on other investigations. "Any ideas who could handle it?"

"Larry Homenick," Perez answered without hesitation. "He's in Witness Security now, but he's a good warrants man. And he knows Boyce. He guarded him during his trial."

"Larry, I'm told that you know Boyce," Safir said the next morning at the Federal Courthouse in Los Angeles.

"Yes, sir. I handled him during his trial and when he had his debriefings with the CIA."

"Larry, I'm going to take you off WitSec for a while and have you working on Warrants for the Boyce case. I don't have to tell you how important this investigation is for the Marshals Service. I've got a DEA plane standing by that can take you up to the prison right away. Look around and see what you can find out. I'll be up there tomorrow.

"I'd start by interviewing Mike Adams, who went to school with Boyce and lives near the prison. He claims he hasn't seen him, but he's a natural. Spend some more time with him."

Homenick, without going home to pack a bag, left for the airport. On the way, he thought for the first time in months about the CIA debriefings.

They had been conducted in great secrecy during a summer heat wave following Chris's conviction in 1977. After weeks of negotiations between the prosecutors and his lawyers, Chris had agreed to tell the agency about the twenty-one months that he and Daulton served as Soviet agents and to disclose what information they had sold to the Russians. Although no promises were made, the prosecutors said that if Chris was cooperative it might help him get a shorter sentence.

On the first day of the debriefings, Homenick picked up Chris at the Federal Correctional Institution at Terminal Island, not far from where Chris had grown up in Palos Verdes, attached the handcuffs and leg irons, and escorted him to an office in downtown Los Angeles. A tweedy, pipe-smoking CIA intelligence officer who used the pseudonym of Jerry Brown and who looked like the actor Ed Asner was waiting with the polygraph examiner. Also in the room were Joel Levine and Richard Stilz, the assistant U.S. attorneys who prosecuted Boyce and Lee, and Chris's lawyers, William Dougherty and George Chelius. After Homenick removed Chris's handcuffs, Jerry Brown directed him unsmilingly to wait in the hall outside, and he left. But a few moments later, Chris was standing outside the room and looking at Homenick.

"I want you in there," he said.

Chris turned to the CIA man who was a few feet behind him and said, "I'm not going in there unless he's with me."

"He can't be there; he's not cleared. Absolutely not," the man said. "He's not cleared to hear what you're going to talk about."

Jerry Brown shut the door, but after a few seconds Chris was back. "Take me back to T.I., would you please?" he said to Homenick.

Dougherty was now standing beside his client. "If you want him in there, it's okay with me, but what's so important about it?"

With affection, and in a softer voice, Boyce said, "He's the only person who works for the government that I can trust, and I want him in there with me."

The CIA man finally acceded, but made Homenick swear that he wouldn't reveal what he heard to *anyone*.

Homenick had met Chris the preceding winter, a few weeks after his arrest, and had been with him much of the spring and summer that followed. He had guarded hundreds of prisoners since becoming a rookie deputy marshal in 1972. He had guarded killers, rapists, dopeheads, other losers whose greed or passions had put them in jail. He had never guarded a spy before, and Christopher Boyce was not what he had expected. During weeks of pretrial proceedings, the trial itself and the debriefings, Homenick discovered his prisoner could talk intelligently, or so it seemed, about any subject in the world—politics, art, literature, current affairs or anything else that Homenick brought up to kill time while they waited for a hearing to start, were on a lunch break or were on their way back to the jail. Except when he was talking about the CIA, Chris was soft-spoken and introspective and had a sense of humor that disarmed most of the deputies and jailers he met.

It is not clear when Larry Homenick and Christopher Boyce began to be friends, but it was probably within the first few days after they met. Boyce was twenty-three and Homenick was twenty-eight. In some ways their lives had followed parallel courses: Homenick had grown up in a middle-class family in the San Fernando Valley of Los Angeles, about forty miles from the more affluent Palos Verdes Peninsula where Boyce lived, but populated by the same kinds of families pursuing the same kinds of dreams.

Like Boyce, Homenick had experienced the classic rites of passage for a teenager in Southern California—cruising Sunset Boulevard on Saturday nights in his customized '55 Chevy, surfing, experimenting with a few forbidden pleasures. Still, by many of the standards of his generation, Larry Homenick was a square.

When he saw more and more of his surfing buddies immerse themselves in the wave of illicit drugs that was sweeping over California during the 1960s, he backed away from them. Later, he saw some of these friends become junkies or alcoholics or beach bums, and he had to arrest some of them. When the antiwar movement erupted in the '60s, he had no trouble choosing sides; he became the only member of his crowd to volunteer for the Army.

The Army sent him to a school for military policemen, and as wars tend to do, it changed his life. Like Tony Perez, who was to become his best friend, Homenick went to Vietnam, and when he returned a year later, he had decided to make a career in law enforcement; he joined the Marshals Service.

While directing security for the trial of Daniel Ellsberg, the man who made public the Pentagon Papers, Homenick was surprised to hear testimony that the United States had misled, even lied to the American people about the war. But he was unprepared for the depth of anger in Christopher Boyce whenever they talked about American foreign policy or the CIA. Boyce claimed that when he worked in TRW's Black Vault he had seen examples daily of how the government was still misleading the American public and its allies, and it was long after the Pentagon Papers had been written.

With memories of Ellsberg's trial still vivid, Homenick wondered how much of what Boyce told him was true, and he wondered how some of his friends might have handled it if, at twenty-one, they'd been exposed to such information. Boyce told him that he had become a Soviet spy almost as a whim, in a blind gesture of defiance against the CIA, and when he had wanted to end the undertaking he couldn't because Daulton Lee was enjoying the money they were making from the Russians so much that he said if Chris didn't continue to provide him with secrets from the Black Vault he would tell Chris's father about what they had done. If fate had been more perverse, Homenick wondered, could he or one of his friends be sitting where Boyce was?

Christopher Boyce liked Homenick because he was an atypical policeman—open-minded, curious about other people's ideas and not dogmatic, unlike the former FBI agents, friends of his father's, who had spent a lot of time in his home when he was growing up. During the spring and summer months of 1977, as the long legal proceedings dragged on, they spent hundreds of hours together, eating; playing chess; talking about their families, women, the world, their attitudes about life.

In the end, Chris's agreement to allow the CIA to debrief him hadn't mattered. Nor did the defense that he offered at the trial, that he had been blackmailed by Andrew Daulton Lee into becoming a spy. The federal judge who heard his trial, Robert J. Kelleher, after suggesting that a death sentence might be more appropriate, had said he thought Boyce had made up his defense "out of whole cloth" and had sentenced him to forty years.

When Chris began his sentence that fall, he and Larry Homenick had parted as friends—or at least as close as a friendship can be when one man is a prisoner and the other his keeper.

Now Homenick had to help put him back in prison.

6

LARRY HOMENICK ARRIVED AT THE SAN LUIS Obispo County Sheriff's Department just as Mike Adams was being escorted into the building by FBI agents. He shook hands with the agents and started to accompany them into an interrogation room. But they blocked his way.

It was a poor beginning for his investigation, he thought.

Mike Adams was the best lead they had. When he was interviewed by deputies following the embarrassing police confrontation outside his apartment, and when he guided Howard Safir on a helicopter tour of the mountains where he had camped out with Boyce, Adams had repeatedly claimed that he knew nothing about Boyce's whereabouts. But he had been unconvincing, and now, four days after the helicopter ride and ten days after Chris's disappearance, he was to be tested on a lie-detector machine.

Homenick had flown to San Luis Obispo in a hurriedly arranged special flight in a government plane to be in time for the polygraph examination, but he had been ostracized to an outer office while it took place.

He looked around and recognized a few faces among the dozen or so FBI agents who were also in the room. They were all dressed in blue jump suits and reading *The Falcon and the Snowman*, a book about the Boyce-Lee case. Several looked up without smiling, giving Homenick the feeling that he was not welcome here. One of the agents, whom he knew from a previous case, handed him a copy of the book and he started to read it. An hour later, the senior FBI agent came out of the interrogation room and said that Adams had passed the test. It appeared that he didn't know anything about the escape, the agent said. Then, coolly, he dismissed Homenick.

Remembering Safir's instructions not to be cowed by the Bureau, Homenick returned Adams to the room for his own interview; the tall, curly-haired carpenter repeated what he had now said many times: he hadn't seen Chris in more than two years, and his friend had not answered a letter he had written to him in prison. Homenick called Safir in Los Angeles and told him about the interview with Adams and his run-in with the FBI, and Safir said that he was flying back to Lompoc in the morning.

At the same time that Adams was taking the lie-detector test in San Luis Obispo, Freddy Gray was sitting in a room at the Lompoc penitentiary being harnessed to an identical polygraph machine. After publication of the newspaper article describing his role in the escape, a steady stream of FBI agents, deputy marshals and Bureau of Prisons investigators had been swarming around him, threatening to indict him for helping a Soviet spy escape from prison. Instead of the nine months left to serve for bank robbery, they warned him, he could be sent away for twenty years for aiding and abetting the escape.

In the questions they had asked, the investigators revealed the frustrations they felt over not being able to find Boyce. Gray sensed correctly that he had the upper hand, and he refused to talk unless they agreed to give him immunity. Without much choice, his interrogators consented. Now, even before he was attached to the polygraph machine, he began to talk about the escape.

At first he was cautious. He spoke slowly and tried to disassociate himself from any personal involvement in the escape, while admitting that he had known beforehand that it was being planned.

But soon his caution seemed to evaporate, and he began to speak very quickly and boast about his part in the drama.

"He started talking about an escape as soon as he got here last summer," he said.

Boyce had previously joined other inmates in several failed escape plots, but, he emphasized, it was only after *he* had agreed to help him that Boyce succeeded.

"Why didn't you go with him?"

"I only had a few months left to go on my sentence."

"Why did you help him? What was in it for you?"

"He needed help. Chris didn't belong in here," he said. "He was a political prisoner; he hated prison."

Gray repeated much of the story that he had told the reporter—about the discovery of a blind spot at the fence, his arranging for Boyce to be transferred to the grounds crew, the theft of the pruning shears and wood for the ladder.

Gray said that it had been his idea to dig out the shallow drainage sump as a hiding place near the fence, and, he boasted enthusiastically, the mannequin had been the key to the scheme's success. Once they figured out how to fool guards into believing Boyce was in his cell at four o'clock, everything else fell into place. The idea for the dummy, he said, came from Hollywood. A movie that had just been shown to inmates, *Escape from Alcatraz,* depicted a convict who had fooled his guards into thinking he was in his cell.

After a guard marked Boyce present for the four-o'clock count, Gray said he had removed the mannequin, smashed it into small pieces and flushed it down a toilet.

"What did Boyce say he planned to do if he got away safely?"

If Boyce made it over the fence, Gray said, he was going to hide in the mountains for a while and eventually make his way to the home of an old friend named "Mark" or "Mike" who lived near the prison. Gray wasn't sure of the name. Then, after a few weeks, Boyce was going to try to obtain false identity papers and make his way to Nicaragua and, eventually, Ireland, where he intended to seek political asylum. His goal, he said, was to find an English-speaking country where there was a war on or there was strife of some sort that would make it easy for him to get lost underground; then, he said, he might write a book about it. Nobody else had helped him, Gray said—not the KGB or the CIA.

"I'll tell you one thing," he continued. "Christopher Boyce hated this place so much that you'll never catch him without a fight. He'll die first before he'll go back to prison."

"Was Chris going to contact Mike or Mark?" the examiner, drawing from a list of prepared questions, asked.

"Yes," Gray said.

The automated pen on the polygraph machine, responding to Gray's emotions, continued to scribe back and forth in an even pattern. There was no indication that he was lying.

"Is Mark or Mike a carpenter?"

"Yes."

No reaction.

"Was Chris going to travel north?"

"Yes."

There was a slight jiggle in the line scribed by the pen.

"Does Chris have any buried documents?"

"No."

The pen, as if jolted by a surge of electricity, made a wide swath across the sheet of graph paper.

An inmate dressed in khaki pants and a white T-shirt was brought into an office at the prison at the request of Howard Safir and Larry Homenick.

Andrew Daulton Lee is small—about five feet, two inches tall—but he is muscular and carries himself with a confident manner some people might consider cocky. The convicted spy gave the investigators an icy stare as he entered the room.

"What can I do for you gentlemen?"

They started with easy, friendly questions designed to lower his guard. Prison officials had said that the two former spies hated each other, and Safir and Homenick wanted to see if they could use the hatred as a lever to persuade Lee to inform on his old friend. Lee patiently answered inquiries about his tennis and prison life in general, but soon grew tired of the game.

"Look, gentlemen, shall we get on with this?"

Safir and Homenick exchanged quick glances and began to fire pointed questions: Who inside the prison had helped Boyce? Who was likely to help him once he got over the fence? Where was he likely to go?

Lee's expression remained emotionless. He claimed he knew

nothing about the escape and that he had been as surprised as anyone else by the disappearance of his former friend, whom he referred to as "Mr. Boyce."

Homenick and Safir tried asking their questions in different ways, but Lee, after fifteen minutes or so of humoring them, said, "Well, gentlemen, if that's all, I have things to do."

"Who do you *think* helped him?" Safir tried once again.

"I'd contact his old employer."

"Who's that?"

"The CIA."

It was an oblique reference to Lee's defense at his trial—that Chris had been a double agent for the CIA and had invited Lee to sell the secrets to the Russians as part of a plot to confuse them about American defense strategy. When he sentenced Lee to spend the rest of his life in prison, Judge Kelleher had ridiculed the claim.

In the social stratification of a penitentiary, no one—not even a child molester—occupies a lower position than a snitch. An inmate who squeals on another inmate for special privilege risks the reprisal of a shank shoved into his heart. Yet in the primeval madhouse of a penitentiary, where inmates are stripped not only of their freedom but of almost everything else they have of worth, information is often the only thing they possess. It is all they have to bargain with, often the only thing they have that those who rule their lives want from them, and despite the risks, some do not hesitate to use it.

Inmates began to flock to the men and women hunting for Christopher Boyce. Brent Pope was one of the first.

He was a convicted confidence man, twenty-seven years of age, who had curly blond hair and a silver tongue. On the outside, Pope had a passion for gold ornaments, flashy cars and expensive clothing. He wore gold chains around his neck, his fingers were heavy with flashy diamond rings, he liked silk shirts and he drove a $60,000 Ferrari automobile.

Behind bars, Pope could no longer express himself in the same way, but he was distinctive in other ways. Among inmates, Pope was considered an operator *extraordinaire*—a glib manipulator who got what he wanted through guile, conning guards into smuggling pot and coke to him and letting him use unmonitored telephones to continue his scams from behind bars.

After Christopher Boyce's conviction for espionage, Pope was his cellmate for almost a year at the Metropolitan Correctional Center, a federal prison in a high-rise building in downtown San Diego. After Boyce was transferred to the maximum-security prison at Lompoc, Pope was shifted to a minimum-security correctional facility nearby, and they kept up a friendship through an exchange of "kites"—letters smuggled illegally between the prisons.

A few days after the escape, Pope sent a message to prison administrators saying that he could deliver Christopher Boyce—for a price.

Homenick and Safir went to hear him out.

Before Boyce escaped, Pope said, the two of them had devised a code to use to communicate with each other if Boyce ever got out of prison. Pope said he wasn't ready to reveal all the details, but it involved placing a classified ad in a newspaper. Boyce would recognize the language in the ad, he said, and follow directions from Pope. "That way, you can set a trap for the Falcon and bring him back.

"I'm going to get out of here in five days," Pope continued. "But when I leave here I've got some state charges facing me. If you help me get out of the state time, I'll tell you the code, and I guarantee it will get you Boyce."

As they drove away from the camp, Safir said he was even more unimpressed with Pope than he had been with Daulton Lee.

"He doesn't know a damn thing," he said.

They drove back to the command post that had been established for the manhunt in a crowded suite of motel rooms in the nearby town of Santa Maria.

Large maps of the Lompoc area were tacked to the walls, and portable blackboards, smudged with notes from earlier strategy sessions, lined the wall of one room. Outside, tracking dogs huddled on the ground with their handlers, and fatigue-clad members of the Marshals Service's paramilitary arm, the Special Operations Group, waited for orders to return to the mountains to look for

Boyce. There was considerable activity, Homenick thought, but nobody seemed to be getting anywhere. Then he noticed that there were fewer blue jump suits around. Even the FBI had realized that the prospects of finding Chris hiding out near the prison were growing slimmer and had reduced its manpower at the scene.

Chris had now been gone almost two weeks, and except for Freddy Gray's claim that he was going to Nicaragua, the Marshals Service didn't have a single lead of value to work on.

The following day, Safir told Homenick, "Larry, I'm putting you in charge of the Boyce investigation."

He said that he had to return to Tysons Corner, but it was vital for the future of the Marshals Service that Homenick find Boyce.

"I need someone full time to take over the case from Tony, and I think you're the best man for the job; your knowing Boyce should be very helpful. I think you can do the job, and I'm giving it to you. Call me twice a day and let me know how it's going; tell me what you need, and I'll get it for you. I think you know how critically important this is for the Marshals Service right now."

"I'll try not to let you down, Mr. Safir," Homenick said.

7

"COULD ANYONE IN THIS CHAMBER TELL ME what has become of Mr. Boyce?" Daniel Patrick Moynihan of New York asked on the floor of the U.S. Senate early in February, eighteen days after the escape.

"We act as if counterintelligence were something that is directed against a fantasy, and yet not five years ago Soviet agents procured from two employees of TRW in California the specifications of one of our most sensitive and important space satellites, compromising a surveillance system important for the verification of a SALT treaty.

"The man who was convicted and sent to Lompoc prison has escaped. How he escaped from a maximum-security prison no one knows, and no one seems very interested in finding him."

That afternoon, Howard Safir got another call from the columned office building in downtown Washington that is headquarters for the U.S. Justice Department.

He responded that the entire resources of the Marshals Service were being focused on locating Christopher John Boyce.

The same day, an unsigned letter, typed and in an envelope postmarked Johannesburg, South Africa, arrived at the Lompoc prison:

> Bloemfontein
> The Orange Free State
> Republic of South Africa
>
> Christopher Boyce
> Escaped Prisoner

Superintendent or Governor:

An American living in this area, whose real name I do not know, has told me that he has been in contact with Boyce and is making arrangements for him to be brought into Rhodesia via South Africa. This fellow knew Boyce in an American prison in 1977.

Homenick sent a copy of the letter to Tysons Corner via a facsimile machine and asked headquarters to notify U.S. authorities in South Africa. Interpol, the international clearinghouse of law-enforcement data, had already been alerted that Christopher Boyce was a fugitive in the United States, and at the request of Tysons Corner, the State Department had sent instructions to U.S. embassies and missions around the world alerting them not to honor his passport and to report any contacts or local reports about him. The message from the State Department read:

WE HAVE RECEIVED UNCONFIRMED CONFIDENTIAL INFORMA-
TION THAT BOYCE MAY HAVE PLANNED TO MAKE HIS WAY TO
MEXICO CITY, FLY TO NICARAGUA AND SUBSEQUENTLY FLY TO
IRELAND WHERE HE WOULD ATTEMPT TO OBTAIN IRISH CITI-
ZENSHIP. BOYCE IS HIGHLY INTELLIGENT AND DEEPLY INTER-
ESTED IN EUROPEAN HISTORY. SUBJECT HAS EXPERTISE IN
FALCONRY. LIFE-LONG RESIDENT OF CALIFORNIA. ATHLETI-
CALLY INCLINED. CONSIDER ARMED AND DANGEROUS. POSSI-
BLY SUICIDAL. HAS STATED INTENTION TO RESIST RECAPTURE.

At the Lompoc penitentiary, Daulton Lee was packing his few belongings. The Bureau of Prisons had ordered him transferred to a penitentiary in Terre Haute, Indiana, that had a reputation for being a frightening zoo ruled by vicious prison gangs. The Bureau said the transfer was for Lee's protection from prisoners at Lompoc because Christopher Boyce's escape had revived the notoriety about his past. Bitterly, Lee complained that the real reason he was being hustled out of Lompoc was to get him out of range of the California news reporters who had showered him with requests for interviews since the escape.

"They just want me out of here," he told a fellow inmate, "because of the bad publicity they're getting because they lost Mr. Boyce." But his protests were unheeded by the Bureau of Prisons.

Once again he could curse Boyce for getting him into a mess. It had been Boyce's idea for him to go to Mexico City; it had been his idea to take the torn computer card from the Black Vault to the Soviet Embassy; and if it hadn't been for Mr. Boyce, he wouldn't have gotten caught. After almost two years of delivering the documents and coming home with bundles of hundred-dollar bills, Daulton had sensed a coldness toward him on the part of the KGB agents, unhappy with the quality of the information Chris gave him, and Daulton had wanted to end the arrangement. But Chris said they should make a final delivery, and when Daulton next went to Mexico City, he was busted by a cop outside the embassy.

When he discussed his past with other inmates, Lee stuck to the story that he'd told since the moment of his arrest: he sold *drugs;* he was a *snowman;* he wasn't a Soviet spy; he was an American patriot working on a plot to feed "disinformation"—phony secrets—to the KGB. He and Boyce, he insisted, were working for the CIA all along. Boyce had used him; he was a pawn in a game of global international intrigue that he didn't understand. How, he repeatedly asked other inmates, could he have crossed the border with secret documents when there was a bench warrant out for his arrest on drug charges? How was it that he could repeatedly meet with Soviet agents, sometimes at their embassy, when the CIA considered the Soviet Embassy in Mexico City one of its most important counterespionage targets in the world?

At approximately the same moment that Daniel Patrick Moynihan was expressing his dismay at the disappearance of Christopher John Boyce on the floor of the U.S. Senate, Charles Edward Loggia was hiking in a densely wooded area along the Manzanita River in the Los Padres National Forest of California not many miles from the ranch of a presidential candidate, Ronald Reagan. About fifty miles east of the Lompoc prison, he saw a dark-haired man in his late twenties dressed in old clothes and sporting what looked like a four-day growth of beard.

"Know any good fishing spots around here?" Loggia asked the man as he approached him on the trail. The man was carrying a water jug and a box of soda crackers. He looked weary.

"I'm a stranger here myself," he said, and looked away. They passed in opposite directions on the narrow path without another word.

Loggia returned home, saw Boyce's picture in the paper and called the police. When a deputy marshal came to his home with a large blowup of the spy's face, he said, *"That's him."*

Within two hours, Homenick had organized a manhunt that would have done the U.S. Marshals Service proud in its glory years: rangers from the national forest provided horses and four-wheel-drive vehicles, and a mounted posse of marshals and Santa Barbara County deputy sheriffs entered the rugged mountains to find the stranger. Helicopters and light aircraft looked from the air while the searchers on the ground dispersed into the primitive wilderness.

On the third day, Deputies Larry Hattersley and David Lange were pushing through a dense pine forest in a jeep when they spotted a hiker about a quarter of a mile away walking along the Manzanita River. Both raised their binoculars to see his face. It had to be the man seen by Loggia, they agreed, and if it wasn't Boyce, he was a dead ringer for him.

They jumped out of the jeep and ran down a rocky hillside to the Manzanita, then splashed along the edge of the river toward the man. As they got closer, they saw that he had a water jug and a box of crackers. His hair was matted and he was unshaven.

"Hold it; police officers," one of them said as they ran up behind him. The hiker stopped and turned around.

It wasn't Boyce.

In San Diego the next day, Deputy John Pascucci visited Larry

Mission, another of Christopher Boyce's high school friends who had shared his love of falconry. "He knew that whole area," Mission said of the mountains around Lompoc. "We spent a lot of weekends trapping there along the Santa Rosa road, which runs between Lompoc and Santa Barbara; I think if he had to, he could survive there for months without any help. He could catch a bird with a little bit of fishing line, a couple of leather straps and some bait; he's so good with birds that he could train one to supply game for him and keep him company. That's how he'd do it—I know him; he'd enjoy himself."

There was, it appeared, no end to the parade of inmates who wanted to talk about Boyce, claiming to know something about the escape and offering to trade what they knew for a transfer to an easier prison or a favorable word to a judge who was considering an appeal. There were dozens, and Homenick and the other investigators interviewed them all. Several claimed Boyce had gotten out by bribing a guard to look the other way when he went over the fence. The guards, they said, would do anything for a few dollars—or love. One inmate said several female guards had taken a liking to Boyce. There was one, he said, who had come into his cell and taunted him by raising her skirt over her thighs. He suggested she might have helped Boyce escape.

Barry Fisk, who made his living on the outside by robbing banks, was interviewed in a bed at the prison infirmary. He'd been knifed in a fight with another inmate. There was a rumor around the prison, Fisk said, that Boyce had forged a set of false identification papers in the prison print shop and planned to use them to get out of the country and then start a new life under an assumed name in a foreign country.

"Which country?" Homenick asked.

"I don't know, but he said he wasn't going to stay in this one."

"Boyce didn't really belong here," Fisk continued. "A lot of the guards hated him because he was so smart and wasn't like the other cons. The guards thought he acted superior to them, you know. He read a lot and talked about politics all the time.

"Boyce wasn't a criminal type; he had a lot of friends here who

47

thought he had gotten a bad rap, and they sort of looked out for him. Everybody knew he was planning to escape. What would *you* do if you had forty years? I'd check with a guy in H Unit that he used to run with. I think he's called Big Larry.''

The deputies began to leave, and Fisk got up from his bunk.

"Remember, you said you'd help get me out of here, to somewhere I can do easier time.''

"No promises, but we'll see what we can do,'' a marshal said.

Not all of the inmates interviewed at Lompoc asked for deals. Some of those who were summoned by investigators glared defiantly when they were brought into the small office and refused to say anything except their names. Many said only that they liked Boyce and were rooting for him.

"I hope you don't catch him,'' said David Worth, a handsome black man who was serving ten years for armed robbery. "He's different than the other guys in here; he's not, you know, a criminal type.''

"Big Larry'' was Lawrence Harold Smith. He was a huge man in his thirties with a slow, lumbering gait caused by a broken hip that had not mended properly; he had dark, wavy hair and a weathered face; he looked as if he worked outdoors. But in prison, as elsewhere, looks can be deceiving. He had made his living indoors, as a master counterfeiter and, occasionally, when he wanted a more direct way of raising money, as a bank robber. And the only sunlight he got in prison was jogging around the prison yard.

When Deputies Lou Stefanelli and Al Villegas called him into the interrogation room, he looked at them with the mixture of contempt and frustration that marks the faces of many men in prison. "Do you want me to get my throat cut?'' he asked.

Shaking and uneasy, Smith denounced the marshals for calling him in for an interview and thus exposing him to suspicion that he was a snitch. Besides, he'd already been interviewed by the FBI and had told *them* he didn't know a thing about the escape. "Sure,'' Smith said, "we ran together; but that's it.'' He had jogged around the yard with Boyce and had liked him enough to look after him in the yard and give him a little protection against

48

the bikers and rednecks who had made it clear they couldn't stomach a Russian spy. But he said he knew nothing about the escape, and then he dismissed the marshals.

Other inmates insisted that Big Larry knew more than he was saying, and a few days later the marshals were back, offering a deal. If he cooperated, they said, a federal judge had indicated to them that his four-year sentence for counterfeiting could be reduced by a year.

"Fuck you," Smith said. "I'm not saying anything until I'm out of here. I don't care what you say or promise; you guys will say anything to get somebody to talk, and then later tell you, 'Fuck you.' "

Smith decided to do some dealing of his own.

"I've heard a few things that may interest you," he said, as coy as a man can be when he stands six feet, five inches tall and weighs more than 230 pounds.

"Did you know he still has a lot of secret stuff stashed away on the outside?"

Boyce, he said, had told him that when he was working as a spy he'd held back some documents, and when he got out he was planning to go after them and sell them to the Russians.

"What's in the documents?"

"I'll tell you what else I know when you get me out of this rathole," Smith said.

8

"My name is Christopher Boyce and I am 25 *years old and I am convicted of committing espionage against my government in the service of the Soviets; it is a crime into which I was blackmailed. . . ."*

Lary Homenick found the handwritten letter in an old prison file, a copy of an appeal Chris had written in July 1978, when he was at the Terminal Island prison, to Senator Frank Church of Idaho, chairman of the Senate Intelligence Committee. *"One afternoon I looked out the window of my cell door and observed the inmate across from me eat his own defecation and then proceed to rub other portions on his walls. . . . Have you any idea what it is like to be locked next to one patient who barks like a dog all night while on the other side a man is screaming that he's going to cut off his girl friend's head (that was in fact his crime) until the late hours while the inmate across from you is carrying out a heated argument with a non-existent Federal judge and none of this is even interrupted until breakfast. Try it for eight months."*

The letter requested Church to intervene so that he could join the main prison population. *"I suffer from insomnia, weariness, depression and inner tension,"* he wrote. *"If I had been sentenced to be executed I would have accepted that judgement as the will of God; but I was sentenced to 40 years imprisonment, not to have my mind dissolved in an unending, 24-hour confinement to a 6' by 8', lockdown cell. . . . I only see the sun two hours in the week and even that is sporadic. Please leave me something to believe in.''*

Homenick found similar letters to Senators Birch Bayh and Charles Percy and Congressman Peter Rodino. Although there wasn't any evidence to indicate what effect, if any, the letters had had, he noticed that a few weeks after they were written Chris was transferred into the main prison population at the Metropolitan Correctional Center in San Diego, and later to Lompoc. Chris, he thought, was learning how to manipulate the system.

The file contained a copy of a report prepared by a probation officer to guide Judge Kelleher in determining what sentence should be given Chris for the espionage conviction. ''The defendant is characterized by an extreme sense of commitment,'' the report noted.

This is manifest in his aggressive attitude towards athletics, his perseverance in falconry, and his study of history. His views appear to be very strongly held. The defendant's social and historical view was disturbed further with the recent revelations of Government corruption. . . . The defendant pursued his understanding of ''corruption,'' and held rather deep rooted opinions . . . and evolved an extremely critical view of central Government, and it is felt that to a large extent the defendant was motivated by a desire to attack that central authority.

The probation officer had accepted the story Chris had told in court—that Chris had originally become a Soviet spy because he had wanted to make public the details of how the Central Intelligence Agency was deceiving Australia, one of its allies, about the secret base the agency operated near Alice Springs, and that Daulton had taken his letter about the deception to the Russians and then blackmailed him into serving as a spy for almost two years.

Homenick noticed a date on the first page of the probation report and looked at the calendar. February 16. Today was Chris's twenty-seventh birthday.

* * *

The hand of Freddy Gray moved slowly across the page in a painful scrawl while he tried to write his thoughts to the reporter who had visited him the week before:

"I made perhaps and undoubtedly the biggest mistake of my life by witnessing a few mysterious undercover actions that I definitely was not to have knowledge of. Unfortunately, there is absolutely no place to run."

Then Gray got to the main point of his letter. What he had told the reporter the week before, he said, had not been the whole truth. The CIA, he said, had broken Christopher Boyce out of jail.

Gray had been confined in a one-man segregation cell since the day after the escape. He had been allowed to place a collect long-distance call to his mother from a pay telephone at the prison.

As a guard eavesdropped, they talked:

"They're probably listening on this line, so don't say anything."

"Honey, are you all right?"

"I'm okay right now, but I can't say anything more on the phone. Boyce has made a fool of the Bureau of Prisons and they've really put the screws on me . . .

"There's something I can't talk to you about now. All I can say is that the administration is extremely embarrassed about the whole escape, but they're going to be a lot more embarrassed—the whole country will—when I tell people what I know."

Then Gray said he couldn't say anything more and hung up.

Two days later, he made another call to his mother, and the guard who monitored the call decided that he was probably close to tears.

"Mom, if anything happens to me, go to the news media and tell them what happened to me. They're going to kill me because I know too much."

Though he had been promised immunity from prosecution, Gray said, he had been double-crossed: Because he had helped Boyce, the administration had taken away his credit for "good time." Instead of nine months left to serve, he had to complete his full sentence—a year and a half. But Gray said he wasn't worried about that: he was afraid he was going to be killed.

"I'm the only one who knows what happened, and I'm expendable. They're going to kill me."

"What happened?"

"About Boyce. If they don't kill me, they'll operate on me; they have an operation on your brain and they take your memory away and make you forget what you know.

"I don't know who to trust; I'm even afraid to eat the food here. I'm scared."

His mother asked if the phone call was being monitored.

"I don't care. I was trying to help the government. Chris is in the CIA, and he was on an undercover mission when they goofed up and he got caught; then they broke him out, and I found out about it."

Gray told his mother that he had witnessed something that he should not have seen—two men in a government car who helped Boyce get away.

"Who were they?"

"CIA. He went over the fence about six, and I bet he was out of the country by eight."

The guard who monitored Gray's call later prepared a report on it, and at the bottom he wrote: *"Either he was a very good actor, or he honestly believed all he said."*

Two days later, Gray called Al Villegas and Lou Stefanelli, the two deputies left behind at Lompoc to pursue the investigation, and said that he wanted to add more details to what he knew about the escape. When they saw him, they were amazed at the difference a few days had made. His face was white and his hands were shaking and his eyes were red. Freddy had just been to see a doctor, but pills he had been given to calm him down were having no visible effect, and he told this story:

One day before the escape, between 11:30 A.M. and 1 P.M., Boyce had made two phone calls and afterward told Gray, "We've got to do it tomorrow." After he removed the dummy from Boyce's bunk he had gone to the prison laundry, to a window where he could see the drainage hole. At about six o'clock that night he had seen a light flash in the darkness beyond the fence. Boyce had then gone over the fence as planned, and a car was there—a green Ford sedan or possibly a pickup truck—with U.S. Government markings on the side. And then it looked as if Boyce got into the car and was driven away.

Gray said he wanted to add one more thing to what he had told them before: Boyce had confided to him before his escape that when he got out of prison, he was going to work again for the CIA.

"They broke him out," he said, and looked at the two men, waiting for their expressions to change.

Villegas walked to the drainage hole and looked over at the laundry. It did not look possible for Gray to have seen Boyce or a car from the laundry: another building blocked the line of sight. Still, a search was begun for a green sedan or pickup truck with U.S. Government insignia.

In Tysons Corner, senior officials of the Marshals Service did not believe the latest story from Freddy Gray. Jerry Brown, the case officer for the CIA, whose headquarters was in the Virginia countryside just a few miles from Tysons Corner, said emphatically that the agency had had nothing to do with the escape.

Still, some deputies in the field remained puzzled by the ease with which Boyce had disappeared—and they were troubled by the implications of Gray's story.

After the interview with Villegas and Stefanelli, Gray returned to his cell and began drafting a letter to the editor of *Playboy* magazine. He introduced himself as the man who had developed the "diabolical plan to break The Falcon out of prison" and offered to sell the magazine an exclusive story about the case. He said there was a spectacular secret about the escape that no one knew yet. *"No one but Christopher John Boyce and myself could ever tell the actual story that left the prison authorities, the F.B.I. and the U.S. Marshals totally baffled. . . . I have had five different offers from other magazines to do stories for them, but they all lack the classical experience of sophistication that only your magazine has to offer. If your magazine is interested in buying my exclusive story, please feel free to contact me."*

At the Federal Courthouse in Los Angeles, Larry Homenick looked over his desk. It was covered with reports from people in a dozen states claiming that they had seen Chris. There were reports of stolen cars, stolen boats, even a stolen horse from a farm near Lompoc, that had to be checked out, and there were still dozens of inmates who had to be questioned.

"I don't know when or how, but I think Chris will contact me eventually," the author of *The Falcon and the Snowman* said.

"Why do you say that?" Homenick asked.

Some investigators in the Marshals Service suspected that the author had helped Boyce escape and might be hiding him.

"During the writing of the book, and afterward, we got to know each other very well. We talked a lot, on the phone and at the prison, and a kind of mutual trust developed. For a while he didn't want to talk to his parents, because he felt he had humiliated them, and I served as an intermediary between Chris and his parents."

Homenick was puzzled by the author's confidence that Chris would call and wondered what else he knew.

Billy Joe Simmons was a month short of his thirty-sixth birthday when Deputy U.S. Marshal Brad Lipner, acting on a request from Homenick, found him in a cell at the Nevada State Prison in Carson City. Simmons had spent more than a third of his life in prison, and he was scheduled to spend most of the rest of it there, too.

He was serving thirty years for armed robbery, and after finishing that sentence in Nevada he faced a life sentence in California for murder, plus seventeen years in a federal prison for kidnapping the customer of a bar he had once held up.

Simmons told Lipner that he'd talk about Boyce if it would help him reduce the time he owed the Federal Government.

"I can't promise you a thing; I don't have the authority to make any deals," Lipner said. Nevertheless, if Simmons provided information that helped find Boyce, it was likely to help him.

"Sure, I know Boyce," Simmons began.

He said that he had had a cell adjoining Boyce's at Terminal Island and he had taken a liking to him, tried to give him tips about surviving in prison. Once he got his forty years, he said, the kid had talked about nothing besides escaping and once even had friends from Palos Verdes smuggle him some hacksaw blades for an escape. But Simmons said that he had aborted the escape himself by reporting the plot to a guard, a woman of whom he had become enamored and who would have been blamed for the escape if it succeeded.

"Did you and Boyce ever discuss his future if he got out?" the marshal asked.

"Yeah; he told me how he would get to Russia eventually."

"Do you think he's in Russia now?"

"No," Simmons replied. "When he leaves this country for Russia, the whole world will know it. Everybody will know it when he leaves. You will know it, and the world will know it, because he told me how he is going to do it."

Simmons' voice began to fade, and Lipner thought he heard the words "Air Force."

"What?"

"Never mind; that's all I want to say."

"Do you know of any connections Boyce may have in Africa or South America?"

"He never discussed Africa or South America. Texas, yes, Mexico, yes, but not South America or Africa," Simmons said.

"Any ideas at all about where Chris might be now or about who helped him get away from Lompoc?"

"Yeah. But I want to deal on my federal time. If you can promise me a deal on my federal time, then I can help you. But otherwise I already said too much."

"Billy Joe, one thing puzzles me, bothers me," Lipner said. "What did you mean when you said the whole world would know when Boyce leaves this country and everybody would know the same day that he arrives in Russia?"

"That's it. I ain't saying any more right now unless you can do me some good on my federal time."

With that, the interview ended, and Lipner decided to report the news directly to Howard Safir.

9

By the end of February 1980, almost seventy people had been interviewed in the manhunt, and Howard Safir had instituted a daily ritual at Tysons Corner. At his staff meeting each morning, he turned to his senior deputies and asked, "Where is Christopher Boyce?"

No one had a clue.

At Lompoc, Freddy Gray told anyone who would listen to him that Boyce had been sprung by the CIA, and it was soon part of prison lore that the Falcon had been freed by the Central Intelligence Agency.

The CIA continued to insist that it had nothing to do with the escape. Safir was satisfied, but not some of his investigators.

The line of sight between the rear fence and the laundry was checked again. Villegas decided again that it would have been impossible for Gray to see Boyce go over the fence and get into a car. A prison psychiatrist was sent to interview Gray, and afterward, he speculated that Gray might have convinced himself that there was a car near the fence out of the despair he felt over losing his early release date from prison or paranoia rooted in something Boyce had told him. Perhaps it was a hallucination linked to a dream of becoming famous because he said he had helped break a famous spy out of jail.

Whatever the reason, the psychiatrist emphasized, *"he believes he saw a car out there."*

Villegas and Stefanelli decided to continue looking for a green Ford.

Meanwhile, it was decided to suspend the search for Boyce in the mountains and hills near the prison.

To Safir and Homenick, Billy Joe Simmons' hint that Boyce intended to make his way to the Soviet Union was interesting. But until they had something to corroborate it, they decided to dismiss Simmons as another inmate who was trying to get something for nothing.

When Homenick received his orders from Safir to head the Boyce investigation, he had been delighted, despite his friendship with Chris, to be able to return to his first love in the Marshals Service—chasing fugitives. Chasing someone he knew only added a different dimension to the job. Some deputies never wanted to leave the WitSec program. Although it had a degree of personal danger, there were many advantages: an undercover car, a predictable routine and several thousand dollars a year in overtime pay. Homenick and his wife, Karen, who had been a secretary in the Los Angeles office of the FBI when they met in a college class on law enforcement, had used some of his overtime pay to buy their ranch-style home, with a backyard swimming pool, in a suburb at the far edge of the San Fernando Valley. But he found the long days confined in safe houses so boring that it was physically draining. Doing nothing, he decided, was the worst job of all, and he never was so tired as he was after baby-sitting a witness in a safe house. Along with many of the younger inspectors who had joined the Marshals Service after serving in Vietnam, he preferred more action.

Homenick enjoyed the challenge of a one-on-one chase. He had gotten his first taste of it not long after he came back from Vietnam and joined the Marshals Service and was assigned to the fugitive squad in Los Angeles. It was years before the Service got its expanded jurisdiction; in the early 1970s, the fugitive squad's principal job was hunting down people who had jumped bail or had dropped out of sight while serving probation. For the most part, they were minor-league criminals too insignificant to warrant the concern of the FBI. Occasionally, though, there were assignments to track down a front-rank drug dealer or other major criminals who had the resources and smarts to make life difficult—and interesting—for the deputies assigned to the fugitive squad. Although Homenick hated hunting or killing animals, he learned that he loved manhunting. The one-on-one chase was as straightforward and as fundamental a challenge as you could find in law enforcement, as basic in the 1980s as it had been in the 1880s. Sometimes it was easy. Many, perhaps most, manhunts ended when a fugitive emerged from hiding to commit another crime and got caught and a fingerprint check revealed his identity. Some fugitives got caught because they ran out of luck or they were simply not very smart. After months on the run, fugitives almost invariably got careless. They might change their names or even change their faces through plastic surgery, but Homenick discovered that most eventually contacted someone from their past. A woman was lurking, Safir once said, behind most wanted men. If a woman didn't lead you to a wanted man, you could often count on someone who had a grudge against him.

Homenick had heard it dozens of times. They all said the same thing. After he had tracked down a fugitive, handcuffed him and eased him into the back seat of his car, the prisoner always asked, "How did you find me?" And almost always, whether the man in his custody had been undone by an ex-wife, an old enemy or his own stupidity, Homenick would keep a straight face and say, "Good police work."

But by the middle of March 1980, Homenick was wondering if it was such a good job after all.

Except for a few footprints in the dirt that were washed away within a day by a rainstorm, there had been absolutely no sign of Boyce since he had been seen wheeling a wheelbarrow across the prison yard at Lompoc on the afternoon of January 21.

Meanwhile, pressure was building up on Homenick—and the Marshals Service—from all sides.

Some members of Congress were starting to say publicly that it had been a mistake to assign primary jurisdiction over prison escapees to the Marshals Service. Newspaper and television reporters were demanding news of progress in the investigation. Judge Kelleher called Homenick into his office and asked for a progress report on the manhunt; and when he didn't have any, the judge let him know that he would have been much happier if the FBI had been looking for Boyce.

There was, of course, the unrelenting pressure from Safir, still demanding daily reports of progress on the investigation. Some of his superiors in Los Angeles resented this direct line to Tysons Corner and warned him that if he didn't find Boyce soon, he'd have to take on other cases as well.

Homenick had seen Christopher Boyce only once since he was sent away for forty years. Boyce had been brought to a trial in Los Angeles to testify in behalf of an inmate who had gotten into some kind of trouble, and he had asked to see Homenick; there were warm handshakes, a catching up on the news in each man's life, then another goodbye. To some extent, time had faded Homenick's fondness for Chris, but it had been rekindled when they saw each other. Now all that he cared about was putting him back in prison.

As the weeks passed without a verified sighting of him, Homenick began to suspect that Chris might be lying dead somewhere in a gully or riverbed in the mountains beyond Lompoc. He checked with the coroner's offices in Santa Barbara and San Luis Obispo counties, and their reports were identical: no unidentified bodies had been found in the wilderness areas around Lompoc since January 21.

A few days later, a new avenue of investigation opened up. A young woman who had attended elementary school with Chris came to see Homenick and confessed that she had mailed several bottles of vitamins to him through an unorthodox channel a few weeks before his escape. She said she had written to Chris and inquired if there was anything she could do to help him, and he'd replied that the prison diet was too starchy and asked her to send four bottles of Thompson Coach's Formula multi-vitamins to the home of a recreational counselor at the prison, who had promised to pass them on to him. *"I feel very inadequate asking a favor of a perfect stranger,"* he had written. *"This is bizarre. You must only listen to me for a while, Martha, and then please wander off from my con-sciousness. Several letters are all I can bear from a free person and like the song: 'I will look away and you must be gone.' "* As she left his office, Homenick decided that the girl had probably fallen in love with Chris.

No vitamins had been found in his cell after the escape. Home-nick decided that Chris had taken them with him for nutrition while he was on the run; he had probably known, when he asked the girl to send the vitamins, that he was going to escape. Homenick began drafting a plan to notify health-food stores in California, and later, outlets for Thompson's vitamins elsewhere across the country, to keep an eye out for Chris.

Later that day, as he was walking to his office in the Federal Courthouse building in Los Angeles, he bumped into one of the prosecutors who had been in the U.S. attorney's office when Boyce and Lee were tried in the same building in 1977. He asked how the manhunt was going, and Homenick brought him up to date.

"You know," the government lawyer said, "if he'd had better luck or different legal advice, Boyce might have walked out the front door of Lompoc legally in a couple of years."

"How?"

Before his trial began, the man explained, government attorneys had wanted desperately to negotiate a deal under which Boyce would testify against Daulton Lee, and in exchange for his testi-mony, they were prepared to offer him a fifteen-year sentence. But Boyce's lawyers, he said, held out for ten years, and the negotia-tions collapsed and he got forty years.

"With good behavior," the prosecutor said. "Boyce would probably have been eligible for parole after doing a third of his time; that means he would have been out legally in 1982."

10

"WARRANTS. HOMENICK."

"Am I speaking to the person who is in charge of the investigation regarding Christopher Boyce?"

"Yes. This is Inspector Homenick. Who am I speaking to, please?"

"My name is Marilyn Mitchell. I'm a psychic, and I had a dream the night before last in which I saw him."

Like policemen around the world, Homenick was accustomed to calls like this one. He was, in the kindest of terms, a skeptic about psychics. He was also desperate.

"Is that right?"

"Yes, I had a vision of him," she said matter-of-factly. "I saw him in a cabin along the ocean. There were boats. I think there were three people in the cabin. . . . I can see a woman picking him up in a car. . . ."

Homenick wondered if the woman really knew something. Maybe she was trying to pass him a tip without implicating herself.

"Did you see any license numbers?"

She thought a moment.

"No, I'm sorry."

"Do you remember the address of the cabin?"

"No, but I think it's somewhere near Monterey."

The woman gave Homenick her telephone number. He asked her to call back if she remembered anything else. As a precaution, he decided to saturate police departments near Monterey, a resort community on the Pacific Ocean south of San Francisco, with Wanted posters of Boyce. But he didn't tell them he was doing so because of a tip from a psychic.

In Tysons Corner, Howard Safir selected someone to head the fugitive program.

Of all the senior officials in the Marshals Service who in 1980 began the task of reconstructing the agency to resume its old frontier mission as government manhunters, Thomas C. Kupferer, Jr., looked the part more than anyone else.

A forty-four-year-old Californian with a broad brow, dark hair and a big mustache, he had a presence that made it easy to imagine him riding up to a frontier bar, tying up his horse, walking through the door and leaving a few minutes later with a pair of desperados in tow. Moreover, Kupferer had a reputation in law enforcement for having little patience for bureaucratic red tape like that of the FBI and most big police departments. In some businesses he might have been called a pragmatist, but in the Marshals Service, some lawmen who preferred the bureaucratic way of doing things had another word for him: "cowboy."

Kupferer had an informal style—even the lowliest deputies under his command called him "Chuck"—that concealed a great seriousness about his job, as well as an intense personal distaste for what he called "scumbags and dirtbags."

After attending college in Southern California, Thomas Kupferer had briefly worked as a fireman, but had found it boring and gotten a job as a policeman. In 1969 he had joined the Marshals Service, where he soon earned a reputation as one of its stubbornest fugitive hunters, who enjoyed staying up all night on stakeouts and keeping after suspects even if it carried him across the country. In March 1980, Kupferer, then the chief deputy in the New Orleans office of the Marshals Service, was picked by Howard Safir to be chief inspector of the agency's enforcement division, the man with overall responsibility for the fugitive program. With his wife, Helen, whom he'd married when he was a cop in West Covina, California, and their three children, Kupferer moved from New

Orleans to Virginia. As he had expected, on his first day on the job Safir told him he was to give his highest priority to finding Christopher Boyce.

At the federal penitentiary in Terre Haute, Indiana, Daulton Lee was unhappy and grieving about his transfer.

"I don't think you really understand the ramifications of the over-all picture at hand," he wrote to a friend in April. *"The business of the transfer is a micro part of the macro scenario. The fact of the matter is that after three years, Boyce got tired of playing the game. His former employers were The Company and I strongly feel they're the ones he's gone back to."*

In Washington, Senator Daniel Patrick Moynihan was still asking about the whereabouts of Christopher John Boyce.

"Why, I ask, is the United States Marshals Service, not the FBI, looking for Mr. Boyce?" he demanded to know at a meeting of the Senate Intelligence Committee in April.

"Having the Marshals Service look for him? That's just like letting him go free!"

William Hall, the director of the Marshals Service, wrote the Senator that his agency was capable of finding Boyce and, given time, it would do so.

Even in his own office Homenick felt the pressure. Whenever another news article reported that Chris was still at large, someone dropped a copy of the story on his desk. Even after work, when he was having a beer with some of the other deputies, kibitzers needled him.

When he was low, Homenick usually got a lift from Tony Perez. They had gone to work in the Los Angeles office within a week of each other and become close friends. Later, when they were partners, other deputies had begun to refer to them as "Freebie and the Bean," appropriating the title of a movie and television series about two cops, one Hispanic, one Anglo, who worked as partners. Perez, the survivor who had fought his way out of a Miami ghetto, had street smarts and a special sensitivity for minorities; Homenick, the product of middle-class suburbia, was soft-spoken and disarming and had a knack for sizing up people quickly and persuading them to talk. Karen Homenick once complained that she thought her husband was closer to Perez than he was to her, and Larry Homenick did not disagree with her. The two men were the best of friends; but nevertheless, they disagreed sharply about Christopher Boyce.

Perez got angry when Homenick used the familiar "Chris"— and got even angrier if he ever said anything favorable about him. Perez had nothing but contempt for Boyce, who had been given every opportunity to succeed in America and then had sold out his country.

"Tony, if things had been different, that might have been *me,*" Homenick told his friend one Friday night late in May at the Revolver Club, a bar at the Los Angeles Police Academy where cops can buy a pitcher of beer for $2 and get away from the civilians who don't share their special pressures.

"That's bullshit; I don't believe it. He's a spy: he betrayed his country; he's no Robin Hood."

Homenick said that he was scheduled to go to a training class soon for Witness Security inspectors and he was looking forward to attending; it was a clean way to get the Boyce case off his back.

"I'm stumped," he said. "I really am."

"Larry, nobody could do any better. He's a smart kid. The FBI's looking for him too. I know they are. They haven't found him either. *You* know him. We'll find him; it's just a matter of time."

The next day, Homenick called Safir and told him that he had decided to stay on the Boyce case and was going to cancel his place in the Witness Security training course.

Marilyn Mitchell, the psychic, called again:

"I see Christopher Boyce in San Francisco. . . . An apartment near Fisherman's Wharf . . . an apartment with an ornate railing overlooking the sea. I see him holding up something to the light, a microfiche, and it says, 'Top Secret.' "

And then she hung up.

Homenick asked Al Villegas and Lou Stefanelli if they had been able to find her. They said the number she had given Homenick when she called the first time was for a pay phone at a restaurant, the Broken Egg, in Santa Barbara, and no one there had ever heard of Marilyn Mitchell.

A few days later, Homenick called Kupferer and asked if there was any word from South Africa.

"Not yet," Kupferer said. But he told Homenick he wanted him to check out a convict at the Missouri State Prison who might know something about Boyce.

"His name," Kupferer said, "is Captain Midnight."

11

LITTLE HAPPENS ORDINARILY ON THE LATE SHIFT at the U.S. Marshals Service Communications Center in Tysons Corner, Virginia. Unless there's a special operation going on that requires coordination from headquarters, most calls are from deputies in the field checking for messages or from police departments around the country checking whether someone they've just arrested is still wanted by the Feds. It had been especially slow on the night of July 11, 1980, when, a few minutes after 11 P.M., Duty Officer Robert M. Brown answered the phone.

"Hello. Is this the United States of America?" a voice asked.

There was an echo on the line, hinting that the call was from overseas.

"Yes, sir," Brown responded. "May I help you?"

"I want to speak to the policemen in Los Angeles, California."

The man had an accent that was vaguely British, but not quite.

"Sir, this is the United States Marshals Service. May I help you?"

"Is this a police department?"

"Yes, it is; may I help you?"

"I want to know if the policemen in the United States still want Christopher Boyce."

"Yes, sir. Mr. Boyce is still wanted in this country. Do you know where he is?"

Brown heard the crackle of radio static in the background. It sounded as if it were in the same room as the caller.

"If I pick him up, will you still want him back in America?"

"Yes, sir. May I have your name and where exactly you are calling from?"

"What is *your* name?"

"Sir, my name is Brown. I am the duty officer for the United States Marshals Service."

"Spell it."

"B R O W N."

"Are you a lieutenant colonel like me, or just what are you?"

Brown wondered if the accent was South African.

The line had faded. Brown could hardly hear the man, and soon they were shouting at each other to be heard.

"I am the duty officer!"

"How much are you paid in your police department?"

"Sir. Could you tell me exactly where Mr. Boyce is at present?"

"If I came to America, would I be well paid in your police department? Could I come there and be a lieutenant colonel?"

"That depends on your education and experience in the field of law enforcement. Could you give me what information you have on Mr. Boyce? Where is he at present?"

"Mr. Boyce has settled in Zimbabwe-Rhodesia."

"Sir. Would you spell that name for me, please?"

The man ignored the question. He had ignored most of Brown's questions.

"Do you have any women in your police department?"

"Yes, sir, we do."

"Let me talk to one, a pretty one."

"Sir, there are none working at the present time. I am working alone right now."

"That's all right. I can't do anything on the phone anyway. You have to grip them just right for maximum effect."

Brown's voice was beginning to show his anger.

"Sir. Could you give me a number where you can be reached concerning Christopher Boyce?"

"Let me tell you what I will do to your women!"

Brown hung up the phone.

Five minutes later, it rang again.

"Hello!" It was the same man, shouting cheerily.

"May I speak to Muhammad Ali?"

"I'm sorry, sir, Muhammad Ali is not here right now."

"I want to talk to the son-of-a-bitch," the voice replied. "I want to fuck him up good."

Brown hung up again. He checked with the telephone company, and an operator told him it was impossible to trace the source of the call.

The call, strange as it was, interested the investigators in Tysons Corner and Los Angeles for two reasons: the anonymous letter received a few days after the escape that claimed Boyce was on his way to Rhodesia, and a remark by Freddy Gray to Homenick: "Chris said that if he managed to get away, after he got to Nicaragua he wanted to go to a neutral English-speaking country like Ireland or Rhodesia, where there was a war going on, or there was political turmoil that would help him get lost." As far as the marshals knew, no one outside the United States knew about the letter, and the call excited the investigative team.

But how do you track down a voice—possibly the voice of a drunk—from halfway around the world? Safir asked the State Department to accelerate its inquiries about Boyce in South Africa.

In Los Angeles, the stack of reports on Larry Homenick's desk from people who believed they had sighted Christopher Boyce was growing. The FBI had refused to place Boyce on its list of the Ten Most Wanted Men because, the Bureau said, he was technically not an FBI fugitive. The deputies hunting Boyce were astonished by the decision, then agreed that it was another snub by the Bureau calculated to make it harder for them to find him. Despite the snub, Homenick spread the word. He distributed thousands of Wanted posters with a photograph of the Soviet spy to police departments around the country, and a police trade journal, *Police Products News*, agreed to publish a copy of it.

Before long, it appeared that Boyce was everywhere—and nowhere.

One policeman reported seeing him on an airliner between Los Angeles and Mexico City. A policeman in Plattsburgh, New York, had picked up a hitchhiker named Christopher John Bryce and reported that he looked exactly like the man on the Wanted poster, causing hopes to soar for a few hours; then a deputy went to Plattsburgh and concluded that it was the wrong man. A state trooper had stopped a Jeep for speeding in rural Mississippi and reported that there had been a young man in the back seat who was the spitting image of the Russian agent. The passenger was tracked down, and he wasn't Boyce. Policemen reported seeing Boyce in Colorado, North Dakota, Florida, New York City and almost a dozen other places; each lead was investigated, but none led to Boyce. Deputies in the far-flung regional offices of the Marshals Service visited wilderness areas to ask local people involved in falconry if any falconers had moved into the area recently. Because Boyce was known to have coveted a rare peregrine falcon, investigators spent extra time in regions where this once nearly extinct bird was still thriving.

Mike Adams had moved to Hawaii to work as a carpenter, and deputies in Honolulu were told to keep him under surveillance. Friends of Boyce's in and around Palos Verdes, including some who local police officials said were involved in drug dealing, were put under surveillance. Freddy Gray was now in federal prison at El Reno, Oklahoma, and deputies visited him regularly to ask if he had anything to add to his story; his mother and sister, who lived near Seattle, were watched in case Boyce ever sought help from them. *Playboy* turned down Gray's idea for an article, but he insisted to his new friends in Oklahoma that he had masterminded Boyce's escape and that someday he would be recognized for his brilliance in helping pull it off. Usually, his new friends immediately went to a guard, claimed to know something about the escape and offered to trade the information for special treatment. The investigators interviewed all of them.

Gray remained the one inmate they knew of whom Boyce had taken into his confidence before the escape, and he remained their best link to him. But with each new telling of his story, it splintered into new directions: one inmate said Gray had told him Boyce was hiding in Guadalajara, in central Mexico; another said he had hinted that Boyce had told him that he was going to go to Seattle and then cross the border into Canada; a third said Gray had told him that Boyce intended to go to Balboa Island, an affluent community located on the Pacific coast between Los Angeles and San Diego, where he was going to board a friend's boat and sail to Mexico and then South America; a fourth said Gray had told him that he had invented a story that the CIA had been involved in the escape in order to deceive investigators and help sell his story to the movies.

One day in the middle of July, Homenick took out the file and reviewed the conflicting stories that Gray had told since January 21, and decided that Freddy Gray was crazy.

Eleven days after the call to Tysons Corner reporting that Christopher Boyce was in Rhodesia, a telephone call was made to another federal agency located in a suburb of Washington. The National Security Agency, headquartered at Fort Meade, Maryland, is perhaps the most secretive of American intelligence agencies. From its base in Maryland, it operates a global network of clandestine electronics listening posts—on land, in aircraft, on ships and on space satellites—to eavesdrop on the communications of foreign countries. With one of the world's most sophisticated computer systems, it then attempts to decode the intercepted messages.

At 10:30 P.M. on July 22, 1980, Vernon Schultz, a night duty officer at Fort Meade, took a call from a man who said that he was calling from the lobby of the Sheraton Hotel in Mexico City.

"My name is Christopher Boyce," he said matter-of-factly. "I'm wanted in the United States for espionage, but I want you to pass on some information to the proper authorities."

Although he was on the run, he said that he wanted the government to know certain things before he disappeared again and asked Schultz to listen carefully.

Schultz set in motion the agency's procedures for tracing phone calls. The caller said that he had just met a stranger in Mexico City named Jay Cook who seemed to be connected with American intelligence and he had admitted that as a U.S. agent he had sabotaged negotiations for an important agreement between the United States and the Soviet Union intended to control the spread of nuclear weapons. The stranger had refused to go into the details of the failed negotiations, but, cryptically, had mentioned two code names: "Tiffany" and "Double-Day." Although he wouldn't say what he had done to sabotage the agreement, he had hinted that it involved a secret space-satellite project, and the caller told Schultz that Cook had told him it meant that the world's two great superpowers were approaching a nuclear war in which 130 million Americans would die.

The duty officer could hear sirens in the background and suspected that the call was originating from an outdoor telephone stall.

"I think he's CIA, but he wouldn't say so," the caller said. "He seems to know a lot about the intelligence community—names, places and dates."

"What did he look like?"

"Slender, brown-haired, about forty years old; five nine, a hundred thirty-five pounds; he said he'd served as a double agent, and that he'd spent some time in a prison camp someplace."

Schultz guessed that the caller was in his late twenties or early thirties and sober, although he tended to ramble, and Schultz wondered if he might be emotionally troubled. Still, he said in his report later, the caller had a basic knowledge about American intelligence operations, and he had repeated his story coherently enough to make Schultz believe he was talking to Christopher Boyce.

Even though the call lasted forty-five minutes, NSA operators were unable to trace it.

The caller said that he was staying in Room 1250 at the Maria Isabel Sheraton, which was near the U.S. Embassy, and he said if Schultz had any further questions about the man he'd met, he could call there later. As soon as Schultz hung up, he telephoned his NSA supervisor at home and told him about the call. They agreed to call the FBI in Washington, and the FBI's night duty officer, after checking with *his* boss, called Kent Pekarek, a senior official of the Marshals Service in Tysons Corner.

Pekarek called Schultz and got a quick briefing about the call. He telephoned the Maria Isabel Sheraton Hotel and asked if a guest named Christopher Boyce was staying in Room 1250.

"No, sir," a clerk said after a few moments. "The guest in Room 1250 is named Roland Cliff. Excuse me a second, please."

There was a pause while the clerk looked over some records.

"Oh, I see that Mr. Boyce had Room 1250 until yesterday, but he's gone. He checked out yesterday."

Pekarek woke up Larry Homenick and told him to have Tony Perez, who spoke Spanish, call the hotel and get more information about the previous guest in Room 1250. The next morning, Chuck Kupferer told Homenick that he and Perez should pack their bags and be ready for a quick trip to Mexico City.

But they never had to fly to Mexico City.

After two days, a senior National Security Agency official told Tysons Corner to forget about the call. The agency had identified the caller as Leo Jones, a former CIA agent with a mental problem. Someone had registered under the name of Christopher Boyce in Room 1250, the NSA man said, but it wasn't Boyce. It was a curious call, and it puzzled the men responsible for finding Boyce. But soon they had something else on their minds.

Kupferer told Homenick to forget about flying to Mexico City for now and to concentrate on Captain Midnight.

12

BOB MERMAN USED TO BOAST THAT JACK NICHolson had called him once to propose making a movie about his life. But Merman had turned him down; he had a turbo Commander waiting at the airport, and there was another load of dope waiting to be picked up at Chihuahua. Nicholson had never called back.

It was too bad, because it would have made a good movie. After they became friends in a San Diego prison, Boyce called Merman a "forty-year-old hippie." In a lot of ways, the description fitted. He was born in 1937 in a suburb of Los Angeles, the son of well-to-do, alcoholic parents who never had much time or love for their son. At thirteen he dropped out of school and left home, and three years later he joined the Marines. At nineteen he was arrested for the first time, on a minor burglary charge, and it started the fitful dance of his adult life, swinging between crime and trying to go straight.

Merman was tall and well built, with blond hair and expansive, friendly eyes. He had a way with automobile engines and other mechanical things, and when he was trying to go straight, he easily found work as a truck driver, mechanic or logger. But conventional jobs bored him. Even in his twenties, the prospect of growing old troubled him. He told friends that he didn't want to die before he had *lived*. Along the way, he had four wives and he couldn't remember how many other women who, attracted by his zest for new experiences, kept house with him for a few days or a few months.

For five years during the 1960s, Merman swallowed a hook dangled at him by middle-class America. He saved enough money to buy a gas station in San Jose, and the station prospered so much that the Junior Chamber of Commerce cited him as one of the most successful young businessmen in Northern California. He gave lectures to delinquent youths, offering himself as evidence that even after a bad start, it was possible for someone in America to make something of himself. But even as he spoke, he had begun spending his weekends with the hippies and drop-outs who were congregating in the Haight-Ashbury district of San Francisco and orienting his life around the drugs they used. He was getting bored with pumping gas in San Jose, and when somebody told him about the excitement and big money to be found in drug smuggling, Merman swallowed a different hook. At thirty-one, he learned how to fly and began his metamorphosis into a legend of the international drug underworld, a bearded pilot known throughout much of Mexico as Captain Midnight.

Flying mostly at night, often a few feet above desert cactus and sagebrush to avoid being detected, Merman during the early 1970s airlifted tons of marijuana in all kinds of airplanes on hundreds of trips between the Sierra Madre mountains in Mexico and desert strips in Nevada, Arizona, Texas and Utah. So that he didn't fly empty southbound, he did a bit of gunrunning to Central America. Before long, his Mexican partners were spreading word of the amazing feats of this *gringo*. No weather was stormy enough to keep him on the ground, no landing strip too short or too rough to keep him from flying. He had cracked up a dozen planes, legend had it, most of them because they were overloaded with pot, but he had survived. In the *cantinas* of Sinaloa, Sonora and Chihuahua, the stories spread about his daring flights, his crash landings, the shoot-outs with the Federales, his women and the millions of dollars he made as a smuggler, and it seemed as if it all would never end.

The end of the saga of Captain Midnight began in the middle of 1974 when U.S. Drug Enforcement Agency investigators traveled to Mexico determined to break up the legendary smuggling ring. Mexican policemen tracked him down, and when they caught him, he said they beat him so badly that two of his ribs were smashed and a lung was punctured. They took him to a military camp in the town of Los Mochis, stripped him naked, gagged him and left him in a pool of water on a cement floor while they tortured him with electric wires attached to his testicles and poured Pepsi-Cola down his nose, nearly drowning him. After forty-five minutes, Merman confessed, and there was a quick trial. He was sentenced to three and a half years in a Mexican prison. But after a few months he was freed because an appellate court ruled that his confession had been extracted illegally, under torture. Mexico ordered him to leave the country within thirty days; but knowing that DEA agents were waiting for him on the other side of the border, he disappeared into the Sierra Madre. After almost a year on the run in the impoverished interior of northern Mexico, he was arrested by the Mexican Federal Police in March 1976. But instead of taking him to prison, the *comandante* of the arresting party offered him a beer and a business proposition: if Merman agreed to make clandestine dope flights for *him* and a group of other Federales, he wouldn't turn him over to the DEA.

Captain Midnight was in the air again—but not for long.

There were, unfortunately for him, two policemen in the state of Chihuahua who hadn't been told that Merman was flying for their own officers, and a few months later they ambushed the Federales' plane at a remote landing strip and riddled the plane—and Merman's legs—with machine-gun bullets. The ambush was followed by months in a Mexican hospital and several operations on his legs. The policemen for whom he had been flying were arrested, and finally, in the fall of 1976, Merman was sent to the Mexican federal prison in Juárez for twenty years.

Merman stayed in the prison only seventeen months. Hobbling on legs permanently and grotesquely misshapen by bungled surgery, he spent five months tunneling his way to freedom. With a screwdriver and empty tuna cans as his only tools, he dug through his cell floor in a month; and then, at a rate of three inches a night, he burrowed a tunnel beneath two buildings and two rock walls to the outside world. The tunnel, in all, was forty-nine feet long. Each night, he hid the rocks taken out of the tunnel in false ceilings he constructed above the cells and flushed the sand and dirt down the drain of the prison shower.

Merman emerged from his tunnel in August 1977, made his way to the border and, determined to forsake smuggling forever, told friends that he was going to get lost among the wheat fields of rural Kansas. But as soon as he entered the States, he was arrested and charged with drug trafficking and sent to the Metropolitan Correctional Center in San Diego, where he became, for several months in 1978, one of many mentors whom Christopher John Boyce found in prison. The long-haired average hippie and the former altar boy who was still an untested new ''fish'' in the prison became close friends, and Merman told him what he knew about drug smuggling, escape and survival.

After several months, Merman was released by a parole board that took into consideration his painful ordeal in Mexico, and he took a bus to the rural Kansas home of his latest sweetheart, a beautiful blonde who was the mother of his young son and had waited for him in Mexico while he dug his way to freedom.

But life in America proved no easier for Captain Midnight than it had been at the end in Mexico. He settled with his girlfriend and son in a small farming town and got a job at $3 an hour pumping gasoline. Within a few weeks, Merman's twisted legs ached so much from standing all day at the gas station that he had to quit and apply for welfare, and it wasn't long before his girlfriend left him, taking their son.

If the story of Captain Midnight had concluded there, it would have completed a morality play that Bible Belt preachers might have used to convince the youthful members of their congregations about the dreadful fate awaiting those who give in to the temptations of drugs and easy money. But it didn't end there.

Not long after Merman applied for welfare, a Kansas City gambler and sometime pimp named Richard Henry Drummond, who was an old friend, asked him for a favor. Whether it was a favor agreed to out of friendship or for some money for Merman to improve the conditions of his life is not known, and perhaps not important. In early March 1979, Drummond, who was accused of murdering four people, was being led down from an eleventh-floor holding cell in the Jackson County Courthouse in Kansas City to a hearing in a sixth-floor courtroom when he told his guard he needed to go to the rest room.

When Drummond and his escort entered the men's room, Merman was waiting with a .38-caliber revolver, and pointing it in front of him, he led Drummond out of the courthouse.

But Captain Midnight had lost his magic. There were a hundred-mile-an-hour chase across town, a blazing gunfight and a few extra minutes of freedom for Drummond. But the fugitives were quickly cornered. Drummond was wounded, and both were arrested.

When Bob Merman was asked at his arraignment the next day if he had enough money to hire a lawyer, the man who had made millions smuggling drugs said, truthfully, "I don't own anything."

His federal parole was rescinded, and a few weeks later, Merman was sentenced to twenty years in the Missouri State Prison. Writing to a friend a few weeks later, Merman said, *"I'm just a truck driver who learned how to fly a plane, and just between you and me, I don't think that man was meant to fly."*

Early in July 1980, Richard Henry Drummond, the man for whom Merman had gambled his freedom and lost, placed a telephone call from the prison in Jefferson City to the local office of the Federal Bureau of Investigation. He said that he wanted to talk to someone about the Russian spy Christopher John Boyce. The FBI passed on the information to Andrew Snyder, a deputy marshal in Kansas City.

A few days later, Snyder looked across a table at a man facing four concurrent seventy-five-year sentences for murder, plus thirty years for escape. He was a man who wanted to make a deal.

Bob Merman, Drummond said, knows where Christopher Boyce is. In fact, he said, Merman had helped set up the arrangements for Boyce to hide out in Mexico, and before he was caught trying to break Drummond out of jail, Merman had been planning to get Boyce out of prison himself in a helicopter flown by a Mexican pilot. "They were going to stash fuel along the route and go to Mexico. Mexico is where he was going to go."

Snyder asked Drummond how he knew about the Boyce-Merman connection, and Drummond explained that Bob Merman was his cellmate, and he talked about Boyce all the time.

Drummond offered to work with the Feds to get Boyce if the Feds helped him. If his information helped locate Boyce, he wanted three things: a lawyer so he could petition the courts for a reduction of his sentence, a private word to the judge that he had helped find him and a transfer to a prison where he could do easier time.

Snyder, saying he couldn't offer any deals, pressed Drummond for what else he knew about Boyce.

"Everything I know comes from Merman," Drummond stressed.

According to Merman, Boyce had been obsessed by a desire to escape, and to prepare him for it if he ever succeeded, Merman had devoted hundreds of hours to teaching him about living off the land as a fugitive in Mexico.

"Did he ever mention anything about Boyce going to work for the Russians again after he got out?"

"He said he thought Boyce, once he got to Mexico, would contact the Soviet Embassy in Mexico City. Merman said Boyce wanted to get a source of information that he could sell, and had some ideas for setting up his own intelligence network in which he'd sell information to different governments."

Merman, he continued, had told Boyce to get out of espionage and go into smuggling, but Boyce, claiming he had allegiance to no country and hated all the great powers equally, had been obsessed with taking on their intelligence services. Drummond remembered one remark quoted by Merman: "He said, 'I cannot tear apart the intelligence sphere, but I can reshape it.' "

Merman liked Boyce very much, Drummond said, but might co-operate with the investigation if there was something in it for him.

"Merman says that Boyce has one weakness. He said he likes the good life and after a while will get tired of running and hiding and having a second-class life. That's his weakness."

Drummond agreed to pump Merman to get more information about Boyce and to report anything new. If his information really helped find the escaped spy, Snyder said, the government would try to help him.

13

LARRY HOMENICK BEGAN TO FEEL GOOD AS HIS muscles loosened up on the dusty, unmarked frontier between the housing development where he lived and the mountainous wilderness just beyond it, from where coyotes and rattlesnakes still wandered out from time to time, unaware that the territory no longer belonged to them.

He liked to run at least four miles a day; but as the summer wore on, he had had less and less time for jogging. Now he needed to relax after spending most of the afternoon on the telephone to Terminal Island, a jetty of land in Los Angeles' man-made harbor that long ago was called Rattlesnake Island because it was infested with snakes. Now it served as a rocky platform for U.S. military facilities and a federal prison.

An inmate at Lompoc had told Homenick that when Boyce was at T.I. he'd been close to a prisoner who had served as a mercenary in Rhodesia and had also lived in South Africa. The informant said he couldn't recall the man's name, but remembered that he loved guns and disliked blacks. After many calls, officials at the prison said that nobody could remember an inmate during 1978 who had been a mercenary, and for Homenick it had been another frustrating day.

In recent weeks, he had begun to have the same dream almost every night: through a misty sky he saw Chris walking or sitting, with handcuffs on; but then Chris bolted and he saw him running away, getting farther and farther, and he wasn't wearing his leg irons or handcuffs. Homenick tried to run after him, but for each step he took Chris took three, and soon he had vanished and Homenick was alone.

He usually woke up at this point in a cold sweat and couldn't go back to sleep.

Chuck Kupferer's arrival at Tysons Corner had made things a little easier for Homenick. Before, all he got from headquarters had been questions. Now, when he had a major problem, or a decision had to be made about pursuing a lead, Kupferer, who had been Homenick's first partner in Los Angeles almost a decade earlier, was there to help him set his priorities and suggest new avenues of investigation. Mercifully, he also acted as a buffer against Howard Safir.

But as the months passed, Kupferer too had begun to grow impatient.

Homenick had to admit that he had made no progress.

Some weeks it seemed as if every single resident of California called to say that he or she had seen someone who looked exactly like Chris driving along a freeway with a falcon on his shoulder. Then there were the crazies who said they had heard Chris talking to them through a transmitter the CIA had placed in their teeth while they were asleep. Someone called to say he had seen Boyce get into a raft near Santa Barbara and row it out to a waiting submarine; but when Homenick checked, the caller turned out to be a hospitalized mental patient. FBI agents called every few days to pass on reports they had received about possible sightings, and Homenick was beginning to wonder if they were playing a cruel game by giving him leads they had invented over their martinis. Still, he checked them out. He traveled to Skid Row hotels, suburban shopping malls and remote mountains and deserts of Southern California, to every place where people said they had seen Chris. He couldn't afford not to. It would be embarrassing if the Bureau gave him a lead and he ignored it and it later turned out to have been legitimate.

The previous night, after working all day trying to identify the Rhodesian mercenary, he had pulled into his driveway after ten o'clock and, too wrapped up in the case to go to sleep right away, had taken a beer from the refrigerator and turned on the Home Box Office channel to watch a movie. The first thing he saw was the face of Clint Eastwood, who was fashioning a dummy of himself. The movie was *Escape from Alcatraz*. He turned to Karen, who had begun to complain that he was spending too much time away from home on the investigation and that when he was home he was often grouchy, and said, "If it wasn't for that movie, I wouldn't be in such a bad mood."

After the movie they went to bed, and Homenick dreamed again about Chris running unrestrained across a field.

The next day, as he ran along the edge of the Los Angeles exurb called Canyon Country where he lived, Homenick, as he often did, searched his memory for details of his conversations with Chris, trying to recall anything he had said that might indicate where he would go. Chris had been his friend, but the friendship had never diluted his determination to catch him. If anything, he felt the friendship should give him an edge in finding him, and now he felt guilty that it hadn't.

Homenick recalled Chris's hatred of the CIA; his sense of doom for the world; the surprising depth of his knowledge about world affairs and history. He remembered his obsession with falconry and birds, and it made him think of the magazines and books about flying that Tony had found in his cell. According to the Flying Book Club, he had ordered two books about flying by mail order, a guide to buying used aircraft and a pilot's guidebook for overwater flying. It made Homenick think of the opening line of "The Prisoner's Song": "If I had the wings of an angel . . ." Perhaps every prisoner in every prison dreamed at least once of having the power to fly like a bird. But he thought it probably went deeper than that in Chris: whenever they talked about his falcons, Chris's blue eyes had seemed to explode with emotion, and when he described their flight it had seemed almost as if he were transported from the court-house into the minds of his birds.

On Homenick's desk were leads placing Chris in South Africa, Mexico, Nicaragua, Ireland, the Soviet Union and more than a dozen states. There was a possibility that Chris had left prison to find a buried treasure of secret documents. There was the possibility that the KGB—or even the CIA—had helped get him out of prison. He thought about Captain Midnight and the books about flying and wondered if Chris had learned how to fly since his escape.

If he had, where would he go? He could be anyplace in the world. Was he smuggling drugs? It was a possibility. One of the biggest puzzles, among many, was how he had been able to support himself. If he was still alive, he had to be getting money from somewhere, someone. There was lots of money to be made in drugs. Every day fugitive reports passed over his desk about drug dealers who took in so much cash that they had to buy machines that weighed it. Chris could make a lot of money smuggling drugs.

The Senate Intelligence Committee had scheduled a closed hearing on the Boyce escape in a few weeks, and Howard Safir had sent word that he wanted some signs of progress to report.

Almost eight months had passed since the escape. As he began to head back toward his home, Homenick reminded himself again that there was not a single piece of evidence to prove that Boyce was even still alive. He had disappeared. It was as if he had gone into a cave on the night of his escape and never come out. Homenick had heard it said many times that almost every fugitive, sooner or later, contacts someone from his past. Yet virtually every person who had ever known Chris had been questioned, and in many cases those interrogated had been kept under surveillance.

Still, there were a few reasons to be optimistic. Homenick remembered a bank robber he had once arrested who had eluded the police for several months, and as he was being led away in handcuffs, he had looked at Homenick and said, "You guys can make all the mistakes in the world; but if we make one mistake, it's over."

Chris, if he was alive, still hadn't made a mistake—or he hadn't been caught at it if he had.

Homenick tried to imagine what he would do, where he would go, if he were Chris. He decided that if he escaped from a prison he would pick a remote town somewhere in the middle of America and get a job, find a girl, start a new life and stay out of trouble. As

83

Homenick was musing over the possibility that Chris might do the same thing, he remembered a remark he had once made. Homenick's recollection was related in some way to his still unresolved curiosity over why a likable, seemingly harmless kid from a fine family had decided to become a Soviet spy. They had been sipping soft drinks while waiting for a pretrial hearing to begin, and Chris, chain-smoking as usual, had said that even though he had been scared when he had smuggled secret documents from the Black Vault, he had enjoyed the excitement.

"Larry, I guess I'm a pirate at heart," he had said. "I guess I'm an adventurer."

Back at home, as he started to turn on the shower, Homenick thought about the remark and wondered if it offered any clue as to what Chris was doing now.

In early August, a cable arrived at the State Department in Washington from the U.S. Embassy in Pretoria, South Africa:

DISCUSSED MATTER WITH APPROPRIATE MEMBERS OF SOUTH AFRICAN AND ZIMBABWEAN POLICE. NEITHER ORGANIZATION HAS KNOWLEDGE OF BOYCE ENTERING SOUTHERN AFRICA. BOTH POLICE FORCES ARE VERY CONSCIOUS CHAIN OF COMMAND. IT WOULD BE HIGHLY IRREGULAR FOR A LIEUTENANT COLONEL TO PLACE A TELEPHONE CALL TO THE UNITED STATES.

Under a brilliant sky at the Poipu Village Resort Hotel on the island of Kauai in Hawaii, Marshals Service Inspectors Larry Hattersley and Bill Friel laid four photographs of Christopher John Boyce on the desk in front of the hotel manager and asked him if he had ever seen the man in the pictures.

He took his time to study the photographs.

"I'm sure he was here," he said. "About a month ago; he was hanging around the hotel grounds and looked sort of suspicious. I checked him out and found he wasn't registered, so I told him to leave."

"Are you sure it's the same man?"

"I think so."

Then the inspectors asked a question to which they already knew the answer, because that was what had brought them to Kauai:

"Do you have a registered guest named Mike Adams?"

"Yes—a carpenter. He's been here for about three months; he's working on some new condominiums down the road."

The manager excused himself and returned a few moments later with a reservation card indicating that Adams had booked rooms at the hotel the following week for three men and a woman.

Hattersley and Friel looked at each other.

"What names did he give?"

"He didn't give any names . . . just four people."

As they were leaving the hotel, Friel spotted a friend from high school who lived nearby. He showed him the same pictures of Boyce, and his friend said he thought he'd seen him hanging around the hotel a few weeks before.

The inspectors flew back to Honolulu and reported to Tysons Corner that Mike Adams might be planning to rendezvous with Boyce in Kauai the following week.

After he had passed the lie-detector test in January, Adams had fallen from prominence as a suspect in the investigation. But his move to Hawaii had renewed suspicions. Kupferer told Hattersley and Friel to stake out the hotel the following week.

When Adams' guests arrived, undercover deputy U.S. marshals were waiting. But the guests turned out to be Adams' three brothers and a girlfriend. They questioned Adams, but he said that he had still had no contact with Boyce.

Hattersley and Friel concluded that the hotel manager and Friel's friend had probably made a mistake. Chuck Kupferer told them to keep Adams under surveillance for a few more days just the same.

At Jefferson City, Missouri, the tubes, electrodes and wires of a polygraph machine were attached to Richard Henry Drummond by a sergeant from the Missouri State Highway Patrol. After a few preliminary questions, he asked:

"Does Bob Merman know where Christopher Boyce is right now?"

"No."

"Has Christopher Boyce contacted Merman since his escape?"

"No . . . I don't think so."

The polygraph examiner concluded that the test indicated Drummond was being truthful and had told the investigators all he knew about the escape, and if they were going to get more out of Merman, they might have to get it directly from him.

Disappointed, Kupferer and Homenick decided to have Drummond work on Merman some more before deciding their next move.

After being promoted to chief inspector, Kupferer had become the person to whom Howard Safir, at ten o'clock each morning, looked across a table at the daily staff meeting and asked, "Where is Christopher Boyce?"

Boyce was only one of some ten thousand fugitives on the wanted log of the U.S. Marshals Service. But no one in the agency doubted that he was the most important one by far. From Congress, the press, snipers in the FBI and everywhere else, it seemed, criticism was growing that the Marshals Service was not up to handling its new assignment. A consensus was growing that if the Service did not find Christopher Boyce, it would lose the fugitive program and revert to its old missions of serving process, transporting prisoners and guarding witnesses and judges.

Safir ordered Kupferer to come up with a plan that could break the impasse, and by midsummer a plan had been agreed on: a dozen or so of the best inspectors in the Marshals Service would be organized into a special task force that would focus exclusively on finding Boyce.

But where should they start looking for him?

Kupferer read and reread the thousands of pages of reports on the case that had been accumulated since January 21 . . . all the interviews with prison inmates and others who knew Boyce, the reports of purported sightings and other material. There wasn't a single item proving that Boyce even existed anymore, no substantive clue pointing to where they should start.

"At least with Patty Hearst," he told Homenick, "the Bureau had pictures of her to prove that she was still alive; we've got a ghost!

"It's purely a judgment call," Kupferer said, "but I don't think he's gone out of the country; I think he's probably still in his own backyard."

To remain on the run for long, Kupferer decided, a fugitive had to have a support system. All of Boyce's friends were in Southern California. Several were drug dealers. He knew the world of dope trafficking from his friendship with Daulton Lee, and even the latest reports from Missouri about Captain Midnight's tutoring in prison pointed to Boyce smuggling drugs.

Kupferer began making preparations for a task force to look for him in Southern California beginning October 1, at the start of the new fiscal year. There would be enough money for the project in the Marshals Service budget then. Kupferer didn't expect that on the following day, Homenick would get an urgent message telling him that Christopher John Boyce wanted to turn himself in.

14

HOLLYWOOD WAS NEVER THE CITY OF GLITTER and glamour that generations of moviegoers imagined it to be. Like the celluloid fantasies that were created in its movie studios, Hollywood really didn't exist. Legally, it was just another neighborhood of Los Angeles that had been subdivided and merchandised by real estate promoters after the turn of the century. In a nice stroke of good luck for the promoters, Cecil B. De Mille, Adolph Zukor and others immigrated to Hollywood and founded the movie industry not far from the intersection of Hollywood and Vine. But as the industry boomed in later years, many of the studios needed more land and moved to the rural San Fernando Valley, Culver City or other suburbs. Columnists such as Louella Parsons and Hedda Hopper nurtured the myth that Hollywood and Vine was the center of the universe into the 1950s, but long before that most Hollywood stars had moved to Beverly Hills or Bel Air, Encino or Santa Monica. In the 1980s, Paramount Pictures was still there, but little else was left of the old Hollywood, and most of the community was gripped by urban decay.

Homenick was awakened late one night in early September by Inspector Bob Dighera of the San Diego Marshals Service Warrants squad. Dighera said that a millionaire Peruvian drug dealer had just tied a string of sheets together, used it to lower himself nine stories down the sheer wall of the Metropolitan Correctional Center and then disappeared. The man's girlfriend, Dighera said, lived in Hollywood, and he asked Homenick to stake out her apartment.

Homenick parked an unmarked Marshals Service surveillance van near one of the most famous landmarks of old Hollywood, Grauman's Chinese Theater (it was now called *Mann's* Chinese Theater), before dawn the next morning.

Nearby, neon signs on porno shops and all-night "adult movie" theaters leered garishly in the darkness, while hookers and teenage boys prowled Hollywood and Sunset Boulevards, offering themselves for sale.

The guy must have had guts, Homenick thought as he looked through a darkened window in the van that allowed him to see out but was opaque from the street.

Just a few days earlier, another inmate had tried the same thing, and he hadn't made it. Homenick had seen a picture of him later. There hadn't been much left after he'd fallen five stories.

The girlfriend lived in one of the few modern high-rise buildings near Hollywood Boulevard. It was conspicuous among the old Spanish-style stucco houses with their faded red-tiled roofs. When Homenick and Deputy Charley Almanza arrived at the building, they told the manager that they were telephone repairmen and got into the garage. They touched the hood of the girlfriend's car. It was warm: she might have driven him from San Diego a few hours earlier.

The sun rose above the Hollywood Hills, illuminating the newly rebuilt HOLLYWOOD sign that looked down on the community. A few tenants left the apartment building, but there was no sign of the Peruvian or his girlfriend. They waited. At 7 A.M., a radio paging device at Almanza's waist beeped. He found a pay phone and called the duty officer in downtown Los Angeles. A few moments later, he excitedly told Homenick, "A guy who claims he's Boyce called the FBI and said that he's in South Africa and wants to surrender. The Bureau wants to talk to you."

Homenick dialed the FBI office on Wilshire Boulevard in Los Angeles, sucked in his breath and asked to speak to the agent who had left the message for him. He tried to sound emotionless. The last thing he wanted was to give the FBI agent the satisfaction of thinking he had solved the case.

"The call came in at two forty A.M.," the agent said. "It was a male; sounded fairly young. He was on the line for only a couple of minutes. The first thing he said was 'My name is Christopher Boyce, and I understand you're looking for me.'

"I said, 'Yes, we are,' and he said he was tired of running and 'At three o'clock today, I'm going to turn myself in at the U.S. Embassy in Cape Town, South Africa.'

"It really didn't sound like an overseas call; sounded like he could be around the corner; but it could be authentic. I asked him where he was calling from, but he wouldn't say. He said we could reach him later by calling him at 2-1-4-2-8-3 in Cape Town. I checked, and that's the number listed for our consulate there."

If the information was correct, the agent said, Boyce would surrender in three to four hours.

The man from the Bureau said that he had already alerted FBI Headquarters in Washington about the call, and an alert had been sent by the State Department to Cape Town. Homenick's heart sank. The Bureau, he realized, was already moving in to claim credit for arranging Boyce's surrender. *They must have been working on it all night. Then, when it's all set up, they call me.*

He hung up and tried to call Kupferer, but he wasn't in his office. Kent Pekarek at Tysons Corner said he would call the State Department to be sure that the consulate was ready to receive Boyce.

Homenick arrived back at the van, waiting now for two fugitives. The beeper signaled again, and he went to the pay phone. It was Kupferer. He had returned to his office and reported that everything was under control in South Africa. He promised to call Homenick as soon as there was any news.

As the hours passed, it got warm in the van and then very hot. There was no sign of the woman or of anyone who looked like the Peruvian, and Homenick kept his eyes on his watch.

He was too anxious to eat lunch. By midafternoon, he realized that Chris should have turned himself in four hours before.

He should have heard from Tysons Corner. There had been enough time for Chuck to relay the word to him.

Finally, he decided to telephone Kupferer to find out what was going on.

Kupferer did not have good news.

"Nobody showed up in Cape Town," he said. "It looks like it was a phony."

Homenick agreed.

But he wondered why, of all the countries in the world, the prankster had chosen South Africa for his prank.

He returned to the courthouse, exchanged the van for his own car and drove home. It had been another bad day: not only was Chris a no-show in South Africa; they hadn't found the Peruvian drug dealer either.

Three days later, an FBI agent relayed a tip to Homenick from the L.A. Police Department that an informant had called a city detective and said Christopher Boyce was planning to leave on a ship from the Los Angeles harbor in the morning.

Homenick called the detective, who was assigned to the Harbor Division of the LAPD, in the port town of San Pedro. He said that a confidential informant whom he considered reliable said he had known Boyce in high school, and that he had been hiding out in Palos Verdes most of the time. He said that the police had nearly caught him several times, and he had decided to get out of the country on a freighter bound for South Africa that was scheduled to depart within a day or two.

"According to the informant," the detective said, "Boyce is supposed to show up tonight at the Lighthouse in Hermosa Beach and finish his negotiations for the trip and then get instructions on how to board the ship; he says some rich kid he grew up with arranged for it; the kid's dad owns the ship, or something like that."

The informant, he added, had promised to find out more about the rendezvous and call back.

It was four o'clock. Homenick looked around the office quickly and picked eight deputies to send to Hermosa Beach, a coastal town between the Palos Verdes Peninsula and Los Angeles International Airport that by day was popular among bathers and by night was one of Southern California's principal drug market-places. The Lighthouse was a popular jazz club a few steps from the surf.

Dressed in the old clothing that most of them kept handy for such stakeouts, the federal agents took up positions around the Lighthouse about four thirty, although it wasn't scheduled to open for several hours. Homenick remained at the courthouse, waiting to hear from the detective.

At six the detective said he hadn't heard again from the inform-ant, so Homenick joined the others in Hermosa Beach.

"Larry, look behind you. Do you see what I see?" a deputy asked.

Homenick whirled around in the front seat of the stakeout car, which was parked in an alley near the Lighthouse.

There were two young men in the alley. One dug into his pocket and produced a handful of bills; the other took the money and handed him a transparent plastic envelope. The deputies were close enough to see that it contained a white powder.

They decided to ignore the drug buy.

"The last thing we need is a bunch of cops coming down here right now," Homenick said.

By seven thirty, shadows were descending swiftly over the Pa-cific surf, rolling onto the sands of Hermosa Beach only a few yards from the Lighthouse. The beeper at Homenick's waist started chirping, and he walked to a phone booth to call his office. The L.A. detective had called, the duty officer said, and had said that while he was out, the informant had called again and left a mes-sage:

"You guys missed the meeting; it's already taken place. But Boyce is still around. He's in the white house on P.C.H."

"Which house? Where is it located?" the desk sergeant had asked.

"The white house on P.C.H. Your guys will know what I'm talking about," he said, and hung up.

The Pacific Coast Highway—the P.C.H.—runs parallel to the ocean. It is the main artery of Southern California's coastal towns, linking the surfing beaches south of Santa Barbara, the million-dollar homes that line the beach in Malibu, the old neighborhoods in Santa Monica and Redondo that Raymond Chandler wrote about a long time ago and other towns all the way south to Mexico.

Homenick hadn't the foggiest idea of which white house the informant was referring to. There were hundreds of white houses along the highway. He and two other deputies drove slowly along the P.C.H., pausing at each white house they saw and looking for anything unusual. Meanwhile, the late summer sun disappeared beneath the horizon.

At midnight, they gave up the search. As Homenick drove home, he wondered if it had been a prank. It was the kind of thing that Chris himself might have done.

The next day, officials of the Port of Los Angeles told Homenick no ships were scheduled to leave from the port for South Africa for more than a week. He called the LAPD detective and asked him if he had heard again from the informant. He said he hadn't.

There's an unwritten rule that investigators exercise exclusive proprietary rights, if they choose to, over their own snitches—not only to protect their identity but, at least incidentally, to ensure that whatever information the snitch provides benefits the investigator's career, not that of another policeman. It's a breach of etiquette for one investigator to ask for direct access to another's confidential informants; but Homenick decided to raise the question.

"We're *really* anxious to get Boyce," he told the detective. "I don't want to screw up any of your investigations, but do you think he would be willing to talk to us?"

"I've got no problem," the detective said. "But I don't know who he is. He just called here. I've never met him."

"I thought you said he was a reliable informant."

"He sounded reliable on the phone."

Three days later, a newspaper delivery supervisor for the *Los Angeles Times* took a telephone call from a man who appeared to think he was talking to a reporter. The caller said that Christopher Boyce had $15,000 and was planning to leave the country soon aboard a ship anchored at San Pedro. He said he would call back. He never did.

A few days later, when Homenick arrived for work in his office at the courthouse a few minutes past 8 A.M., there was a woman with a smile and a self-confident air that Homenick did not find appealing sitting at his desk.

"I'm waiting for Larry Homenick," she said.

"Hi. I'm Larry Homenick."

The woman introduced herself as an investigator for the California Attorney General. "I think I have some information that will help you find Christopher Boyce," she said. "I have a confidential informant who may be able to lead you right to him."

15

"I CAN'T GO INTO EVERYTHING RIGHT NOW," the woman said, "but I think he knows what he's talking about."

Homenick wondered to himself: How could *you* know that he knows what he's talking about?

"How much do you know about the case?" he asked.

"Only what he told me."

His interest began to wane.

Homenick had interviewed so many people who claimed to be able to break open the case that he was now more than skeptical. He had become more cynical than he would have thought possible nine months earlier. Still, her confidence was persuasive. He asked her to explain.

"I can't tell you any more now," she said, "but you won't be disappointed."

Without another word, she left his office.

An hour later, a Secret Service agent whom Homenick knew came to his office. "Larry," he said, "we just busted a guy on a counterfeiting case who says he knows a lot about Christopher Boyce."

When the agent said that he was working with a female investigator for the state A.G.'s office, he realized that they were talking about the same informant.

He knew his friend would be more communicative than the woman.

"What's his name?"

"Pope . . . a guy named Brent Pope. Says he knew Boyce in prison.

"He got busted over the weekend with eleven million dollars in funny money. He's on his way up from Palm Springs to be arraigned. Says he's willing to talk about Boyce."

When Homenick walked into a holding cell at the courthouse an hour later, he recognized the silver-tongued confidence man he and Howard Safir had interviewed during the first week of the investigation. Expensive clothing and Palm Springs hairstylists had done wonders for him. Instead of prison dungarees he was wearing shiny, tight slacks and a silk shirt with the three top buttons open. His hair was darker, and he'd had a permanent wave; his head was a bundle of curls. If it weren't for his mustache he would have looked like Shirley Temple. On a table, in a cellophane property bag, there was a pirate's fortune in gold—two necklaces, a huge medallion with some kind of Inca inscription, several rings and a watch.

Nine months earlier when Safir and Homenick had interviewed Pope they'd gotten nothing. Safir hadn't thought much of him. But there was a new element in the equation now: As an ex-con, Pope faced twenty years for counterfeiting. If he knew anything about Boyce, he would probably want to make a deal.

"Hi, Brent. Remember me?"

Pope looked at Homenick and squinted.

"I know I've seen you before," he said. "You look familiar, but I can't place you."

"Howard Safir and I talked to you up at Lompoc about Chris Boyce."

"Oh, sure," he said enthusiastically. "Now I remember. Say, I want to talk to you guys about Boyce."

"Fine. When you're done with your processing, let's talk."

Pope was even more friendly when they met a few hours later.

"Larry, I've got all kinds of shit that I think will help you. But you've got to help me.

"I *know* I can tell you how to find him; when we were at

M.C.C., we worked out a way to contact each other if he ever got out. I've got all kinds of stuff for you. If you'll help me."

Pope's eyes looked anxious, as if he were searching Homenick's face for a sign of interest in him. At that moment, the Secret Service agent and the woman from the Attorney General's office walked into the room and told Homenick that they had to take Pope to Palm Springs, where he was to help set up the arrest of one of his partners in the counterfeiting operation. The partner had a familiar name: Larry Harold Smith—"Big Larry"; another of Chris's friends from Lompoc. Homenick asked the woman if he could accompany them to Palm Springs, but she turned him down.

Encouraged for the first time in weeks, Homenick called Kupferer in Virginia and told him the news. They agreed that this might be the break they had been waiting for.

Then Pope disappeared.

Homenick had expected him to call the next day or to hear from one of the investigators. But the only times his phone rang were a call from Kupferer, asking for a report of his progress with Pope, and one from a woman who lived in a Los Angeles suburb to report that she had seen Christopher Boyce buying tacos at a restaurant. Three days passed, and still there was no call from Pope or the other investigators.

Homenick did some checking with friends and discovered that Pope, wearing a miniature tape recorder under his silk shirt, had had a meeting with "Big Larry" in Palm Springs and easily persuaded him to admit, on tape, that he had printed the counterfeit cash. Smith had been arrested, and, he learned, Pope had then posted bail and been released. But after that Pope's tracks disappeared. Homenick's friend from the Secret Service and the woman from the A.G.'s office refused to help: they told him only that Pope was involved in an undercover operation that they couldn't discuss with him.

Many weeks later, Homenick discovered that Pope had been placed in hiding by the Attorney General's office, first in Palm Springs and then in Las Vegas, in what was ultimately a failed attempt to penetrate a ring of organized-crime operators who commuted between the two cities.

But as he waited anxiously to talk to his promising new informant, no one told him that.

Less than a week later, on October 1, a dozen inspectors from
regional offices of the Marshals Service around the country converged on a Holiday Inn that rises from among a cluster of indus-
trial and office buildings on the edge of Chinatown in Los Angeles.
Nobody called it a posse, but in many ways, that is what it was.

In early September, Chief Inspector Thomas C. Kupferer, Jr.,
had sent each of them a copy of every investigative report that had
been written about Christopher Boyce since his disappearance on
January 21. The file weighed almost fifteen pounds and was two
feet thick. Kupferer told them to reevaluate every conclusion in the
reports, to question everything that had been done so far in the investigation.

For most of the inspectors, two puzzles emerged from the thick
mound of paper.

One was the question of whether Christopher Boyce was dead.

Most accepted as an article of faith that all fugitives, if they are
on the run for very long, leave a trail of some sort. His absence after nine months, without a single piece of evidence to show that he
was still alive, suggested that Boyce might have died somewhere in
the mountains near the prison—or that he might have gotten on a
plane shortly after the escape and flown to Russia.

The second question involved the CIA.

Some cops don't trust anybody—not their partners, not their
wives. From the beginning, many of the inspectors who gathered
at the Holiday Inn in the first week of October 1980 believed that
the escape and flight of Christopher Boyce had gone off too easily.

Kupferer emphasized that CIA officials had told him and Howard Safir that the agency had had nothing to do with the escape, and
he said he believed them.

But the possibility that another federal agency had broken one of
its agents out of prison as part of a grand scheme of deception of
which they were never to be told hovered like a cloud over the task
force, adding an unseen prism to the investigation through which

every piece of information about Boyce and the escape would have to be scrutinized.

"My guess is that he will try to avoid falconry. He's a man of considerable intelligence; it's likely he'll figure out that's exactly what we would be looking for."

The speaker was a tall, balding man in his early forties.

"However, I think there's a good chance that he'll go into something related to falconry by finding a substitute, such as flying, hang gliding or scuba diving. He seems to enjoy taking risks, and he relates closely to birds."

Kupferer had invited a psychiatrist who he knew had served as a consultant to the Los Angeles Police Department during several investigations of political terrorist organizations to prepare a psychological profile of Christopher John Boyce. A few weeks before the task force assembled, Homenick had boxed up the few items that Chris had left behind in his cell, copies of the investigative reports given to members of the task force, a copy of *The Falcon and the Snowman* and a few superficial reports about Chris made by prison psychologists and had sent them, along with a transcript of the trial, to the psychiatrist. A few days later, the doctor called to say that he had become so fascinated with Boyce that he wanted to serve as an unpaid, ex officio member of the task force. He insisted, however, on anonymity. In official records of the investigations and on tape recordings made of their meetings, he was to be referred to only as "Joe."

"Dr. Joe," as he was soon dubbed by members of the task force, explained to the investigators at their first meeting that there were gaps in what he could deduce about Boyce without a personal interview. Nevertheless, he said that he felt he understood a good deal about him. "If I could define Chris in one word, it's 'deceptive.'

"What he appears to be thinking or doing is not necessarily reality. He has a good deal of charm, which helps him manipulate people. He's got a strong ego. It appears his father is an important figure to him; his father was an achiever, and I think he'd like to outdo his father, to get recognition, even if it means becoming famous in the way he has.

"He's a type of person, I think, who will try to be the leader of whatever he does. He'll get other people to do his dirty work, as he did with Daulton Lee. He'll use people. I don't think he's violent; if he has to support himself in the underworld, I think he would probably go into something like drugs or counterfeiting. I don't think he's prone to violence or would use firearms, but he might if he were cornered. He's a fugitive to whom freedom really means something. Most people rebel at the idea of captivity: it's the natural thing to do. But Chris seems obsessed by it; that's why he started planning to escape right after he got to prison.

"His obsession with birds suggests that he relates strongly to flying, free flight. It's interesting that he chose falconry. The falcon is a loner, one of the few birds that doesn't fly in a flock; falcons depend completely on themselves to exist, and I think he's the same kind of person . . . a loner who can get by on his own without needing other people. He's smart, but he's like all of us; I think he'll make a mistake sooner or later; his ego may betray him.

"Of course, he could have fallen into a crevasse and be dead by now."

Kupferer had a decision to make: should the task force operate covertly or publicly?

Dr. Joe suggested that they go public. Christopher Boyce, he said, seemed to enjoy tweaking the nose of the Establishment. It might not work, but why not lay down a public challenge to him to see if it smokes him out?

16

HOWARD SAFIR KNEW THE QUESTION.

He had asked it himself almost every day for nine months: "Where is Christopher Boyce?"

This time, the question was directed at him in a hearing room on Capitol Hill.

"We are investigating the possibility," Safir testified, "that he is hiding out near his home in California, where he'd have the best chance of finding a support system, and we've had reports that he could have fled to Mexico, Ireland, South Africa and several other countries; we're checking them all out. So far, we've checked over a hundred leads and we're still at it."

The members and staff of the Senate Intelligence Committee, holding a classified, closed-door hearing on the disappearance of Christopher Boyce, were not impressed.

"Can you tell me what the probability is that you will ever catch Mr. Boyce?" Senator Walter Huddleston of Kentucky asked.

"I can't tell you, sir," Safir said. "All I can say is that we are applying every resource we have to finding him."

Safir did not add that he had absolutely no basis on which to make an estimate about the probability of finding Boyce because there was not a single substantive clue to his whereabouts. Nor did he admit that he was convinced the ability of the Marshals Service to survive as a bona fide law-enforcement agency might hinge on its ability to find Christopher Boyce.

* * *

Tony Perez coined the motto for the task force: *No Hay Piedra sin Vira.* No Stone Unturned.

Virtually everyone who had been interviewed in the investigation, Kupferer decided, must be interviewed again: the guards and staff at Lompoc; the convicts who knew him; the members of his family; his co-workers at TRW; his friends from childhood, high school and college. The transcript of his trial and the FBI files on his espionage activities were brought to the suite at the Holiday Inn that had become the nerve center and command post for the manhunt. A wide range of other data was brought in, including hour-by-hour meteorological reports showing weather conditions in and around Lompoc after the escape and every report of a stolen car, boat, plane or horse in Central California in the weeks after the escape. The highest priority was given to investigating several of Chris's friends who were involved in drug dealing to find a possible connection between them and Bob Merman and his contacts in Mexico; to Brent Pope and other friends in prison such as Billy Joe Simmons, the inmate who had said he was going to Russia, and Larry Harold Smith. Finding the former Rhodesian mercenary who was supposed to have served time with Boyce at Terminal Island was also high on the list. And, of course, there were Freddy Gray and the psychic, Marilyn Mitchell, wherever she was.

Nine months after his escape, Christopher Boyce had all but disappeared from the news. Kupferer saw to it that his face was seen again. On the basis of his speculation that Boyce was hiding out in Southern California, and the psychiatrist's suggestion that a challenge to his ego might bring him out of hiding, Kupferer tipped off reporters about formation of the task force and depicted Boyce as a "loser," who had remained at large for so long because he had been lucky. In interviews, Kupferer urged the public to report any information they had about Boyce to a special telephone line set up by the task force. The number was 628-CLUE.

It may have been a mistake.

How many calls were made to the CLUE line is not recorded. But there were hundreds, and they were all checked out. The posse of marshals was dispersed across the plains of Southern California.

A Los Angeles County Sheriff's Department artist made sketches of Boyce wearing dark glasses, with a mustache and with a variety of beards and hairstyles. These were distributed to local police departments and to the press.

A famed plastic surgeon who was on the faculty of the UCLA School of Medicine was interviewed about the possibility that the missing spy had changed his appearance through plastic surgery.

"In my opinion," the surgeon said as he studied the features of Christopher Boyce on a Wanted poster, "no reputable plastic surgeon would touch him."

Nevertheless, he conceded, a desperate man could go to certain places in Mexico where, for about $2,000, a plastic surgeon could give him a new face. It would take twenty minutes or so; he would probably do it, the UCLA plastic surgeon continued, by implanting silicone into Boyce's cheeks and around his chin and eyes.

He used a pencil to sketch on a Wanted poster where the silicone could be implanted and how it would create a face that was fuller and more rounded than Boyce's own features. He would not look the same.

"It would last for about five years before the silicone would start to move, and then his face would become deformed," the surgeon said. "But I suppose that would give him enough time, for his purposes."

"Larry, it's for you," someone said, holding up a telephone.

Homenick recognized the purring voice of Brent Pope.

"Larry, I'm sorry I didn't call sooner; I've been helping the Secret Service and the A.G.'s office. They wouldn't let me talk to you. I wanted to, but they wouldn't let me.

"Larry, I think they're going to burn me. I'm giving 'em all kinds of help, but I don't think they're going to do a damn thing for me. Larry, you promised to help, didn't you?"

"Brent, I meant what I said: you help us, we'll help you."

"Good deal, Larry. I'll get back to you real soon."

* * *

Each night, members of the task force met in the Holiday Inn and reviewed the day's events and, afterward, adjourned to a table in the bar downstairs.

As the days, and then the weeks, passed, Homenick was bemused. During the first few days of the task force, the out-of-towners in the group had regarded him with suspicion when he referred to "Chris." Now, as the other deputies were getting to know the fugitive through their interviews with his former neighbors and friends, they were doing the same thing—except for Tony Perez.

Homenick had had mixed feelings when Safir made the decision to establish the task force. At the least, it meant that he had failed in the assignment Safir had given him a few days after the escape. Now there was the possibility that someone else would follow up on a lead that he had overlooked and find Chris, making him look like a fool. But on the other hand, he decided, if they did find him, he would be grateful.

October 23 began routinely for the task force with a call from a woman who stated matter-of-factly that Christopher John Boyce was hiding out in the California desert with a "Manson-style gang."

When asked how she knew it, she said she was psychic and had had a dream about it. The inspector who was on duty thanked her and waited for the next call on the CLUE line.

As usual, there were several dozen calls from other people, placing Boyce in various corners of California, several other states and three foreign countries.

Two deputies boarded a Greyhound bus in Conway, Arkansas, just before noon after someone called to report that Boyce would be on the bus. He wasn't. In Los Angeles, preparations were made to impanel a grand jury to hear testimony from several of Chris's old friends who were in the drug business.

Brent Pope called again. He told Homenick that it was urgent that he intercede for him with the assistant U.S. attorney who was prosecuting the counterfeiting case. Homenick didn't tell him that he couldn't promise anything because there was a feud going on between government lawyers. The assistant U.S. attorney who was handling the Boyce investigation was in favor of making a deal with Pope if he helped find Boyce, but the prosecutor in charge of the counterfeiting case didn't want to make any deal that would let Pope escape a prison sentence for helping to counterfeit $11 million.

Lou Stefanelli and Al Villegas returned to the prison at Lompoc to interview a convicted bank robber named Eddie Mack Moore, who, prison informants claimed, had been a good friend of Boyce's before the escape.

In January, Moore had refused to talk. But in early October, he sent word to Homenick that he wanted to make a deal.

Two weeks before Boyce disappeared, Moore admitted, he had joined him and three other inmates in an escape plot which had to be aborted when someone snitched to the hacks about it.

"Did he say where he planned to go if you'd gotten out?"

"After we got out, we were all going to split. Chris said he was going to Santa Barbara, where he had a friend, and get some money. Then he was going to head for Seattle and leave the country. That's all he said."

"What was the name of the person who was going to help him?"

Moore said he didn't know.

There was a long pause. Then he reversed himself:

"I know. And I know which country and city he was going to go to. But I won't tell you until you help me. I want to get out of this place and get transferred to a state institution. This place is a madhouse."

The two deputies said they couldn't promise him anything, and the interview ended.

Homenick received a report of the interview by telephone. It had been another typical day, he thought. Mirrors, illusions, but no Boyce.

That evening, a telephone rang in a suburb of Los Angeles. The call was from Christopher Boyce.

17

"HOW YA DOIN'?"

There was silence.

"Chris?"

"Man, is it good to hear your voice."

The author of *The Falcon and the Snowman* didn't inquire where he was calling from, and Christopher Boyce didn't volunteer the information.

"I don't believe it," the author said. "Your mom and dad will be glad to know you're still alive. They thought you were dead."

Chris laughed. "Tell 'em I love 'em."

The call lasted perhaps seven minutes. Chris said he was well, that he jogged several miles a day and that he had never been happier.

"How are you surviving? Do you have money?"

"Yeah. I'm fine." There was a pause. "I've got friends. Did you ever talk to Freddy?"

"Yeah. I couldn't figure out if he's a flake or if he's for real."

Chris laughed. "He's a nice kid, a little screwed up."

"You know, he's telling everybody that the CIA broke you out of prison. And some people are saying it was the KGB."

Chris laughed again. "I did it myself. I used a dummy. We got the idea from *Escape from Alcatraz*. They showed it at the prison."

"Freddy said you went after some documents buried in Arizona after you escaped."

"Freddy makes up things."

"Where've you been?" the author asked.

"I've been everywhere. After I got out, I was out in the wild for a while; I lived on insects, berries, moss off the trees, anything I could find. I was a real Euell Gibbons. They got pretty close a few times. . . ."

"Do you know you're in the news again? They've got a task force of marshals looking for you all over town. Remember Larry Homenick? He's in charge of finding you."

Chris said he hadn't heard about the task force.

"Chris, I'm going to have to tell them you called."

"Wish you wouldn't."

"Aren't you worried about making a call?"

"I hope your line's not bugged. It doesn't matter; I'm leaving here in a few minutes. I'll be gone. I'm getting out of here." The impression he left was that he was at an airport, ready to jump onto a plane.

"Chris, I really will have to tell 'em about you calling."

"Do what you have to do. I gotta go now. God, it's good to hear your voice again. Do what you have to do."

The phone call had an electrifying effect on the men who were searching for Christopher Boyce.

As Chuck Kupferer would recall many months later, "Until the phone call, we didn't even know he was alive. We didn't have a damn thing. He changed from being a ghost to a fallible individual who wanted to make contact with his old life. It showed he could make a mistake, and it stimulated everybody. If he hadn't made the phone call, we might have run out of gas."

"Well, I guess the theory that Chris fell in a crevasse was wrong," Dr. Joe joked at a hastily called meeting of the task force less than two hours after the telephone call.

He was convinced that Chris had taken the bait the task force had set out for him. Regardless of what he had said on the telephone, he must know about the task force and must have called to taunt the people who were looking for him and the Establishment that he despised. They would be wise, Dr. Joe added, to believe nothing that he had said during the call.

"I find it difficult to believe that Chris engineered the escape by himself and lived off of berries," he said, as spools of a tape recorder rotated on a table in front of him.

"That may be true," he continued, "but right now I find that less appealing than the fact that he had assistance and he made it and he left the Lompoc area as soon as possible. I just prefer to assess the facts in this way and put it together this way, but recognizing that I could be wrong, I would, right now, tend to believe that he was still in the L.A. area. Either he heard or read about the task force or was informed by his friends, and this call to Lindsey was Chris's way of attempting to throw us off the trail with the idea that he's leaving the area."

News reports about the telephone call generated dozens of new tips about the fugitive's whereabouts, and morale soared on the task force. They had blasted Boyce out of hiding, and with new energy, they moved out to find him.

Tony Perez, Lou Stefanelli and all the other deputies who had spent days slogging through the muddy hills behind the prison trying to track his footprints or find other evidence of him in the wilderness said they agreed with Dr. Joe. As far as they were concerned, he hadn't been there. It seemed impossible. He would have been spotted; he couldn't have survived alone for more than a few days without food. The claim that he had done so was probably a ruse to take them off the scent. But the next morning they were warned not to make so quick a judgment.

"Last year there was an exceptionally good acorn crop, and there's plenty of water up there," a senior ranger in Los Padres National Forest told Stefanelli. "There are some pretty rugged, isolated areas up there where someone with experience in the outdoors could probably support himself for several months pretty easily on acorns, berries, wild lettuce and other plants. If he didn't mind the blandness of the diet, a person could probably live indefinitely on these plants. He would be competing with other creatures of the forest and would have to keep moving to find more food, and he'd have to deal with a lot of psychological stress, living in isolation like that; but it's possible.''

As Stefanelli was talking to the park ranger, Mrs. Noreen Boyce told Inspectors Bob Dighera and Larry Hattersley at her home in Palos Verdes that she was happy, naturally, to know that her eldest son was still alive. But she said to them what she had said to Larry Homenick many times since January 21: ''I have no idea where he is.''

''Would it be like Chris to make contact with Bob Lindsey now to challenge us and say, 'Here I am. I'm really not dead; I really haven't left the country; I'm here'?'' Hattersley asked.

'' 'Come and get me'?''

''No, not necessarily 'Come and get me,' but just kind of a challenge?''

''Well, you know, Chris was a great one for climbing up the tallest tree. If there was a bird that nobody else had caught, or nobody else had climbed the tree, he'd climb it. If the bird was up on a cliff, he'd climb the cliff. Once he went out on a hemp rope and climbed out to get a bird and put it in his pocket; he's moving out on the rope and he starts sliding down, burned all the flesh off his hands, fell in poisonous sumac. I had to take him to the hospital. Another time, he fell out of a forty-foot tree up in Santa Maria, and fortunately he fell on a wet riverbed with a lot of leaves on it, and he compressed his fourth and fifth vertebrae; but I mean, he would take a chance. I know of three times when he fell, but I can't tell you how many other times he didn't fall. So maybe there's something to the possibility that he's asking to be caught; but you know, I don't believe it.''

Dighera asked how she thought her eldest son would react if he was cornered.

''I think Chris would take his own life if threatened rather than go back. Maybe I'm completely and totally wrong, but it was such a devastation to him, and degrading, and you know what goes on in those places for a kid. And we're just plain, ordinary people. We're not wealthy. We're not pretentious. This was a part of life that Chris was not familiar with. He wasn't in on this corruption until this Daulton Lee thing. I mean, we had a good, moral, Christian, loving family. He's not a violent person. He's very tender and very caring, and I really do not feel that he would try and maim or kill or harm somebody if he was cornered and there was no way out. I think that he would kill himself rather than that."

At almost the same moment that Hattersley and Dighera were saying good-bye to Mrs. Boyce, an anonymous telephone call was made to the prison at Lompoc.

"Please listen to me carefully," the caller told the duty officer.

"Christopher Boyce is hiding out near San Diego; he had friends who are planning on taking him over the border into Mexico tomorrow. He's with a man named Norm Black who hates cops and has had a lot of trouble with the police, and he's going to give Boyce an M-16 rifle when they go into Mexico."

Boyce, he said, would be either at Black's home in San Diego or at the home of a friend who had done time with him at Lompoc. The man's name, the caller said, was Marvin Thomas.

He gave the duty officer an address in a suburb of San Diego where he said Boyce was hiding, and then he hung up. The duty officer called Stefanelli in Santa Maria, and within hours a raiding party was being organized to go after the fugitive they all wanted to find in San Diego.

18

CHUCK KUPFERER WAS IN TYSONS CORNER AND furious that he had chosen this weekend for a hurried trip to headquarters to review investigations that were under way elsewhere in the country. He advised Howard Safir about the call and said that the task force had determined that Marvin Leroy Thomas had served time at Lompoc when Boyce was there and that Thomas had a close friend, Norman Black, with a long record of firearms arrests. It appeared, Kupferer and Safir agreed, that the strategy designed to smoke Boyce out of hiding had worked. Of course, they did not know then about Marvin Leroy Thomas.

Within three hours of the call, Inspector Bob Dighera had rousted a U.S. magistrate from his bed in San Diego and obtained a warrant to search the suburban San Diego home that Black shared with his parents.

Before dawn the next morning, a Sunday, almost a dozen deputy U.S. marshals armed with automatic weapons and the paramilitary Special Weapons and Tactics (SWAT) team of the San Diego County Sheriff's Department raided the home of Norman Black as a police helicopter hovered several hundred feet in the sky.

The tip received at Lompoc, coming so soon after Chris's phone call, had convinced Homenick and Kupferer, who jointly coordinated the operation from Los Angeles and Tysons Corner, that they had found him.

Instead, all they found was a great deal of embarrassment.

Homenick, tired and anxious after a night without sleep, got the news in a short phone call from Tony Perez:

"He wasn't there, Larry; if he was ever there, he got away."

The next day, the Associated Press reported from San Diego:

> A 64-year-old woman with an aged, ailing husband says officers with "machine guns pointed at us" stormed their home in a futile search for escaped spy Christopher Boyce. She said they were awakened by a telephone call and "someone told me in a very loud, nasty voice that the house was surrounded and ordered that everyone should walk out with their hands up. I have severe high blood pressure and was terribly worried about my husband. He's very ill, senile and virtually confined to bed."

The failure of the raid, after spirits had soared so high, plunged the task force into depression.

In fact, the anonymous tip had come from Marvin Thomas himself. He had invented the story that Boyce was at his friend's home. And it was not the last tip from him that the U.S. Marshals Service would pursue in its search for Christopher John Boyce. He peppered newspapers, television stations and federal and local police agencies with anonymous calls and tips that led them onto false trails. He had never met Boyce, but after reading a book about him, Marvin Thomas had decided that he was the alter ego of Christopher Boyce, and he had set upon a plan to help him stay free.

On Monday morning, members of the task force, depressed and tired, arrived at the Federal Courthouse in Los Angeles. They looked silently at each other; then, slowly, they began asking one another what they should do next.

The only thing to do, they decided, was go over the old material again and look for something they had missed before; and, of course, there were tips still flooding the CLUE line . . . calls from health-food stores reporting what seemed like a startling number of people who looked like Boyce that used Thompson's Coach's Formula vitamins . . . from a retired CIA employee who said he had met a stranger in the High Sierras who liked mountain climbing,

112

followed the Pritikin diet, drove a yellow Volkswagen and looked like Boyce . . . from a policeman in Sheridan, Wyoming, who said someone who looked like Christopher Boyce had robbed a local bank of $20,000 . . . from an elderly nurse in Long Beach who called to say that when she had been in Seattle the previous May she had seen a young man with "electrifying blue eyes" who was unquestionably Christopher Boyce. When they neared the bottom of their list of old leads, they launched a new campaign to find Marilyn Mitchell, the psychic who had called from the Broken Egg restaurant in Santa Barbara before disappearing. Meanwhile, another psychic appeared at the task-force headquarters and announced that Christopher Boyce was being hidden out in San Diego County by members of a religious cult and when he went out in public he wore women's clothing. Meanwhile, there was still more digging to do among the inmates who had known him in prison.

Eddie Mack Moore sent word to Homenick that he wanted to talk.

Moore was the bank robber who three weeks earlier had told Lou Stefanelli and Al Villegas that he was convinced he knew where Boyce would go after the escape because Boyce had confided it during preparations for an earlier escape plan which had to be abandoned. Moore had said Boyce would make his way to Seattle and then a foreign country, but then he refused to identify the country. Moore had been transferred from Lompoc to the federal penitentiary at Lewisburg, Pennsylvania. Asking prison officials to relay his message, Moore sent word to Homenick that he was now willing to talk because members of the Mexican Mafia, one of the gangs that run life in most American penitentiaries, had put out a contract on his life because they claimed he was a snitch. If the marshals helped him get transferred to another prison, he said he would tell them Boyce's destination.

Much of what he told Inspector Joe Gaughan at the Lewisburg prison was familiar. He recalled how he, Boyce and three other inmates had had to abort their escape from Lompoc in early January after a snitch turned them in and that during the planning for the break Chris had said that he intended to head for Seattle if they got away. He had wanted, Moore said, to become a spy again, and after reaching Seattle, he was going to make his way to Russia.

Inspector Roger Archiga was a large, soft-spoken man with such an easygoing style that it bordered on shyness. He had a reputation for having a quick mind and was considered one of the best investigators in the Marshals Service. Kupferer had imported him from Minneapolis for the task force. In reviewing the growing file of interviews in the case, Archiga began to notice what he regarded as a pattern suggesting that Boyce might have fled into the Pacific Northwest or points farther north. Freddy Gray, Boyce's last contact in prison, lived near Seattle; there was scuttlebutt among the inmates that Gray had asked his family to help Boyce. And several inmates said they had heard Chris talk about heading for Washington, Canada, Alaska or the Soviet Union.

Archiga decided to reinterview Billy Joe Simmons, the lifer who was close to Boyce at Terminal Island and had said, when he was interviewed in February at the Nevada State Prison, that Chris was going to make his way to the Soviet Union. Simmons was the inmate who had made the cryptic remark that when Boyce got to Russia "the whole world will know it" and then refused to say any more.

Simmons was now in Folsom, a California penitentiary tucked away in the dry, rolling foothills of the High Sierras not far from the spot on the American River where gold was discovered in 1848 and touched off the California Gold Rush.

When Archiga and Inspector Tony Sereda arrived at Folsom, Simmons balked at seeing them.

But after an hour, he sent out a message: he said he would talk if the Feds agreed to help him get his sentence reduced—and that if there was a cash reward for Boyce and his information helped find him, he got a piece of it.

Archiga promised to help if Simmons told them something that they didn't already know, and the interview began.

Simmons recounted his earlier story about having joined with

Boyce in an aborted escape plot when they were in Terminal Island, and said:

"Chris told me that if we got out of T.I. he could get some money from the Russians to help him travel. He said they couldn't help him pull off the escape in any way, but if we got out of the country, they would take care of us in Russia."

"How was it going to work?"

"After we got out, we were going to hide out with a friend of Chris's in L.A. for a while, then go north to Alaska."

Once they reached Alaska, he said, they were going to make their way to the Aleutian Islands and hijack a small plane and force the pilot to fly across the Bering Strait to Siberia, across an island called Big Diomede.

"Do you think he would still try to do that?"

"Definitely, but only if he had to, if he was forced into it. He really loves his family and probably wouldn't want to cut himself off from them. He likes the freedom in the United States. And I don't think he has the makeup to hijack a plane with a gun. I think he'd know it was the absolute final decision and there wouldn't be any turning back. But I think he'd do it as a last resort, definitely."

Archiga's tape recorder jammed, and he paused to adjust it.

"When you were at T.I., did you ever hear of a white mercenary from South Africa or Rhodesia that Boyce might have known?" Archiga asked.

Simmons thought a moment.

"That would be Riley. He was at T.I. for selling a phony Luger that he claimed belonged to Hermann Goering. Got several thousand bucks for it."

"Do you remember his first name?"

"No."

"Do you remember much about him?"

"Intelligent, but a little crazy. Hated blacks. I heard he went to Georgetown University. Chris and he had opposite personalities, though. I don't think they were close. Chris was more quiet and interested in books. Personally, I think if you're going to find Boyce you have to think of him as an intellectual, not as a criminal who needs liquor, women and dope."

On their way back to Los Angeles, the two deputies were jubilant. They had found the South African connection, or so it seemed. Archiga called Bob Dighera at the task-force command post in Los Angeles, and within a few hours Dighera had confirmed that an inmate named Frank Burton Riley had been at T. I. in 1977 at the same time Boyce was there.

The prison's records indicated he had been transferred from Terminal Island to the federal prison at Leavenworth, Kansas, in early 1978. From there Archiga traced him to a state prison at Thomaston, Maine, where he had been sent to serve a federal sentence for stabbing a prisoner in a fight. He had been sent there because that prison had relatively few blacks and Riley, because he had a reputation for hating blacks, was considered unsafe in a federal prison. When Archiga checked with officials in Maine, he learned that Riley had been released in December 1979, listing his forwarding address as South Africa, his occupation as "soldier of fortune" and his next of kin as Frank Burton Riley, Sr., Tenafly, New Jersey.

Archiga asked Inspector Joe Heil in Trenton to see what he could learn about Riley in New Jersey. Then he asked Janice Brown-Martin, a deputy in Anchorage, Alaska, to warn FAA, state police and airport officials in the state that Christopher John Boyce might attempt to hijack a plane in Alaska to be flown to the Soviet Union.

Within a few days, Wanted posters were hammered up on the walls of airport hangars from the Canadian border to the Arctic Circle, marked with a special warning: "BOYCE MAY BE SUICIDAL, WILL NOT SURRENDER, BUT WILL ATTEMPT TO FLEE."

Within hours of the request from Archiga, Heil had discovered a few essentials about Frank Burton Riley, Jr.: he was a thirty-seven-year-old native of New Jersey who had a criminal record several pages long, had served as a mercenary soldier in the Rhodesian Light Infantry in the early 1970s and sometimes used the alias of "Schmeiser."

The day after Archiga and Dighera made the connection in California, Heil knocked a the door of a modest frame house on a tree-lined street in Tenafly, and an elderly woman answered the door. She explained that her husband, Frank Riley, Sr., had recently died, although her son, Frank, Jr., was upstairs.

116

A man in his late thirties with curly brown hair came down the stairs. Heil sensed that he was nervous. It wasn't an unusual response from an ex-convict who was being visited by a policeman.

"I'll be glad to help you, but I really don't know much about Boyce," Riley said. "I knew Boyce when I was at Terminal Island in '77. We were in the same unit."

"Did he ever mention escaping?"

"Everybody in prison talks about escaping; he may have, but I don't remember him specifically ever talking about it. The only thing he talked about, most of the time, was falcons. He was a friendly guy who made friends with everybody. That's really about all I know."

In Los Angeles, members of the task force were not satisfied with the answers; they asked Heil to return the next day.

"How easy would it be to get into South Africa without papers?" Heil asked on his second visit.

"I really don't know. I couldn't tell you. I have no experience at that."

Riley spoke with a curious accent—part nasal twang from northern New Jersey and part clipped European.

"If Boyce made it to South Africa, where could he get employment?"

"I don't know, but it wouldn't be difficult."

"If Boyce ended up as a mercenary, would they tolerate him knowing his background?"

"No, of course not; but it would be hard for them to find out."

"What is his chance of survival in South Africa?"

"Good."

"What do you know about the Orange Free State? Is it white-ruled, and is it easy for an American to wander around?"

"It's part of South Africa and it's anti-Communist. But it's easy to wander around there. I've done it. I was there for a couple of weeks."

Again, Riley said he didn't have a clue to Boyce's current whereabouts, but said if he had to place a bet on it, he'd guess

Boyce had gone to a European country like Italy or Sweden. There, he said, English-speaking immigrants can easily blend into the population and get lost.

Later the same day, FBI officials in San Diego dispatched a message to FBI Headquarters in Washington. It said that a confidential informant who had been incarcerated with Christopher John Boyce at the Metropolitan Correctional Center in San Diego in 1978 prior to his transfer to Lompoc wanted to discuss Boyce with the FBI, and was refusing to discuss the case with representatives of any other agency:

> THE INFORMANT SAID THAT HE CAN FURNISH THE IDENTITY OF INDIVIDUALS WHO FURNISHED BOYCE FALSE IDENTIFICATION WHICH HE MAY PRESENTLY BE USING; LOCATIONS OF MONEY DROPS WHERE BOYCE RECEIVES MONEY FROM UNNAMED SOURCES; THE LOCATION OF A SAFE HOUSE BOYCE IS POSSIBLY USING; THE NAME AND LOCATION OF A FAMILY IN MEXICO ASSISTING BOYCE AND FINALLY A METHOD FOR RUNNING A NEWSPAPER AD TO WHICH BOYCE WOULD RESPOND.

Sitting at his desk in Los Angeles, Larry Homenick put down the telephone, laughed and turned to Tony Perez:

"That was the Bureau. They've got an informant who they claim can break the Boyce case wide open, but the guy doesn't want to talk to the Marshals Service. Guess who it is."

"Who?"

"Good old Brent Pope."

Pope, unhappy that he hadn't yet been able to cut a deal with the Marshals Service, was now trying to trade the same information to the FBI.

"He's like a rug merchant," Homenick said. They laughed, and Tony finished packing for a visit to Captain Midnight.

19

"IF BOYCE IS NOT IN MEXICO, THEN HE'S A fool," Robert Merman, former daredevil of the Mexican skies, told Inspectors Tony Perez and Andrew Snyder in a drafty office in the Missouri State Highway Patrol barracks at Jefferson City on the morning of November 6, 1980. Merman had been brought there from the nearby state prison where he was serving twenty years. Captain Midnight had found religion and repentance in prison, and he told the two inspectors that his friend Richard Drummond, the Kansas City pimp whose plea for help had put him back in jail, had persuaded him to reveal everything he knew about Christopher Boyce.

"Basically, I taught Chris everything I knew," Merman began, as the spools of a portable cassette tape recorder whirled quietly on a desk. "We had almost four months together in San Diego, and I taught him everything I knew about smuggling drugs and living in Mexico. He said to me, 'I'm not going to spend forty years in here; I'm either going to escape or die trying,' and he meant it. He was a nice kid, highly intelligent, certainly not your normal convict, and I took a liking to him. He pumped me, and I taught him all I knew. I gave him the names of all my contacts. These are people who would give him absolute protection if they knew he was my friend. I told Chris they would love to have someone like him, an American who could market the dope and bring back their money. I was

119

washed up. I told him he could take my place; what I told him was enough to make him a *kingpin* in smuggling."

The interview lasted more than eight hours over two days. Merman drew detailed maps of ranches and remote airstrips tucked away in the mountains of rural Mexico to which he had directed Chris and where he had told him he would never be found. He gave the deputies names of his former partners in Mexico, ranchers, businessmen, judges, corrupt soldiers and other people he knew. "I told him, 'As long as you keep your mouth shut, people won't care who you are.' That's the kind of place it is. I don't know of a better place in the world where a man who wanted to get lost could hide out."

Merman's long hair was now almost completely gray. He was forty-three, but he looked like a sixty-year-old hippie. He walked with a limp, and he looked weary, except when he interrupted his narrative to tell the deputies about his newfound love for Jesus and to express his sadness and remorse for wasting his life before he found Him.

"If he's not in Mexico," he repeated, "he's a fool, because he would never get caught there.

"But sometimes I've wondered whether he'd actually go there; I know he'd like the money, but I don't know if hiding out down there would fit his personality. It wasn't what he really *wanted* to do."

What Chris really wanted to do, Merman said, was become a spy again.

"Chris claimed that the documents he sold to the Russians really didn't do any harm to the country. He hated both the CIA and the KGB, and he had this plan to screw up the world intelligence system by selling forged information to different countries."

."Do you think he had any documents hidden on the outside?"

"I think he said once that he had some documents left over someplace that were outdated, but mostly he said he was going to manufacture secrets, using microdots and microfilm, and then recruit people to serve as couriers to sell the information to foreign consulates and embassies. He said the intelligence community would just gobble it up."

"Did he expect to make money out of it?"

"He said if he made money, 'fine,' but mostly he wanted the money to move his people around the world. He was going to start by giving the foreign agents a taste—for instance, he'd give people in the Middle East a taste of things they may want to hear from Russia and China and give the people in Australia a taste of what *they* wanted to hear. He thought he could destroy the intelligence community, because people would no longer know what was real and what wasn't real."

Perez tried to fix the point in time at which Boyce would have made these plans. It was the middle of 1978, when he and Merman had known each other at the Metropolitan Correctional Center in San Diego, more than a year after his arrest and more than a year before his escape. It was a preposterous thought: an escaped spy trying to sell fabricated secrets to the intelligence services of the world.

But then, he thought, it was preposterous that two Americans not long out of high school could even get access to some of his adopted country's most prized secrets and then sell them to the Russians.

"If you ask me, their whole espionage caper was clumsy and asinine," Merman said. "I don't think he'd even be worth chasing now if it weren't for the fact he wants to do it again."

Merman said that he'd liked Chris so much that he'd promised, if he ever got out of prison, to help him get out, and he would have done it if he hadn't had his trouble in Kansas City.

"We were going to wait until he was transferred to an institution with a yard big enough for a helicopter to come down in. Chris had read someplace about a Bureau of Prisons regulation that says guards aren't supposed to shoot at a helicopter because there may be hostages inside. I was going to get a Mexican fella I know who knows how to fly a helicopter to pick him up, and Chris said he would be able to get some money to pay for the escape. Unfortunately, I had some trouble of my own before I could do anything for Chris. I felt bad about it, but he got out without me."

"Did he ever mention anything to you about hijacking a plane in Alaska and flying to Russia?"

"No, I don't think he'd go to Russia under any circumstances. He hates the KGB as much as he hates the CIA."

Perez turned off the tape recorder. He told Merman that the Marshals Service would report his cooperation to Missouri officials.

"God bless you," Captain Midnight said.

Larry Homenick looked with amusement at the thick file sent to him by the FBI. Brent Pope obviously knew how law-enforcement people think. He had been trying to play off one agency against the other. After the assistant U.S. attorney who was prosecuting the counterfeiting case had resisted giving Pope probation and said that he should go to jail, Homenick had told him that he couldn't guarantee probation. Pope had sent a six-page letter to the FBI offering to help the Bureau find Christopher Boyce and asking the Bureau's help in obtaining probation. The tone of the report prepared by the FBI agents who had been sent to interview Pope indicated they believed he knew something about the escape.

"Living together in an area six feet by ten feet for any period of time you get to know someone pretty good," Pope had written to the FBI. *"After the time I spent with Chris I knew him better than I did friends I had known for five years on the outside."*

Pope depicted Christopher Boyce as a man possessed by the thought of escape from the moment they met at the Metropolitan Correctional Center in 1978. Chris was so obsessed, he wrote, that he evaluated everything he touched for its possible utility in an escape. Once he had decided that if he had enough dental floss, he could drop it ten stories down the side of the prison and use it to lift up rope tied to it by a friend, and then use the rope to rappel himself down the wall of the skyscraper like a cat burglar. He had even tried to smuggle a gun into the prison. *"I told people at M.C.C. that Chris Boyce would escape, one way or the other; he just spent too much time planning it. He was totally obsessed with getting his freedom at all costs, even if it meant his loss of life in the process."*

After several months, the letter from Pope continued, Chris had confided to him that the full magnitude of his espionage scheme had never come out before. Besides selling secrets to the Soviet Union, he said, he had also sold CIA secrets to Communist China.

Also, he said that Daulton Lee had not been the only one involved in the espionage.

"*He told me the Russians, along with the Chinese, had an appetite to buy anything at all. He referred to the computerized cards programming the KH-11 surveillance satellite, a simple card with a date in one corner and a simple 'N.S.A.' for the National Security Agency. He told me he made them up and would give them half and sell the other half anywhere from $5,000 to $50,000. He said he had several couriers prior to Daulton. He referred to himself as the center of a wagon wheel, with the outlying spokes as information routes. He told me for the most part he only used a courier very few times because the K.G.B. agent contact would try to turn them very quickly. . . .*"

Pope said that he and Boyce had devised a method to communicate with each other using coded messages in newspaper advertisements; he was ready to discuss it, along with other important things about Christopher Boyce, if the FBI helped him get probation for his counterfeiting arrest. Pope said he doubted that Boyce would respond to the ad, but it was possible that he might. "*I don't feel any law enforcement official will ever get close to Chris. I have a feel for Chris I don't think any one reading reports could get, not knowing him. I don't feel that Chris is that far away!!!!*"

The FBI, however, following procedure, sent the file on Brent Pope to the Marshals Service.

Homenick and Perez found Pope living in an expensive condominium apartment overlooking a golf course in Palm Springs. Outside was a long Lincoln limousine that he had leased, along with a Rolls-Royce; inside, the silver-tongued Brent Pope, laden with gold, said, "Larry, I *know* I can help you find Chris."

Pope was still fighting attempts to return him to prison. He was now free on bail, but his lifestyle, his cars and his gold were in jeopardy. He had pleaded guilty to the counterfeiting charge and was scheduled to be sentenced soon. His only hope of staying out of prison was persuading the judge to give him probation, and for that he needed a recommendation for leniency from the Justice Department. Concealing his disappointment that the FBI had turned him over to the Marshals Service, he said, "It's going to take a lot of work, but you're good, Larry, and I can help you find him."

For the next three hours, Pope retold the story he had presented in his letter. The only thing he added was that besides going to Mexico, Chris had talked about hiding out in Costa Rica, Chad, Bali and South Africa.

"My guess," he said, speaking slowly for emphasis, "is that Chris is living in Southern California, dealing drugs."

He had spent months, Pope confirmed, at the San Diego prison being tutored about smuggling and where to hide out in Mexico by an inmate with the improbable name of Captain Midnight, who had promised to break him out of prison using a helicopter.

"Now I've helped you; you've got to help me."

"Brent, like we said before: if you help us find Chris, we'll help you."

During the two-hour drive back to Los Angeles, Homenick and Perez went over their conversation with Pope feeling a mixture of satisfaction and uneasiness. Pope was desperate and had known Boyce well. But they didn't believe he had told them everything he knew.

"You know," Homenick said as their car headed north through Riverside, the town on the edge of the California desert where Chris had been arrested for espionage almost four years earlier, "it sounds like he knows a lot, and maybe he does; but when you analyze it, he hasn't given us a lot we don't already know. We already knew about Captain Midnight. He could have made up some of the other stuff. But who knows what he's holding back? Maybe he's giving us just enough so we'll help him get probation but is keeping quiet about the stuff that will really help us."

Then the conversation turned to other things. In two days, they were going to attend a wedding.

20

OF HIS EIGHT BROTHERS AND SISTERS, CHRISTOpher Boyce had been closest to his sister Barbara, who was five years younger. She had always shared some of his irreverence for convention and authority, and when they were both children, they had sometimes collaborated in family pranks. In the autumn of 1980, the men and women who were pursuing Christopher Boyce had decided that if he were ever to come out of hiding, it would be to attend her wedding, which was scheduled to take place on November 22 at St. John Fisher, the family parish in Palos Verdes.

The wedding was followed by a reception at the Elks Club in San Pedro, the port town situated between Terminal Island and the southern flank of the Peninsula, and along with the wedding party and their guests, several teams of deputy U.S. marshals were at the reception. Tony Perez, wearing workman's coveralls, patrolled the fringes of the reception posing as a maintenance man. Larry Homenick, to ensure that he wasn't spotted by Chris, took a place at the bar where he could keep an eye on the reception from a distance. Deputies Jan Axthelm and Jim Moss, posing as a married couple, mingled with the guests. Other deputies were staked out in cars nearby. On a hill overlooking the Elks Club, Deputies Bob Dighera and Gerald Smith sat in Smith's Ford pickup truck and watched the building through a starlight scope, an electronic device that amplified dim light and helped surveillance teams penetrate the darkness.

In the months after he began looking for Chris, Homenick had found himself unconsciously studying the faces of people wherever he went—in airports, on the street, in supermarket checkout lines or in the lobbies of movie theaters on those rare nights that he was able to steal from the investigation for an evening out with Karen. Now, as he sat at the bar of the Elks Club, drinking beer and talking to the lodge brothers, it was second nature to keep up a conversation while his eyes explored the crowd. All he could see was a large and seemingly joyous Boyce family and relatives of the bridegroom, and it pleased him that despite the troubles and embarrassment Chris had caused his family, everybody seemed to be having a good time. In fact, he found himself enjoying the music and the warmth of a close family, even as a spectator.

Outside, almost a dozen sets of eyes were on the entrances to the Elks building, but as the evening progressed, the only thing of interest anyone noticed was a succession of young couples leaving the wedding reception for a romantic interlude in their cars.

Gerald Smith was a large man with a gaunt face, intelligent dark eyes, metal-rimmed eyeglassses and a stark bald pate that some of his friends compared to Yul Brynner's. Some called him "Skull." Others called him "Grand Jury Gerry," a reflection of his proclivity for handing out grand-jury subpoenas to anyone who refused to answer his questions.

Like Smith, Bob Dighera had been assigned to the task force from the San Diego office of the Marshals Service. And probably more keenly than any other member of the agency except Larry Homenick, he had made finding Christopher Boyce a personal obsession.

Dighera had the kind of physical presence that made people look him over almost by reflex when he entered a room. He stood well over six feet, weighed 250 pounds and had the thick shoulders of a National Football League linebacker. His dark salt-and-pepper hair was curled in a rich harvest of ringlets, matching a bushy mustache that curled several inches down both cheeks. Dighera was a native of Fresno, in the San Joaquin Valley of Central California. After attending college briefly and getting married, he had spent a year in Vietnam as door gunner on a medical evacuation helicopter. When he came home, after being wounded, in 1971, he had been unable to afford to return to college and had begun looking for a job. Impressed, like Tony Perez, with the frontier glories set forth in recruiting brochures, he had joined the Marshals Service in Fresno and prepared to hunt desperados. Instead, he had found himself transporting prisoners in his car between the county jail and the Federal Courthouse at 10 cents a mile.

Some people who work in large bureaucracies adapt easily to the conformity and discipline of an organization, the necessary tolerance of red tape and others' inefficiencies and the need to follow an order even when it is unreasonable. Dighera was not that kind of person. Before he had been in the Marshals Service very long, he had acquired a reputation as an impatient rebel against the encrusted old bureaucracy, interested more in results than in form. In Fresno, it didn't take him long to get himself assigned to the district's small fugitive detail. Dighera was so good at hunting down fugitives in the San Joaquin Valley that he was soon transferred to the larger office at San Diego with orders to establish a fugitive squad. San Diego was soon achieving one of the highest rates of apprehensions in the Service.

But success made Dighera more impatient for improvements in the agency. He saw how the better-paid FBI agents wasted money on investigations while the Marshals Service had to do everything on a shoestring. After an agent from the Bureau interviewed a witness, he went back to his office and dictated his report into a recorder and it was neatly transcribed by a stenographic pool. When Dighera had to file a report, *he* typed it. Still, Dighera believed that the Marshals Service was on its way to reclaiming its old importance as a front-line federal law-enforcement agency.

When Christopher Boyce went over the fence at Lompoc in January, Dighera, like Howard Safir, had felt instinctively that the case would be a watershed in the evolution of the agency. Now, ten months later, he was perplexed and depressed by their utter failure to make any progress. Over drinks at the Holiday Inn, Dighera had said, again and again, that it shouldn't be difficult to find a twenty-seven-year-old prison escapee who had been arrested only once in

127

his life, who had no street smarts and had grown up in the cushioned shelter of a suburban paradise.

For several months, Dighera had been pursuing leads on his own. There had been a few promising ones, but they had taken him nowhere. When he heard that Kupferer was organizing a special task force to find Boyce, he had volunteered for it. Now, after more than a month, and more and more leads that had turned to dust, he was feeling the same frustrations and failure that had haunted Homenick, He was also beginning to feel a compelling curiosity about the man they were seeking. What puzzled him most was that as each day passed, and he interviewed more people who had known him before he went to prison, absolutely *no one* said anything unfavorable about Boyce. Friends, members of his family, almost everyone who knew Boyce described him as likable, hardworking and charming—the least likely man in town to become a Russian spy. Dighera thought of himself as a patriot, and what little he knew about what Boyce had done as a Soviet agent made him loathe him. But sometimes, after a long day of interviews that carried him into the world Boyce had once inhabited, he felt at odds with himself, unable to put into focus the picture of Chris presented by the people who knew him and the reality of his treasonous acts. For the first time in his career, Dighera had begun referring to a fugitive by his first name. But more than that, he had become consumed by his desire to find Chris Boyce. Many months later, he observed, "I broke a rule: I got wrapped up in him personally."

"Look," Dighera now said to Gerry Smith.

A van was approaching the Elks Club. In the front seat there were two dark-haired young men, one of whom, through the starlight scope, looked like Christopher Boyce.

The van slowed and edged past the building, as if the driver were looking for a parking place. He suddenly accelerated and sped away.

The two federal agents looked at each other. Quickly they attached a magnetized red light to the top of the pickup truck, and the truck surged forward. A few blocks later, they pulled in behind the van, and responding to the red light, it stopped. The young men got out. Neither was Boyce, and the rear of the van was empty.

The pursuit of the van was the only moment of excitement that night. At about the same time that the musicians in the band were packing up their instruments to go home, the deputies also decided to go to bed.

Brent Pope's betrayal of Larry Harold Smith, his partner in the counterfeiting scheme, had finally started to thaw the federal prosecutor's adamant insistence that he go to jail for his part in the scheme to distribute millions of dollars in counterfeit money. The prosecutor was now assured of Smith's conviction. If Pope really helped on the Boyce case, the prosecutor said, he was willing to consider recommending to the judge in the counterfeiting case that Pope be given probation, not a prison sentence.

Homenick was hesitant about making a deal. Pope was a glib salesman who knew how to manipulate the justice system. Did he really know how to contact Boyce, or was he trying to bargain his way out of a prison sentence by dangling an illusion? There was an even more perplexing problem: supposing he *did* know where Boyce was—how could Homenick be sure that Pope had told him everything he knew?

Pope, announcing that he knew how to prove himself, volunteered to take a lie-detector test. The test, he said, would prove that he *was* telling Homenick everything, that he knew a way to make contact with Boyce and that he was sincere in his promise to work closely in the weeks ahead to help run him down.

"Let me prepare you for this guy," Homenick told a polygrapher from the Los Angeles County Sheriff's Department before Pope arrived from Palm Springs for the test. "He's your consummate con man; he'll come in here with his shirt open at least three buttons down his chest, he'll be wearing more gold than you've ever seen and he'll try to charm your feet off you."

"I get a lot of guys who think they can fool the machine," said the man who would administer the test, "but not many do."

Watching them an hour later through a one-way glass, Homenick was reminded of two street hustlers trying to outscheme each other at an open-air market.

"Those fucking Feds; can you believe they're making such a federal case out of this young kid?" the Sheriff's Department sergeant asked. "I don't have time for this shit, I'm used to dealing with big cases—murders, *multiple murders,* things like that. These guys waste my time."

It was a technique many polygraphers use, a kind of foreplay to soften up a subject and gain his confidence before hooking him up to the machine and beginning the test.

"These marshals are the poorest excuses for investigators I've ever seen."

He reviewed the questions that he was going to ask Pope when the machine was turned on and continued trying to soften him up.

But, Homenick noticed, Pope, with at least as much guile, was trying to do the same thing: he asked the sergeant for details of the big cases he had worked on, seemed genuinely interested in him and tried to flatter him. When the sergeant went over the questions about Boyce that he was going to ask, Pope showed no sign of uneasiness; he was a model of self-confidence who responded to everything the sergeant said as if he hadn't a care in the world.

After almost two hours of this informal banter, the polygrapher excused himself to go to the rest room.

"Larry, how important is it to polygraph this guy?"

"Very important. Why?"

"What does he have to gain from this?"

"A lot. He wants probation on a counterfeiting charge. He was caught with eleven million dollars' worth of counterfeit money."

"Larry, let me give you some advice. You're going to lose if we polygraph him. This guy is a con man; he's so good there's no way you can win. The result will show that he was telling the truth; he'll beat it, and you won't know what the truth is."

They decided to call off the test.

The sergeant returned to the room where Pope was waiting, said that he had been summoned away to do some *real* police work and then left him there, still unattached to the lie-detector machine.

Pope had been deprived of his chance to lock up a recommendation for probation by proving his truthfulness on the lie-detector machine. But he had an alternative plan. When he returned to Palm Springs that afternoon, he called a newspaper reporter in a nearby town, Riverside, and confided that he had just provided important information that would help the U.S. Marshals Service find Christopher John Boyce, the escaped Soviet spy.

The newspaper ran a long story about the interview and it was picked up by the wire services. The next day, Pope called Homenick. Almost shouting over the phone he said, "Larry, have you seen the paper? What the fuck did you do to me? Who burned me? There's a story out that I turned in Boyce. You *can't* let me go to prison now. I go in the joint now and everybody knows I'm the guy who fingered Chris. A snitch is a dead man."

Homenick later discovered that Pope himself had been the source of the article. But the silver-tongued ex-con's strategy worked. A few days later, still promising to give the seekers of Christopher Boyce any help they wanted, Pope went before a federal judge in Los Angeles. On the recommendation of the U.S. Attorney's office, he was granted probation on the counterfeiting charge. Then, once again, he disappeared.

Except for a call from the owner of the condominium he had rented in Palm Springs complaining that Pope had stolen some of the furniture when he vanished, Homenick didn't hear anything about Pope until it really didn't matter anymore.

21

No one wanted to admit it at the nightly sessions in the Holiday Inn bar, but a sense was growing among the members of the task force that they had failed. Kupferer seemed to acknowledge as much in an interview with the *Los Angeles Times* in late November. He told a reporter that the task force had done a "significant job," but said he was considering closing it down because of its high cost and manpower needs elsewhere. "There always has to be a bottom line someplace," he said. "We didn't expect an instant arrest; that would be foolish; but we feel it has been productive.

"Whatever we do," he added, "the investigation will continue. We don't abdicate."

The task force was dismantled in the first week of December. A dozen men had worked two months without a day off, often for sixteen hours a day. When Kupferer added up the results, he admitted to Homenick, except for a lot of loose ends tied up and a lot of old ground retraced, there was pitifully little to show for it: the phone call that confirmed Boyce was still alive; Roger Archiga's identification of Frank Burton Riley as the ex-convict who knew Boyce and had fought in Rhodesia; the still unexplained telephone call that had led to the raid in San Diego; the equally curious stories of Brent Pope; perhaps most promising, the leads supplied by Bob Merman, and reinforced to some extent by the involvement of some of Boyce's friends in drug dealing, that indicated he was supporting himself as a drug smuggler; the vague clues that he was on his way to Russia . . . or South Africa . . . or Mexico . . . or a dozen other places.

What Kupferer hadn't told the reporter was that he had hopes that Boyce would come out of hiding soon: the Christmas holidays made even the wariest fugitive want to reestablish, if only briefly, emotional contact with loved ones. Nor did Kupferer tell the reporter that he was thinking about organizing another task force which, without the publicity of the first, would concentrate on finding Boyce in the drug underworld.

Six days before Christmas, Homenick got a telephone call from an executive of a magazine called *U.S. Hang Gliding* who said that she had just read *The Falcon and the Snowman* and the name of Christopher Boyce had struck a familiar chord. She had checked the magazine's list of subscribers, she said, and discovered that one was named Chris Boyce.

Homenick's first reaction was the obvious one: Chris was too smart to have signed up for a magazine subscription under his own name. Still, the first lesson of fugitive hunting is that everyone makes a mistake sooner or later. And he remembered Dr. Joe's prediction that Chris, in lieu of falconry, might try flying or hang gliding as a substitute.

"Where is the subscription sent to?"

"Australia."

It was an English-speaking country large enough to hide out in, and Chris's disclosure at his trial that the CIA was manipulating Australian labor unions had created a sensation in some segments of the country's press. It had probably made him a hero to some left-wing Australians.

"Where in Australia?"

"A place called Alice Springs."

"Are you sure that his name is Christopher Boyce?"

"Yes, it's Christopher J. Boyce."

"Are you sure it's Alice Springs?"

"Yes."

Alice Springs is a remote town in the Outback of Australia. When Christopher Boyce was working as a code-room clerk for

TRW, he was in touch with Alice Springs daily. He must know people there. Alice Springs was the site of a secret base where photographs and data collected by Rhyolite spy satellites were transmitted to a network of huge microwave antennae. Chris couldn't have picked a better place to resume his espionage activities, Homenick thought. Kupferer, when he called him at Tysons Corner, was also dubious that Boyce would use his own name on a magazine subscription. But he had seen other fugitives make stupid mistakes. He said he would check with Duke Smith, a Marshals Service inspector based in El Paso, Texas, who had contacts in the international law-enforcement community, and decide how best to follow up on the tip without alerting Boyce that they were looking for him in Australia.

At eleven o'clock on the evening of December 23, a telephone rang in the suburban Virginia home of Howard Safir. The call, from California, had been patched through to his home by the Communication Center at Tysons Corner. It was a woman who said excitedly, "I want to report that my cousin Christopher Boyce just called me."

She identified herself as a cousin of Boyce's who lived in Los Angeles.

"Did Chris say where he was?"

"No, he didn't," she said, "and I didn't ask. I just want to do the right thing and let you know he called."

The young woman—who had been close to Chris when they were children—gave Safir a brief summary of the call, and he told her that an investigator in California would contact her shortly. Within a few minutes, she was talking to Larry Homenick.

"What did he say?" he asked.

"It was mostly about family matters. He just called and said, 'How's my favorite cousin?' and said he wanted me to call his parents and wish them Merry Christmas and tell them that he loved them. I said he ought to call them himself, but he said, 'I can't do that.' "

"Did you hear any coins drop when he called?"

"No. The whole conversation only lasted three or four minutes."

Except for Chris's saying that he was happy and in good health, she said they had talked only about his parents and his sisters and brothers. "I asked if he knew about your task force, and he said he didn't. I told him that I'd have to report his call. He didn't say anything when I told him that. He said, 'I have to go now; I love you, and please call my parents,' and he hung up."

The call indicated three things to Homenick and Kupferer: the task force had succeeded again in smoking him out of hiding; he was lonely at Christmastime; and there was a chance he would try to contact his parents on Christmas Day.

A Personals-column ad in the *Los Angeles Times* caught Homenick's eye the following morning. He had been watching the ad columns in case Chris tried to send a holiday message to his parents. The ad he spotted read: "I miss you. Have a nice Christmas. The K.M.A. Kid." He had no idea what the initials stood for, but it could be a family joke. He walked over from the courthouse to the newspaper office and showed his star to an official in the classified-advertising department. The office manager summoned the clerk who had taken the ad.

She had no trouble remembering the ad. "It was placed by a young lady who originally wanted to put something else in it and I had to tell her it was against our policy. I suggested something else," she said.

"What did she want to put in the ad?" Homenick asked.

The girl blushed slightly.

"She wanted to sign it 'The Kiss My Ass Kid.' I told her we couldn't do that, but I suggested she use 'K.M.A.' instead, and she liked that."

On Christmas Day, a van was parked all day on the tree-lined street in Palos Verdes where the Boyce family lived. But it proved another waste of time. Chris didn't come home for Christmas.

22

BEFORE HE LEFT HOME ON THE MORNING OF JAN-
uary 21, Larry Homenick patted Karen's belly with affection and
said he wouldn't be surprised if their second child, who was due in
two months, arrived earlier than Karen's obstetrician had predicted. The baby, at least, was something they could talk about
without arguing. It helped release the tension developing between
them and divert their thoughts from Christopher Boyce.

They kissed, and Homenick, feeling beaten and depressed,
drove a few blocks to the Antelope Valley Freeway and began his
daily hour-long drive from Canyon Country to downtown Los Angeles. Karen had reminded him that his thirty-second birthday was
the following week. Even the thought of a small party hadn't
brightened his mood. He parked his car in a lot near the Los Angeles County Jail and walked the remaining few blocks to the Federal Courthouse, a granite monolith at the edge of the city's
downtown district, past Olvera Street and the old adobe buildings
where two hundred years earlier a handful of migrating Mexicans
and Spaniards had founded the city. As he sat down, he saw that an
anonymous needler had left another clipping on his desk. It was a
long article, with two photographs of Chris, noting that the day
was the first anniversary of Boyce's escape. Federal agents, the article pointed out, were no closer to finding him than they had been
a year earlier.

The long days that often ended with him crawling into bed at midnight after Karen had fallen asleep; the family get-togethers he missed; the weekends when he was away from home chasing leads that never led anywhere were causing an increasing strain on their marriage.

Karen, he thought, was probably much more patient than most wives would be with a husband who was seldom at home. She understood how much he and Tony enjoyed their jobs and why they enjoyed them, and she accepted the fact that his wasn't an ordinary job. But after a year he could feel her patience ebbing away, and he resented it—not so much because she was wrong as because there was nothing he could do to change things. Homenick was soft-spoken and in the past had rarely raised his voice. Now, under pressure at home and on the job, he struck back often, exploding angrily when she complained and, increasingly, causing her to cry.

"Remember, you have a wife and a son too!" she had sobbed after he told her early in 1981 that he would be away on still another weekend after other members of the task force had gone home.

"Look," he shouted. "I've got enough problems at work. You don't have to make it harder for me."

"Why do *you* always have to go out on these calls?"

"Because it's my case."

The truth was that on some of the nights when he came home late, Homenick hadn't been chasing leads about Chris. Often, these days, there weren't any leads left to pursue. After going through the old files one more time, he and Tony Perez would go to the Revolver Club to share several pitchers of beer. Tony understood his torment and offered a sympathetic ear. He had a theory— just a feeling—that someday they would find Boyce hiding out near the water; Larry still thought he was hiding somewhere in a small town under a new identity. They talked about how easy it was for someone in America to get false identification papers and blend into a new community; birth certificate, driver's license, Social Security card, alien registration card, U.S. passport—they could all be purchased for a few hundred dollars in almost any big city.

"At least now you know it's not you who's to blame for not finding him," Perez said. The sounds of Havana still accented his voice, but they were fading. "We had some of the best investigators in the Marshals Service on the task force, and they couldn't find him either. You can't blame yourself. Nobody else could find him either."

It made Homenick feel better, for a while.

But later, when he was alone, he realized once again that he was the one who was responsible for finding Christopher Boyce.

One morning in mid-January, Tony hung up his phone, walked over to Larry's desk, clicked his heels and said, *"Achtung!"*

Homenick looked up from his papers.

"How would you like to go to Germany?"

An American prisoner, a suspect in a multimillion-dollar fraud case, had been arrested in Frankfurt, and headquarters had assigned Homenick and Perez to fly there in a week or two to bring him back. It was big news. Neither Homenick nor Perez had ever been to Europe, and a trip to Frankfurt would provide a chance to forget Chris Boyce for a while.

A few hours later, as Homenick was reading the anniversary newspaper story spotlighting the Marshals Service's lack of success—*his* lack of success—in finding Christopher John Boyce, he looked up and noticed a handsome, dark-haired man with dark glasses standing at the front counter in the office apparently trying to get his attention. The face was vaguely familiar.

The man at the counter was Don North, a television correspondent whose face had appeared in hundreds of reports from Vietnam battlefields and scores of other places around the world. North had a reputation as a stubborn journalistic investigator who undertook difficult, out-of-the-ordinary challenges, like trying, as he once had, to track down the celebrated international assassin known as "Carlos the Jackal." He had left network television and now worked as a free-lance journalist in Los Angeles and was looking for another big story. When he sat down with Larry Homenick, he told him that he believed he had one. He said he believed he had found Christopher Boyce.

He explained that someone whom he trusted had introduced him to a stranger, a soldier of fortune who lived near Fresno, California, when he was not fighting wars as a mercenary someplace overseas. The stranger, he continued, had told him he had seen Christopher Boyce recently in a country "down south" and had had a number of interesting things to say about him.

Homenick was skeptical. If someone really knew where Chris was, why would he take the information to a reporter instead of a law-enforcement agency? Nevertheless, he wanted to know what this reporter knew. North, however, only teased him:

"I'm starting a three-part series on this guy tonight. I think you'll be interested in what he has to say."

Homenick watched the ten-o'clock news on KTTV, Channel 11, that night, and indeed, he was fascinated.

Much of North's report was familiar. There were a review of Boyce's espionage trial and escape, a report about the inability of the special federal task force to find him, the speculation that he had been helped by the KGB or the CIA and a reference to Chief Inspector Thomas C. Kupferer, Jr.'s, theory that Chris was holed up in Southern California and smuggling drugs. Then North dropped his bombshell: Christopher Boyce wasn't smuggling drugs; *he was smuggling guns.*

He told viewers that he had investigated the escape and had uncovered a man named Tommy Roger Harmon, an American Vietnam veteran, who had recently seen Christopher Boyce in Mexico City.

And then he introduced him.

A husky man in his mid-thirties with a square face covered mostly by a black, gray-flecked beard appeared on the screen long enough to say, "He tells me he's smuggling, off and on, to make a few bucks. But I know for sure the Cubans are financing him. . . ."

It was compelling television. On the ten-o'clock news the succeeding two nights, North completed his series. Harmon, an articulate man with the sound of rural Arkansas in his voice, reviewed some of his exploits as a soldier of fortune and demolition expert who performed free-lance jobs for the CIA, or anyone else who would pay for his services , in Central and South America. But the most startling part of his account concerned Christopher Boyce and Mexico City, the city where Chris and Daulton Lee had sold their secrets to the Soviet Union.

Harmon said that while he was dealing with his contacts in Cuban intelligence, he had met Boyce twice at the Cuban Embassy in that city—first in June, six months after his escape, and again during the previous November. At their second meeting, Harmon said, Boyce had told him who he was and disclosed that he was smuggling guns to Central American revolutionaries. The guns came from Cuba, but he said he suspected they originated in the Soviet Union. Besides gunrunning, which he did for the adventure and for ideological reasons, Boyce said he also had a profitable sideline: smuggling pre-Columbian art objects and artifacts from Central American jungles and selling them on the international black market.

Both times they had met, Harmon said, Boyce was accompanied by a large black man who he presumed was a Cuban bodyguard. Boyce, he said, had been delighted to meet someone from California and was hungry for any news about life in his home state.

"He wants to come home," Harmon said in the third of the episodes. "That's all I can say. He's a very unhappy man . . . a very unhappy man—"

"Sounds like a man who's prone to making mistakes," North said.

"—and it's going to kill him," Harmon interjected, waving his hand emphatically. Then Harmon's face vanished from the screen and North said that he had left California, where the interview had been filmed, "for another rendezvous with Christopher Boyce in a Central American republic. Their plan was to smuggle twelve thousand pounds of small arms that originated in Havana to the rebels in El Salvador."

Homenick didn't know what to make of the series.

Harmon's reference to Central America was intriguing. From the earliest days of the investigation, Freddy Gray had claimed that Chris planned to go to Nicaragua; Brent Pope had mentioned that he might flee to Costa Rica, the nation south of Nicaragua, because of something he had read about a tradition of political asylum there that made the government reluctant to extradite people accused of political crimes.

Homenick decided he would be wise to do some research on Tommy Harmon—if that was in fact his real name.

23

WITH A SENSE OF EXCITEMENT, DON NORTH looked at a telegram shown him by the man called Tommy Harmon a few days after the series ended. The telegram, dated January 7, 1981, had been sent to Harmon in Fresno from San José, Costa Rica. It read:

CANCEL MEETING IN MEXICO CITY. CHANGE TO SAN JOSE, COSTA RICA. MUST SEE YOU.

C.B.

North was in pursuit of a big story, too big for the independent station in Los Angeles that had broadcast his three-part series. After seeing the telegram, North placed a call to a friend at NBC and said that he wanted the network to back him on a mission to find Christopher Boyce. The NBC official told him to stand by, that he would take up the proposal with senior news executives at the network and let him know their decision.

While North was awaiting the decision, a second task force was being organized to find Christopher Boyce in Southern California, but without the publicity or the buoyant self-confidence of the first one.

In early February, Bob Dighera rented a condominium apartment a few blocks from Christopher Boyce's former home in Palos Verdes. It was to be the command post for an attempt to penetrate the community's drug underworld from the inside. For the next few weeks, many residents of the condominium complex would wonder about the curious goings-on in the apartment, which was shared by five men and two women.

Homenick had little difficulty discovering the real identity of Tommy Harmon. The previous September, an FBI agent in Fresno had interviewed a man named Thomas Frederick Lynch after receiving a tip that he had hidden a cache of explosives near the Fresno home of his ex-wife. Lynch, who admitted in the interview that he had worked overseas as a mercenary, denied having placed any explosives, and none were found. The agent filed a routine report of the interview. When Homenick found the agent, it took little time to establish that Tommy Harmon was Tommy Lynch.

After members of his family complained to a local congressman about his transfer to the prison in Indiana, where it was difficult to visit him, Andrew Daulton Lee had been transferred back to Lompoc.

As January ended and February began, he waited impatiently each day for the mail to arrive. He had applied to the U.S. Parole Commission in Washington for early release. He was optimistic. For months he had been telling other inmates and his family that he would be out of prison within a year, two years at the most. Despite being harassed by some inmates as a traitor, Lee avoided trouble and was regarded by guards as a well-behaved prisoner who might qualify for an early parole. Now, he waited anxiously for the word that his good conduct had been rewarded.

The letter arrived in early February: A four-member panel of the Parole Commission denied his application and said it would not reconsider his parole request before January 1991.

In Los Angeles, Don North was also the recipient of news, but it was more welcome: NBC agreed to finance his expedition to find Christopher Boyce.

* * *

Larry Homenick and Tony Perez also got some news. The legal formalities had been completed, and it was time for them to fly to Germany to pick up their prisoner. They boarded a plane for Frankfurt determined to forget the missing spy for a while.

In an obscure federal building not far from the U.S.–Mexican border, a senior inspector in the U.S. Marshals Service named G. Wayne Smith drafted two messages regarding Christopher John Boyce.

Smith was a large man in his early thirties who wore gold-rimmed glasses and spoke with a Florida drawl. He had been called "Duke" by his friends since childhood, when he had performed a highly successful imitation of John Wayne. The nickname had stuck as he grew into a man almost as large as Duke Wayne. His first career choice had been opera. Smith had a powerful voice that had prompted some of his teachers to encourage him to study music; he went away to college, studied voice for a while, but ultimately decided his chances of success were better in police work than in Puccini. After working for several years as a policeman in Miami and North Carolina, he joined the Marshals Service in 1974, spent several years guarding government witnesses and was then spotted by Howard Safir as an up-and-comer with management talents. He was sent to Texas as the Marshals Service's representative at the El Paso Intelligence Center (EPIC), a computerized repository of data about major crimes and criminals that is operated jointly by federal law-enforcement agencies.

Most of the men and women who began to revitalize the Marshals Service in the 1970s were young, polyestered, dedicated lawmen from middle-class families who relaxed with beer or bourbon. Duke Smith preferred French and California wines. This was regarded as pretentious and stiff by some of his colleagues, who, as they ordered a beer with their dinner, chided Smith for laboring over the wine list. A few deputies found him too formal. But there was no doubt that he was marked for greater things in the agency.

The two messages Smith prepared were addressed to places half a world apart.

One was a cable to a senior officer of the federal Drug Enforcement Agency at the U.S. Embassy in San José, Costa Rica. Smith wrote that a tip had been received in the United States that Christopher Boyce might have fled to Costa Rica, and he asked DEA agents based in that country to keep an eye out for him.

The second message was to senior police officials in New South Wales, Australia. According to information developed in America, he wrote, a resident of Australia named Christopher Boyce, "the most sought-after fugitive in our country," subscribed to an American magazine for hang-gliding enthusiasts. According to the magazine, Boyce had lived in Alice Springs and recently sent a change-of-address notification indicating that he had moved to Thirroul, New South Wales.

Boyce is an aerophile. Prior to his conviction for espionage, he was a falconry enthusiast and a subsequent psychological profile . . . determined that he has a predilection for aerodynetics. Hence, our inquiry concerning the subject living in Thirroul.

Two days after the messages left El Paso, an unsigned letter arrived at the United States Embassy in Pretoria, South Africa:

January 28, 1981

Will you please pass the following information on to authorized personnel in the United States. Christopher Boyce, the Soviet agent who escaped from an American prison, was in South Africa between February and June, 1980. He was helped into the country by an American whose surname is Schmeiser. Schmeiser supplied Boyce with an American passport under the name of Hollenbeck with a forged South African visa. I am certain that Boyce also has a Canadian passport, too. Boyce left South Africa and went to Bophuthatswana. He had a job working in a hotel in Montshiwa. He may still be there or he may now be in Mozambique. He did, however, return to America in about October or November,

1980, and then came back here. It is important that you not
mention receiving this letter to Schmeiser. He will definitely
know that I informed on him and he may kill me or my family.
He is very familiar with this country. He and Boyce were
good friends in some American prison.

In San Diego, Bob Dighera's wife, Betty, was starting to feel the
same kind of loathing for Christopher Boyce that Karen Homenick
did. After spending most of the previous autumn in Los Angeles on
the Boyce task force, her husband had returned home, and they had
resumed a normal life. But she learned that he couldn't let the case
alone. After he returned to Los Angeles to take command of another task force, Betty Dighera decided that it would be a good
time to go on a diet. She lost forty pounds. In retrospect, the success of her diet was the only positive thing to come out of the
Boyce investigation in early 1981.

With the help of Duke Smith and the computer system in El
Paso, Dighera began cross-checking data about hundreds of people
whose lives had touched that of Christopher Boyce—friends who
were suspected of drug trafficking; people whose names were in
his address book when he was arrested as a spy; the convicts he had
known in prison; drug dealers associated with Daulton Lee; the
scores of people in Mexico who Bob Merman had said were involved in smuggling and would give Boyce refuge. For each person on the list, his criminal record, a list of his friends and travels,
in some cases a log of his telephone calls were filed in the computer
and compared. The goal was to score a "hit," a connection between two or more of the people that pointed to a conspiracy in
which Boyce might be involved, or otherwise pointed the investigators in new directions.

The analysis took weeks. In time, thanks largely to the information provided by Captain Midnight, it produced a finely etched
portrait of a major segment of the dope-smuggling underworld in
the American Southwest. But it didn't lead to Christopher Boyce.

Bob Dighera, however, didn't know where it was leading when,
in early February, he was distracted from his work on the drug investigation by a telephone call. A man identified himself as a pro-

fessional television news cameraman and said that he wanted to give the U.S. Marshals Service a tip about Christopher Boyce.

He said that Don North, a television newsman with whom he worked, had departed on an airliner the night before for San José, Costa Rica, where he was going to interview Christopher John Boyce for NBC's *David Brinkley's Journal.* Before he left, the cameraman revealed that North had shown him a telegram sent by Boyce from Costa Rica. With a bitterness rooted in losing at least $5,000 in wages—not to mention a few days in a pleasant Central American city—the photographer said *he* had been scheduled to go on the secret mission to film the interview, but that on the eve of the departure, North had hired someone else and left him behind.

The other cameraman, he said, was named George Murray, and he was scheduled to leave for Costa Rica in the morning aboard a Pan American World Airways plane.

After several days of looking, George Richardson, a deputy marshal based in Fresno, found the home of Tommy Lynch in the High Sierras, in a town with a one-gas-pump general store and little else. Neighbors pointed out a shack where, they said, Lynch lived from time to time, but when Richardson went to the home he wasn't there.

Richardson left a message, asking Lynch to call him when he returned.

Bob Dighera decided that the television cameraman was probably telling the truth, and it was clear to him what had to be done.

In its long history, the U.S. Marshals Service had pursued fugitives over prairies, deserts and mountains, but not across international borders. Even Wyatt Earp had had to stop at the Rio Grande. But Dighera realized that if Don North was going to interview Christopher Boyce in Costa Rica, the Marshals Service had to be there when he did.

Dighera dispatched Roger Archiga to stake out George Murray's house. He called Kupferer, but he was in the air on his way to Washington. Howard Safir was in Salt Lake City, also temporarily

146

out of reach. He called Duke Smith in El Paso and told him what he knew about North's trip.

The question didn't have to be stated. It was on the minds of both men: *Should we go to Costa Rica?*

"Let me call down there," Smith said.

He telephoned the U.S. Embassy in San José and asked for Fred Kramer, a DEA agent he knew, and had him pulled away from a diplomatic reception. Smith told him about North and said, "If we decide to come down there and look for Boyce, what kind of support do you think can we anticipate?"

Kramer said that if the State Department approved it, he could assure him of all the help he needed. Smith thanked him and said he would call him back.

Before Smith could hang up, Kramer said that he had received an earlier message from Smith about Boyce and had shown his photograph to DEA informants around town.

"We've got an informant here who's been fairly reliable who thinks he's seen an American who looks like Boyce," Kramer said. "He says he's seen him several times in San José—just the other day, in fact. He thinks he may be able to help find him."

When Kupferer arrived home about 9 P.M., he had a message to call Duke Smith. With Bob Dighera participating from California, they held a three-way conference call that lasted only a few minutes. They concurred that it was urgent to get someone to Costa Rica. Kupferer tracked down Howard Safir in Salt Lake City, and he agreed.

Within a few hours Duke Smith was on a plane bound for San José. And with his departure, the first international expedition in the history of the U.S. Marshals Service had begun.

No one stopped to consider how they would get Boyce back into the United States if they found him.

Sixteen hours before the three-way conference call, at two o'clock the previous morning in Los Angeles, Larry Homenick and Tony Perez had ended a grueling trip home from Germany and deposited their prisoner in the county jail. Perez, who had survived two crash landings of helicopters in Vietnam, hated to fly and had not been able to sleep during the long flight from Germany. Homenick was also exhausted, and they sacked out at Homenick's home in Canyon Country. In the morning, Perez got up early, picked up his girlfriend and left for a camping trip near San Diego—and some rest.

Homenick, feeling sheepish about having been away for so long again, was happily mending fences with Karen that evening when the telephone rang.

"Hey, my friend," Kupferer said, "don't unpack; you're going to Costa Rica."

Kupferer briefed him on the tip from North's former cameraman. He said Duke Smith was already on his way to San José, and Homenick and Perez were booked on Pan Am Flight 415 in the morning along with Gerry Smith. George Murray, Don North's new cameraman, had a reservation on the flight. They were to follow him to San José, Kupferer said, and be there if Boyce showed up for an interview.

Homenick found Tony at a campground in San Diego that, fortunately, had a telephone booth.

"Yeah, bub, what's up?" his surprised friend asked.

"We're going to Costa Rica, buddy."

"Fuck, what? I'm too tired to go anyplace."

But the next morning, along with Grand Jury Gerry, the Skull, they were on the plane.

24

LARRY HOMENICK HAD TOLD KAREN THE NIGHT
before that their headaches and heartaches of the past year might
soon be over. They now had their first solid lead in a year. NBC
wouldn't send a team to Costa Rica unless it was reasonably sure
that Christopher Boyce was there. It made sense that Chris was in
Costa Rica, he said. The warfare and political strife of Central
America would give him a cover; in El Salvador and other countries, Boyce had once told him, a poor peasant class was rebelling
against a rich ruling class supported by the United States. The Russians, according to the newspapers, were behind the peasant rebel-
lions. If that was true, he said, the Soviet Union would be glad to
have Boyce's services again. And, Homenick thought, remembering his long talks with him, Chris would rationalize it all. He
would be working for the Russians, but really helping the poor
people of Central America.

The three deputies tried to get seats in economy class, but it was
fully booked, and so they had to sit near George Murray, the cameraman, in the first-class cabin. Network union contracts generally
guarantee first-class air travel for technical crews, if not always for
the correspondents whom they photograph. To avoid having their
cover blown, Homenick, Perez and Smith agreed to act like strangers and avoid eye contact with each other and with Murray.

George Murray was a tall, middle-aged man. He seemed to
fancy himself attractive, and only a few minutes after their Boeing

lifted away from Los Angeles International Airport and turned south over Santa Monica Bay, he began asking one of the stewardesses for a date in San José.

At Guatemala City, the Pan Am jet landed to discharge and board passengers. As it taxied to the terminal, Homenick looked out his window in the first-class cabin and saw uniformed soldiers with automatic weapons on both sides of the runway. It was his introduction to the political realities of Central America.

While kerosene was being pumped into the big jet, a stewardess encouraged the San José–bound passengers to remain aboard. A door in the forward section of the first-class compartment was opened to take on commissary stores, and Murray got up and walked over to look outside. A moment later, Gerry Smith got up and followed him, as if he wanted to share the fresh air.

Homenick looked nervously at Perez. They had agreed not to approach Murray.

"What takes you to Costa Rica?" Murray asked the Skull.

"Just a vacation; some friends and I just decided to go down there on a lark."

"Where you going to stay?"

Smith didn't answer. They hadn't made any hotel reservations.

"Don't know; we just decided to go down on the spur of the moment."

The refueling was completed quickly. One of the flight attendants started to close the door, and another announced over the public-address system that passengers should return to their seats.

"How long you guys been in the CIA?" Murray asked Smith with a conspiratorial grin. His journalistic antenna was vibrating.

Perez and Homenick overheard him and tried to bury themselves in their seats.

"CIA?" the Skull replied. "We're in the real estate business."

Murray had apparently deduced that Perez and Homenick were his friends, although they weren't sitting together.

"Why do you think we're in the CIA?"

"I don't know; you guys look like it. I'm in the news business, and we always think we're being followed by the FBI or the CIA."

At the San José airport, Don North was waiting for George Murray. At the edge of the crowd, Duke Smith and several American and Costa Rican drug-enforcement agents were watching North.

Homenick lingered after most of the passengers had left the plane and showed his badge to the stewardess to whom Murray had paid attention. Homenick said only that he was working on an investigation that he couldn't discuss, but asked for her help.

"Did he say," Homenick asked her, "why he was in Costa Rica?"

"He said he was here to film an important interview and to do a story on gunrunning."

"Did you make a date with him?"

"No."

Homenick thanked her and ran out to catch up with Smith and Perez. To avoid being recognized by North, he put on a baseball cap and dark glasses and tried to blend into the crowd. By the time he reached the front steps of the terminal, Perez was sitting behind the wheel of a Chevrolet Malibu rented for them by Duke Smith. From the front seat of the car they watched North and Murray load Murray's equipment into a taxi and drive off toward the center of San José. Then they dropped into traffic about fifty yards behind them, with the Costa Rican and U.S. drug agents following in another car.

In the twilight of a hot Saturday night, Homenick was reminded of Saigon. There were the same kind of narrow streets clotted with traffic; the same kind of gaudy neon signs advertising bars and massage parlors and shining down on streetwalkers wearing heavy lipstick, dresses slit to the waist and the same hard look that he'd seen in Vietnam. There was even the same pervasive smell of diesel fumes in the air. A modern city with palm trees, surrounded by a jungle and filled with Kentucky Fried Chicken outlets and McDonald's hamburger stands.

The fast-moving taxi in front of them maneuvered adroitly through the heavy traffic, its taillights vanishing several times into a glittering horizon of cars, trucks, motorcycles and buses. Perez leaned on the horn and bulled his way forward through the traffic until he found it again. If North was headed for a meeting with Boyce, they were not going to miss it.

About a mile past the heart of San José, the taxi stopped at a big stucco building overgrown with weeds. A sign on the building said it was the Playboy Hotel.

They watched North and Murray enter the hotel and followed a few minutes later. The inside of the hotel was still under construction, and only the lowest three floors were occupied, but already the place looked very worn and old. The desk clerk told the Costa Rican agents that the two *norteamericanos* had been given a room on the third floor, but said he hadn't noticed any other *gringo* on the premises that day. Perez and Homenick asked for a room on the third floor and went upstairs to wait for Boyce to arrive or for North and Murray to leave.

From the airport, Duke Smith had gone to the American Embassy, where a diplomatic reception was under way. He was introduced to several of the mission's senior officers who were sipping cocktails at one corner of the room, and he suspected that they were waiting for him with apprehension. They greeted him cordially and listened to him patiently as he explained his mission. Within a few minutes the conversation turned to a sensitive issue: if in fact Boyce was in Costa Rica, how were they going to get him out of the country?

American agents had no powers of arrest in Costa Rica, Smith was told. Even if they found Boyce drinking a beer down the street from the embassy, the diplomats said, they had no legal authority to put handcuffs on him. It was essential, Smith was reminded, that nothing be done that would embarrass the United States or the government of Costa Rica, especially now when the country was in the midst of an important presidential election campaign. Costa Rica, the officials explained, was an increasing rarity in Central America—a peaceful, democratic country friendly to the United States.

"Just don't play Cowboys and Indians," one of the most senior diplomats said. Costa Rica, he continued, was a critical listening post in a politically volatile region of the world, and the United States couldn't afford to lose it. If there came a choice between losing Boyce and embarrassing Costa Rica or the United States, good relations with Costa Rica had to take precedence.

Smith agreed.

Costa Rican authorities, the embassy officials said, would have to be involved in the search for Boyce and be given the opportunity to make the most important decisions about his arrest.

Fred Kramer, the DEA official, had set aside his regular duties to work on the manhunt, and he said he was more than confident that the Costa Rican authorities would cooperate, at least unofficially. In a country whose people hated Communism, he said, there should be no difficulty in obtaining their help in running a Soviet spy to ground. He suggested that they quietly approach senior officers of the Bureau of Narcotics for Public Safety, whose agents were already helping him unofficially on the case. The chief of the bureau, a colonel who was a friend of his, was out of the city conducting an investigation in the south of Costa Rica. Their first step, Kramer said, should be getting him in on the manhunt. Everyone agreed to the plan, and an urgent request was sent to the Costa Rican policeman urging him to return to San José as quickly as he could to coordinate the arrest. The next morning he agreed, and a light plane was dispatched to pick him up.

It was left undecided what was to be done with Boyce once he was caught. Using conventional extradition procedures, legal experts at the embassy stressed, would be risky. Costa Rica had often refused to extradite Americans such as Robert Vesco, the fugitive millionaire wanted in the United States who had found refuge there. The U.S.–Costa Rican extradition treaty, which had been drafted in the 1920s, was antiquated and cumbersome to use. The Minister of Justice, in a lame-duck administration, was unlikely to move fast enough.

They agreed to discuss it later.

At the Playboy, a wedding reception was under way on the ground floor, and Homenick and Perez, two stories above it, could hear the music. Both were still weary from the European trip and lack of sleep the night before. But they kept a vigil down the hall from North's room, waiting for the newsmen to make a move and watching the door of their room through their own barely opened door.

After midnight, they saw the lights go out under the door and decided that North and Murray had gone to sleep. Outside, two Costa

Rican agents remained in their car, watching the entrance to the hotel, and Homenick and Perez decided it was safe to sleep for a few hours.

North and Murray didn't leave the room at all the next day and opened their door only for Room Service.

Over breakfast that morning at Fred Kramer's home, Duke Smith met the DEA informant who said he had seen Boyce in San José.

He was an American in his thirties with long hair that only partly concealed the large gold earring hanging from his right ear. Smith showed him several photographs of Boyce, and the man repeated what he had told Kramer—that he thought he had seen him several times in the Key Largo, a San José bar popular among American expatriates. Smith didn't feel good about the man's identification of Christopher Boyce. He claimed to be sure of himself, but he hadn't talked to the man he said was Boyce, and the physical description he gave was too vague to be convincing. Still, Smith encouraged the informant to move around the city and report to Kramer when he saw the man again.

When he returned to his room at the Irazú Hotel, which was several miles away from the Playboy near the center of San José, Smith was informed that a major breakthrough in the case had just occurred in California. Chuck Kupferer called to report that Deputy George Richardson had finally tracked down Tommy Lynch, the mercenary who had been "Tommy Harmon" in Don North's television report, in the High Sierras. After being promised a reward if he helped find Boyce, Lynch had agreed to "roll over" on him and cooperate.

Lynch, Kupferer said, had given a statement to Richardson detailing his relationship with Boyce that seemed to confirm that Boyce was in Costa Rica. He'd asserted that he had had a third meeting with Boyce—in Costa Rica—and that they had agreed to go into business together to run guns and smuggle artifacts out of Central America. Lynch disclosed that he had just returned from San José, where they made the final arrangements; and he said that the meeting had been requested by Boyce in a telegram a few weeks previously. Lynch had shown the telegram to Richardson.

According to Lynch, Boyce wasn't living in San José. Although he visited the capital occasionally, he was afraid of being spotted there and had built a "hooch," a primitive canvas lean-to, in the jungle near the town of Cañas in the state of Guanacaste. Boyce was likely to resist arrest with firepower, Lynch said. He had two guns—a 9mm semi-automatic pistol and a .44 revolver—and Lynch said that Boyce had told him repeatedly that he wouldn't be taken alive. George Richardson, Kupferer said, was bringing Lynch to Los Angeles to be interrogated by Bob Dighera.

After dark that evening, DEA agents relieved Homenick and Perez at the hotel and they parked their rented car near the Key Largo, the bar where the informant said he had seen Boyce. The Key Largo was a dark, noisy place with a nautical decor. Yachting pennants hung from the ceiling and were draped above the bar. As the two men walked in, a half-dozen young women, some in their teens, converged on them in a flying wedge. Homenick and Perez ignored the hookers, ordered beer and pretended to be interested in a movie, *Close Encounters of the Third Kind,* that was playing on a television set over the bar.

There were several Americans in the crowd, but not Boyce. After an hour, Homenick and Perez left the bar and decided to show his picture to some of the hookers on the street outside. When this didn't produce any results, they began stopping in at massage parlors in the neighborhood. There were lots of them, but no one recognized the picture in their hands.

At El Caballero, Perez said, "I'm tired of these places; why don't *you* try this one?"

Posing as a customer, Homenick went inside. "Do you speak English?" he asked.

"Yes," a man with a sweet-sounding voice answered.

"How much is a massage?"

"About ten dollars." He was smiling.

Trying to be casual about it, Homenick said that besides wanting a massage he was looking for a friend, another American, who might have come into the place, and he produced a photograph of Chris. The man spent a great deal of time examining the photograph but finally looked up and announced that he had never seen him. Then he placed a friendly hand on Homenick's shoulder and said, "Why don't you stay and enjoy yourself now?"

Homenick had noticed that several young men in the room were looking at him, and he decided that what was in their eyes was affection.

Realizing that he had been set up by Tony, he said, "Excuse me, I've got a friend outside; let me go get him."

The attendant was pleased and urged him to return quickly with his friend.

Homenick found Tony in the front seat of their car doubled up in laughter.

The following morning, Homenick looked out the window of their room and was reminded again of Saigon. The streets were noisy and busy with traffic. There was the familiar smell of diesel fuel spewed out by trucks making deliveries. Perez joined him at the window, and at that instant, both spotted North and Murray. They were near the front of the hotel, getting into a taxi. Murray was loaded down with his camera equipment.

"They're leaving!" Tony shouted. The two deputy U.S. marshals sprinted down three flights of stairs to the ground floor.

Tony wrote down the license number of the taxi, but before they reached their car the taxi had disappeared in the noon-hour traffic. Homenick then noticed that a car was accelerating away from the curb in pursuit of the taxi. It was one of the cars driven by the team of Costa Rican agents who were assisting them.

The Costa Ricans kept up with the taxi for several blocks, but then they lost it in traffic near the Royal Dutch Hotel in downtown San José.

Two hours later, as Homenick and Perez waited helplessly at the Playboy, a taxi pulled up to the hotel and North and Murray got out. No one had any idea where they had been. When the Costa Rican detectives showed a picture of Boyce to employees at the Royal Dutch Hotel, no one recognized him.

Three hours later, at four o'clock Monday afternoon, Duke Smith had a strategy session at the embassy with Fred Kramer and senior diplomatic officials. The purpose was to resolve the difficult question of how Boyce was to be expelled from Costa Rica once he was captured.

Everyone agreed that he should be returned to U.S. territory as quickly as possible after his arrest. But no one knew how the lame-duck Minister of Justice, in a country with a tradition of political asylum, would respond to a request for the extradition of a fugitive who claimed to have spied because of his disaffection with the American government. Some people in Costa Rica, they agreed, might regard him as a political dissident. From Washington, Justice Department specialists on international law, after studying Costa Rican laws and legal precedents in political-asylum cases, had said it was possible that the Costa Ricans would agree to extradite him only if the United States agreed not to make him complete his sentence for espionage, a "political" crime. He could still be returned to the United States to face a lesser charge—stealing government documents—but it carried a maximum sentence of only ten years. It could mean that he would have to be released in six or seven years.

A consensus emerged: if they were going to get Christopher Boyce out of Costa Rica, they would probably have to kidnap him. They decided on a Black Bag Job—and they weren't referring to the body bag that Kupferer had had sent down from Tysons Corner in case Christopher Boyce was killed in the operation.

25

SOMEBODY, DUKE SMITH SAID, WAS WATCHING them.

In a meeting at the Playboy, he told Larry Homenick that he had seen two European men in business suits tailing him during several of his trips between the hotel and the embassy.

"Tony and I thought we saw some guys pulling a surveillance on us," Homenick said, "but we thought we were getting paranoid."

"I don't think so," Smith said.

Kupferer called from Tysons Corner to report that Bob Dighera was impressed enough with Tommy Lynch to recommend bringing him to Washington for a lie-detector test.

Don North and George Murray seemed to be camped out permanently in their room at the Playboy, surrounded by almost a dozen American and Costa Rican agents deployed, with walkie-talkies, at strategic points within the hotel and in the neighborhood outside.

In Room 306, Homenick hunched over a radio provided by the DEA and coordinated the surveillance. It reminded him of movies he had seen about World War II resistance fighters broadcasting secret messages from garrets in occupied France.

Tysons Corner approved the Black Bag Job, which was soon referred to by everybody concerned as the BBJ.

If Boyce was found in Costa Rica, according to the plan that was agreed upon, he was to be flown out of the country in a small executive jet painted black without any identifying markings. As soon as he was caught, senior officials in the Justice Department would be notified, and the unmarked jet would leave the United States and fly to a remote airstrip near Cañas, the small town not far from the mountainous jungle where Boyce was supposed to be hiding. Boyce would be bound and gagged if necessary and be airlifted immediately to one of several possible locations—Guantanamo Naval Base in Cuba, Miami, Puerto Rico or the Virgin Islands.

In case any trouble developed, two contingency plans were devised: an American ship was to be placed on station in the Atlantic to wait for Boyce's delivery by a U.S. helicopter flight from Costa Rica; if poor weather or other problems interfered with this plan, he was to be taken through the jungle in a four-wheel-drive vehicle to Panama. The goal was to have Boyce out of Costa Rica within twenty-four hours of his apprehension.

The Costa Rican police colonel said he agreed fully with the plan. "But," he added, "I have one requirement: if Christopher Boyce is injured or killed during the operation, you must agree that you will put him on your plane and fly him out of Costa Rica *immediately,* regardless of his physical condition."

Later that day, Tysons Corner agreed to this stipulation.

Headquarters was less happy about another message it received that day from Costa Rica. Security officials at the embassy warned Smith that all long-distance phone calls from Costa Rica were being monitored by the KGB and that it was too risky to use conventional phone lines. Instead, they directed the visiting manhunters to communicate with Tysons Corner via a secure, encrypted telex line at the embassy.

Kupferer, always unhappy with what he regarded as bureaucratic constraints that stood in the way of getting a job done, agreed with the need for more secure communications. But he said he had his own ideas for dealing with the eavesdropping Russians; Smith and other members of the team, he said, could not afford to be constrained during the final hours of the operation by having to drive back to the embassy through San José's heavy traffic every time they had to confer with headquarters. Coordinating the logistics of the BBJ, he said, demanded the flexibility of a telephone.

With a pragmatism rooted perhaps in the frontier heritage of their service, Kupferer and his deputies devised a code to use in their telephone conversations between San José and Tysons Corner: "Let it snow" meant that it was time for the jet to leave the United States for San José; if someone said "I have a present for you," it meant Boyce; "basketball team" referred to the Russians; "wine" to California; "hat" to Panama, and so forth. Some of the professional spooks at the embassy were distressed by such an informal method of communication, but they agreed it was functional and should do the job. It was never established what, if anything, the KGB agents who were monitoring the calls to the United States might think about it.

In downtown San José, North and Murray remained in their room for a third day.

Now that the American agents in San José were aware that they were being followed, they found it easier to spot the strangers who kept them under surveillance as they kept North and Murray under surveillance.

Duke Smith concluded that they were KGB. Homenick and Perez suspected CIA. They all agreed that they were playing on a stage where they did not know all the actors. The San José newspapers were filled with stories about how Cuban and Russian agents were suspected of moving guns through Costa Rica to antigovernment rebels in Nicaragua and El Salvador and CIA efforts to stop them. If Chris had been a double agent all along, what better stage was there for his work than Costa Rica? At the embassy, however, CIA representatives impressed Duke Smith as being as intent on finding Christopher Boyce as the marshals were.

One CIA agent observed that it was probably not a coincidence that Boyce was in Costa Rica. The KGB agent who had controlled the Boyce–Lee espionage conspiracy during its last months had been transferred from Mexico City and was now in San José. The man, Boris Grishin, was under surveillance.

* * *

At one o'clock Tuesday afternoon, Fred Kramer called Duke Smith from the embassy and said that North had just telephoned there and asked for an appointment with the political officer. North said that he wanted to talk about Christopher Boyce.

Four hours later, Kramer called back and said that North had kept the appointment and had asked people at the embassy if *they* knew where Boyce was. If North was waiting for a secret meeting with Boyce, Kramer asked Smith, wasn't it strange that he would go to the embassy and ask about him there?

"Good question," Duke Smith replied.

What the U.S. agents had not known when they boarded the airliner in Los Angeles with George Murray, when they had followed North and Murray from the airport and when they had maintained their twenty-four-hour-a-day surveillance at the Playboy waiting for Boyce to appear was that Don North had also been waiting. He was waiting for Tommy Lynch.

In Los Angeles, North had given Lynch $1,000 of NBC's money for expenses to fly to Costa Rica, and Lynch had promised North that he would meet him in San José and lead him to Boyce. But now Lynch couldn't meet him; he was in Washington, taking a lie-detector test.

After almost a week in San José, Duke Smith decided that he was tired of being tailed by the two strangers. Either they weren't very good at their jobs or they didn't care that he knew he was being followed. He walked into the Playboy one afternoon and spotted one of the men following not far behind him across the red tile floor of the lobby. He doubled back toward the front door. The man saw him and abruptly picked up a magazine from a newsstand and started to read it. Smith walked up to within a foot of his shadow and said in English, "Excuse me, sir; your fly's unbuttoned."

The man looked down the front of his pants, then looked up into Smith's impassive face. He put the magazine back on the rack and walked away. After that, the U.S. deputies never saw the stranger behind them again, and many months later, they were still wondering who had followed them in Costa Rica.

* * *

After Don North's visit to the embassy, the Americans lost interest in him rapidly, and the following day they ended the around-the-clock surveillance at the Playboy. The decision to give up on North was given added impetus by a call from Tysons Corner: Chuck Kupferer said that Tommy Lynch had passed three lie-detector tests and was on his way to Costa Rica.

"Safir's skeptical about him," Kupferer told Smith, "but we put him on the machine with the DEA's best polygraph expert and he passed with flying colors. He says he's as good as gold."

Lynch, he added, was already on a plane for San José with Bob Dighera. Meanwhile, a memorandum was being drafted recommending a reward for him if he helped them find Boyce. Until the operation was concluded, Kupferer said, he was going to spend nights on a cot in his office at Tysons Corner.

Homenick was at the San José airport at midnight on the morning of February 21 when Bob Dighera walked off a plane accompanied by the same man whom he had seen on Don North's television series about Chris. "I can take you where he's holed up in the bush, or you can wait until he comes into town and take him at the Soda Palace," Lynch said.

The Soda Palace, he explained, was a café in the center of San José that they had used for rendezvous in the past. "When one of us is in town looking for the other, we check the Soda Palace at ten in the morning; if he's looking for me and I'm not there, he's supposed to check back at two, and then six, and vice versa."

Lynch's confidence was contagious, and his motivation was crystal-clear. He said that he realized now that Boyce was a major spy, and he expected a big reward for turning him in.

Because Homenick was the only deputy who knew Boyce personally, Kupferer told him to question Lynch closely about him. "Did he have a beard?" he asked.

Chris's mother had told Homenick that his facial hair was too thin for him to be able to grow a heavy beard.

"No, he couldn't grow much of a beard," Lynch said. "It was light and thin."

"What color are his eyes?"

"Blue; really penetrating blue eyes."

All Lynch's answers were consistent with what they knew about Boyce.

"Was he really going to give an interview to North?"

"No, it was bullshit. When I asked Boyce about it he got all excited and said, 'Hell, no; fuck, no.' "

Each of their previous meetings in Costa Rica, Lynch said, had been preceded by a telegram. He asked Duke Smith to have George Richardson in Fresno send a wire addressed to "C.B." at the San José telegraph office stating: "Leaving earlier than expected. See you soon. Tom."

Kupferer, coordinating the operation from Tysons Corner, rousted Richardson out of bed, and the cable was sent.

The following morning, Tony Perez, who blended easily into the crowd of Costa Ricans that patronized the café, was waiting at ten o'clock at the Soda Palace, a restaurant favored by young people, in case Boyce came looking for Lynch. He was there again at two and six o'clock. But if Boyce was in town, he was not looking for Lynch.

They would have to go after him in the jungle.

26

THEY LEFT FOR CAÑAS AT DAWN IN A CARAVAN OF three jeeps: Larry Homenick, Duke Smith, Fred Kramer, two more DEA agents, three Costa Rican policemen and Tommy Lynch. Tony Perez went to the Soda Palace, ordered a cup of coffee and waited for Boyce to show up there.

The road to Cañas offers to those who travel it a microcosm of the spectacular beauty of Costa Rica, a nation of two million people about the size of West Virginia with a diversity of color and terrain as rich as that of any nation in the Americas. After leaving scattered shantytowns at the outskirts of San José, the road plunges into Costa Rica's bountiful Central Valley. Seldom out of sight of lush mountains, the road is flanked by groves of sugar cane and coffee, fruit trees and pastures in alternating shades of beige and green so lovely that they might have been painted by an artist. Along with some of the world's most beautiful beaches, Costa Rica contains dry, windswept plains reminiscent of the American Southwest, and this was the territory through which they now passed before approaching a jungle as dense and as primitive as any in the world.

"Did we just pass a cemetery?" Tommy Lynch, in the first of the three jeeps, asked Kramer almost three hours after the caravan left San José.

"Maybe," he answered, and squinted into the mirror to check the road behind them. He started to slow up.

"Was there a road near the cemetery?"

"Yeah. It looks like a little dirt road."

"This is it, I think," Lynch said tentatively as he twisted around in his seat.

Kramer stopped the jeep and made a U-turn. The two jeeps behind followed him. They drove a mile or so back to where a few granite gravestones jutted out of the earth in a neatly kept cemetery beside the narrow highway. There were a gate and a narrow road that rose up a gentle, nearly barren slope and then disappeared several miles farther on into a mountainous, dark green rain forest. Lynch opened the gate, and the caravan followed the dirt road up the mountain until it became a trail and then ended abruptly in front of an almost opaque thicket of trees and greenery. Lynch, Fred Kramer, the other DEA agents and the Costa Rican policemen got out of the jeeps; collected canteens of water, some military rations obtained at the embassy and a walkie-talkie, and disappeared into the jungle.

The remaining members of the group drove back down the hill. After a few minutes, they found the airstrip where the BBJ jet was to land. The runway was no more than three or four thousand feet long and was pocked with holes, but it seemed usable. For about forty-five minutes, they vicariously accompanied the others into the jungle via walkie-talkies lent them by a CIA officer in the embassy. Supposedly, the KGB wouldn't be able to eavesdrop on them. Kramer reported that they were approaching the top of a mountain, and Lynch said that he would find Boyce's hooch near the bottom. After that message they lost radio contact, and there was nothing left to do but complain about the heat. It was almost midday, and the temperature had long since passed 90 degrees. Someone joked about wanting to send the message "Let it snow," and they went to a *cantina* to buy a cold drink. When that didn't cool them off, they bought a watermelon from a vendor and split it open with a big knife and shared it.

After two hours of waiting, Homenick befriended a group of Costa Rican youngsters who were puzzled by the *gringos*. He bought snow cones for the children from a pushcart peddler and borrowed the bicycle of one of the youngsters to explore Cañas, a hamlet on the edge of the jungle that reminded him of a frontier town in the Old West.

In single file, members of the raiding team crossed the mountain, forded a river and, near the top, ducked under a waterfall that cascaded more than seventy feet down a steep chasm scented by red and yellow blossoms. On the down slope of the mountain, the jungle grew thicker and darker; spider monkeys and birds high in the canopy of trees above chattered a warning of their approach, and on lower limbs of the trees, Lynch, Kramer and the others spotted brilliantly colored snakes sliding away from them. They saw armadillos and anteaters and, several times, the fresh tracks of a jaguar. But they didn't find a trace of Christopher Boyce, or the campsite where Lynch had said he had spent the night with him.

"No sign of a hooch."

Fred Kramer was the first to speak as they walked out of the jungle six hours after it had seemed to swallow them up.

All six members of the raiding party were caked with mud. Their armpits were stained with perspiration, and their pant legs darkened to their thighs. They had been so exhausted by the heat that they could hardly talk.

"I just couldn't find it."

Tommy Lynch sat in a *cantina* near Cañas, downing one beer after another and apologizing again and again. "I was only there once; I just couldn't find it again. It's a mess in there, a maze, it all looks the same. I know he's in there. I just couldn't find him."

"He's right," Kramer said. "It's a mess."

"You tried; you did your best," one of the deputies said, trying to make Lynch less disconsolate.

While they waited in the *cantina*, the Costa Rican policemen showed photographs of Boyce to shopkeepers, street vendors and others in the town, but no one recognized his face.

The drive back to San José took almost four hours, and on the way home no one said much.

In the morning, however, Lynch was optimistic again.

He said that if they were patient they'd find Boyce at the Soda Palace. He was sure of it. At least once a week, Boyce took a bus to

As teenagers, Christopher John Boyce and Andrew Daulton
Lee flew their falcons and camped in the hills near Lompoc,
California.

Convicted as Soviet spies, both young men were sentenced to the Federal Correctional Institution at Lompoc, where Boyce began work on a book about prison life while planning his escape.

The hollowed-out hole found by investigators on the morning after Boyce's disappearance and the grate that had covered it.

Guards discovered a crude pine ladder made of two-by-fours near the prison fence, which had barbed wire and lethal razor-wire at the top to prevent escape.

U.S. MARSHALS SERVICE

U.S. Department of Justice
United States Marshals Service

WANTED
BY U.S. MARSHALS

NOTICE TO ARRESTING AGENCY: BEFORE ARREST, VALIDATE WARRANT THROUGH NATIONAL CRIME INFORMATION CENTER (NCIC).

UNITED STATES MARSHALS SERVICE NCIC ENTRY NUMBER: (NIC/ W224966144).

NAME: CHRISTOPHER JOHN BOYCE

AKA(S):

DESCRIPTION:
SEX:	MALE
RACE:	WHITE
PLACE OF BIRTH:	SANTA MONICA, CALIFORNIA
DATE(S) OF BIRTH:	FEBRUARY 16, 1953
HEIGHT:	5'9"
WEIGHT:	160
EYES:	BLUE
HAIR:	BROWN
SKINTONE:	
SCARS, MARKS, TATOOS:	
SOCIAL SECURITY NUMBER(S):	566-94-9235
NCIC FINGERPRINT CLASSIFICATION:	16 04 TT 10 03 16 54 TT 04 05

ADDRESS AND LOCALE:

WANTED FOR:	ESCAPE	T 18 USC 751
WARRANT ISSUED:	LOS ANGELES, CALIFORNIA	
WARRANT NUMBER:	19347-148	
DATE WARRANT ISSUED:	JANUARY 21, 1980	

MISCELLANEOUS INFORMATION: BOYCE was convicted of ESPIONAGE in LOS ANGELES, California on June 20, 1977. Sentenced to 40
VEHICLE/TAG INFORMATION: years. Escaped from FCI Lompoc, Ca. 1-21-80.

IF ARRESTED OR WHEREABOUTS KNOWN, NOTIFY THE LOCAL UNITED STATES MARSHALS OFFICE.
(TELEPHONE:).
IF NO ANSWER, CALL UNITED STATES MARSHALS SERVICE COMMUNICATIONS CENTER IN WASHINGTON, D.C.
TELEPHONE 703-285-1100 : NLETS ACCESS CODE IS DCUSM0000.
(24 Hour telephone contact)

FORM USM -132
(EST. 5/79)

The face of Christopher John Boyce looked out from thousands of Wanted posters distributed around the world by the U.S. Marshals Service.

Boyce's friend Larry Homenick was ordered to find him.

The manhunt was directed by Howard Safir (at right) and Thomas C. Kupferer of the Marshals Service.

G. Wayne (Duke) Smith, who headed investigations in Costa Rica and South Africa, at the Playboy Hotel.

Gloria Ann White, who built her home with her own hands, said that she would have felt more comfortable in the nineteenth than in the twentieth century.

ROBERT LINDSEY

Christopher John Boyce, before escaping from prison at Lompoc, vowed that he would never be taken alive.

town to buy groceries and visit a bordello. If they waited long enough at the Soda Palace, he'd show up there looking for Lynch so they could go ahead with plans for the gunrunning operation.

At the American Embassy, senior officials told Duke Smith that they worried about having so many Americans in Costa Rica for so long on a secret mission. Too many things could go wrong. If the operation couldn't be ended, it was time to reduce its size.

Kupferer agreed reluctantly and decided to bring Homenick and Gerry Smith home, leaving Tony Perez and Duke Smith, because they both spoke Spanish, and Bob Dighera, the case agent for Tommy Lynch.

Homenick and Gerry Smith flew from San José to Mexico City, but their plane was an hour late, causing them to miss connections with a flight to Los Angeles. The delay gave Homenick time to buy a ring for Karen at an airport jewelry store—a peace offering, because the investigation was not over yet.

Tony Perez thought of himself as Dr. Pepper. Three times a day—at ten in the morning, two in the afternoon and six in the evening—he and Duke Smith staked out the Soda Palace. They did it every day for a week. But Boyce did not appear. When they weren't drinking coffee at the Soda Palace, they showed his picture to people in restaurants, bars and bordellos; at the airport, bus stations and taxi stands—to anyone who would look at his photograph. No one admitted to having seen him.

Dighera returned to the hotel late one night after canvassing the bars in search of Boyce and unlocked the door of the room he shared with Lynch. Through the half-opened door, he spotted the flesh and dark hair of a young woman. She looked up at him and quickly pulled the covers over her body.

"Excuse me," he said, and started closing the door.

"Wait a second!" Lynch shouted. He got out of bed, put on his pants and walked over to Dighera with a troubled look on his face.

As usual, he reeked of perspiration.

"Can you help me out?" he asked. "I owe her fifty bucks. I don't have the money. Can you be a buddy and help me out?"

Dighera gave him $50 and left.

* * *

Don North was still waiting at the Playboy for a call from Lynch. It had now been almost two weeks since NBC had sent him to San José to find Boyce, and the network was getting impatient. If he didn't find him soon, NBC said, it would have to stop paying his expenses.

North was mystified. He couldn't understand what had happened to Lynch. In California, he had promised to call North at the Playboy the day after he arrived. After two days, North began telephoning people in the United States who knew Lynch to find out what had happened to him. None of them knew where he was.

North was a resourceful and persistent reporter, however, and he managed to obtain from one of these friends the name of someone Lynch knew in San José, a Costa Rican named Carlos. When he found him several days later, Carlos told North a puzzling story.

In early January, Carlos said, Lynch had called him from Fresno and asked him to send him a telegram from San José with a brief message: "Cancel meeting in Mexico City. Change to San José, Costa Rica. Must see you." Carlos said he didn't recall why Lynch had asked him to send the telegram, but he thought it might have had something to do with problems he was having with customs or immigration officials. Carlos remembered only one other thing about the telegram: "He asked me to sign it 'C.B.' "

North left San José shortly after that.

During the day, Tony Perez was starting to wonder what drinking so much coffee at the Soda Palace was doing to his kidneys. At night, he worried about running out of money. When they weren't checking the bars for Boyce, Smith, Dighera and Perez played poker with Lynch in the hotel, and most nights, Lynch won.

The big pots that Lynch scooped in every night while urging the marshals to be patient about finding Boyce was only a minor cause, however, of the stresses that had begun to develop in the relationship between him and his poker companions. In conversations over the poker table, the three federal agents had begun to catch him in disconcerting contradictions. One night he mentioned that besides a 9mm semiautomatic, Boyce carried a .38 revolver. But a week

168

earlier, he'd said that he had a .44, not a .38. Another time, he said that he had never taken the bus to Cañas with Boyce.

The daily ritual of staking out the Soda Palace continued, but at night Smith, Dighera and Perez began to give Lynch the cold shoulder. Complaining that he was being ostracized, Lynch reacted angrily and then refused to talk. He began to sit for hours at a time on the edge of his bed, wearing his Levi's and T-shirt with a Harley-Davidson motorcycle logo on it, and sulk.

"You guys don't believe me, do you?"

There was silence in the hotel room.

"Then fuck you. If you don't believe me, the hell with you."

At an airport in the United States, an all-black jet aircraft was waiting to make a hurried flight to Costa Rica. But in San José and Tysons Corner and Los Angeles, where Larry Homenick awaited word of the investigation, a tacit consensus was growing that they would not need the plane. After almost three weeks of dealing with him, they were starting to believe that Tommy Lynch, despite the validations of his veracity by one of the best polygraphers in the DEA, was a liar and a hoaxer.

On Sunday, March 1, with Lynch still insisting that they could find Boyce if they waited one more day at the Soda Palace, the U.S. Marshals Service ended its first manhunt outside the United States.

At the San José airport, as Duke Smith was about to board a plane for El Paso, the manager of the airport restaurant rushed up to him breathless and said that he had seen the man in the photograph Smith had shown him a few days earlier. The man in the picture, he said, had left San José the night before on a flight to New Orleans.

There was nothing he could do about it, Smith decided, and he got on his plane. Bob Dighera and Tony Perez flew back to California, and so did Tommy Lynch, using a ticket paid for by the U.S. Government.

A few weeks later, Don North returned to San José and visited the offices of the *Tico Times,* one of San José's two English-language newspapers. He told a reporter about his search for Christopher Boyce and a curious story that had been told to him by a former mercenary who had once promised to lead him to Boyce in Costa Rica and then vanished.

North had found Tommy Lynch at his home near Fresno. Lynch, he told the reporter, had told him a bewildering tale. He said that he had flown to San José to meet North, but had been kidnapped by American agents on his way to the Playboy Hotel. They had held him captive in a hotel room for two weeks while they grilled him about the whereabouts of Boyce. Lynch insisted that he had not betrayed his friend, and that while he was being held captive, Boyce had managed to slip away. Lynch said he had no idea where he was now.

The reporter for the *Tico Times* wrote an article that filled much of the newspaper's front page the next day but ended inconclusively: "Was Boyce in Costa Rica running guns? Did U.S. authorities trail two free-lance reporters and commandeer their contact on the case? Or did the Falcon lead the Feds on a wild-goose chase?"

In Los Angeles, Larry Homenick looked at the old leads on his desk and wondered what to do next.

27

THE NEWS FROM AUSTRALIA WAS BAD:

> We have conducted inquiries into the information given in
> the attached memo received from G. Wayne Smith, inspector
> with the U.S. Marshals Service, and found that Christopher
> James Boyce was up to a few months ago residing at 18
> Jennifer Crescent, Thirroul. This person does not appear to be
> identical with the man wanted in the United States. . . .

The writer, a detective in Wollongong, New South Wales, Australia, said that he had learned that the man in question had lived in
Alice Springs before moving to New South Wales. He said that he
had not interviewed the man directly, but on the basis of his inquiries to former neighbors it appeared that he was simply an Australian named Boyce who was interested in hang gliding.

Tysons Corner was not convinced and asked the detective to
make further inquiries.

In the weeks following the debacle in San José, Homenick spent
much of his time in the air, traveling to the East Coast, Honolulu
and elsewhere to interview prison inmates, ex-cons, former guards
and others who might know where Chris was. He managed to be
home for the birth of his second son, Brett; but during the spring of
1981, he was often in a hotel room far from home. Almost every

171

night, he was awakened, in a sweat, by the same dream that had tormented him for more than a year: he saw himself catch Chris and lead him handcuffed back to prison, but then Chris, inexplicably, was suddenly free again and running away from him.

After returning from San José, Bob Dighera had moved back into the condominium in Palos Verdes and tried to put his heart again into the efforts to find Boyce in Southern California. He dispatched investigators to Kansas, New Hampshire, North Carolina, Texas, Hawaii, Alaska, Arizona and other places trying to forge a connection between Boyce and the drug underworld and Captain Midnight's associates in Mexico.

In a rural town in New Mexico, a deputy found the passenger who had boarded a New Orleans–bound jet in San José the night before Perez, Dighera and Smith left Costa Rica. It took the deputy who found him five seconds to realize that the man did not look at all like Christopher Boyce.

Boyce's photograph was now staring out from a Wanted poster on hundreds of walls across America. Homenick sent it to colleges, health-food stores, state driver's-license agencies and any other place where he imagined Boyce might appear.

Chuck Kupferer said that if there wasn't a break in the investigation soon, he would organize a task force in El Paso and use it as a base to go after Boyce in the hinterlands of Mexico where Captain Midnight had said he would hide out.

What had been a personal nightmare for Homenick had become a collective nightmare for the U.S. Marshals Service. Its drive for a more important future was mired in its failure to locate Christopher John Boyce.

Just a month earlier, rumors had circulated in Washington that Boyce would soon be run to ground in Costa Rica. Now there were rumors that the Marshals Service had been taken in by a crazy ex-mercenary who could easily have involved the United States in an embarrassing international incident. There was talk on Capitol Hill that Christopher Boyce had done far more damage to American national security than had been publicly revealed, and there were proposals for legislation that would force the Justice Department to give jurisdiction over escaped prisoners back to the FBI.

To build the best possible case for the Marshals Service if it was called before Congress, Kupferer ordered Homenick to prepare a complete special report of the investigation that proved the lengths to which the Service had gone to find Boyce. To get away from the distractions of his own office, Homenick drove down to San Diego to write the report.

The Marshals Service offices in San Diego are hidden among a warren of courtrooms in the U.S. Courthouse, a sleek modern building of brick and glass located between the city's salty strip of topless joints and tattoo parlors which has long catered to the Pacific Fleet and the sand-colored spire of the Metropolitan Correctional Center, where Boyce had spent almost a year. When Homenick arrived there one morning near the end of April 1981, Bob Dighera gave him a briefing on the progress of the second task force and showed him a copy of the anonymous letter that had arrived at the U.S. Embassy in Pretoria while the two of them had been in Costa Rica. The letter asserted that Boyce had been in South Africa between February and June of 1980, had received help from an American named Schmeiser and was using a forged passport under the alias Hollenbeck.

Dighera said the embassy had since reported that South African immigration authorities had checked their records but couldn't find evidence that any U.S. citizen with either name had entered the country in 1980.

The letter was probably another hoax, they agreed. Still, they thought it had a ring of authenticity.

"Wait a second," Homenick said.

He looked through a copy of *The Falcon and the Snowman* and found a passage about Boyce's family.

"Hollenbeck! That's Mrs. Boyce's maiden name; I knew it was familiar."

Then he leafed through the case file that he had brought to San Diego and located a report of the interview the previous November with Frank Burton Riley, the former New Jersey mercenary soldier who had done time at Terminal Island when Chris was there.

"Francis Augustus Schmeiser! That's one of the aliases Riley uses."

Over the next three days, Deputy Beverly Bargamian from the Newark office and Inspector Joseph Heil from Trenton assembled a large file on Frank Burton Riley, based on interviews and a review of federal, state and local law-enforcement files. It described a violent career criminal with a passion for guns and an obsessive hatred of blacks.

Riley had been in and out of prisons since the age of nineteen. His rap sheet was almost three pages long. It listed arrests for bank robbery, the attempted murder of a policeman, mail fraud, illegal possession of a machine gun and other crimes. Riley, the report indicated, was from a family of substantial wealth, but money had not kept him out of trouble. There were newspaper clippings reporting that when he was still a high school student he had been arrested for robbing a bank to finance what reporters called a "neo-Nazi group." Several years later, he was jailed for attempting to shoot it out with a policeman, and in 1974 he was ejected from the Rhodesian infantry for stabbing another member of the mercenary army. After this incident he had returned to the United States and tried to recruit other mercenaries to fight black insurgents in southern Africa. At home he got into trouble again. He established a mail-order business purporting to import illegal machine guns into the United States, and after some customers claimed they had not received what they'd ordered, he was convicted of mail fraud and sent to Terminal Island.

Almost incidentally, the report noted that Riley often used his mother's maiden name, "Schmeiser," because it was German, and "he fancies himself of the Aryan race with a penchant towards the Nazi ideals."

Looking at the report in his office at Tysons Corner, Chuck Kupferer, using his favorite appellation for a criminal, turned to one of his aides and said, "This guy's a real asshole."

As he weighed his next move, a cable arrived from the U.S. Ambassador in Pretoria. South African immigration records showed that an American named Frank Burton Riley had visited South Africa from February 1 to February 13, 1980, barely two weeks after

Christopher Boyce's escape, and had returned a year later, on January 26, 1981. On this trip, he had listed his occupation on immigration papers as "anthropologist."

Kupferer called the Newark office and ordered: "Find Riley and sit on him."

Beverly Bargamian and Joe Heil discovered that Riley had recently been released from a hospital in northern New Jersey, where he had undergone double-hernia surgery. At his home in Tenafly, his mother told them that he had moved and rented a place in the nearby town of Closter; she did not have his address. New Jersey motor-vehicle registration files indicated that the owner of a 1979 Buick named Frank Burton Riley lived in Closter. The next day they drove up to a large old white wooden house in Closter that was partly hidden behind a fence and a row of maple trees. The motor-vehicle registration papers indicated that he lived in a two-story red house behind the white house. Behind the red house was a small shopping center, and across the street was the Closter Boro Hall, which housed the Closter Police Department. The car registered to Riley was at a curb near the house. They parked nearby and placed the red house under surveillance.

In Los Angeles, Larry Homenick placed a package on a Newark-bound jet that contained a grand-jury subpoena to the New Jersey Bell Company for Riley's telephone toll records. At Tysons Corner, Kupferer ordered the Newark Warrants squad to give the surveillance of Riley precedence over all other cases.

On the morning of May 21, Bargamian and Deputy Cosmo Alagna, Jr., were waiting in a car near Riley's home when, at about nine o'clock, he came out the front door and walked quickly over to a nearby diner. He ordered breakfast and, twenty minutes later, got into the Buick and drove off. The two deputies tried to follow, but lost him in traffic.

Disappointed, they drove back to his neighborhood and parked. But after he didn't return in a few minutes, they decided that they were wasting their time and went back to their office. Before leaving, Alagna walked over to a heavy brown plastic trash bag that was lying on the ground near a curb and picked it up, and they took Frank Riley's garbage to their office in Newark. They placed the bag on a desk and started digging.

There were kitchen scraps, tin cans, a recent issue of *The New York Times*, discarded medical bills, a pair of torn shoelaces, a single corroded razor blade and pieces of junk mail. As they dug deeper into the bag, the lode became more interesting: an empty plastic sheath for a handgun sold by a Harrington Park, New Jersey, gun shop; a Diners Club charge receipt from the Rand International Hotel in Johannesburg, South Africa, signed by Frank Riley and dated February 1, 1981; almost a dozen spent .38-caliber cartridges and eight pieces of white stationery on which someone had been composing a letter.

Whoever had written the letter was a poor typist. It appeared that the author had repeatedly made typographical errors, discarded the partly finished letter and then tried again, typing the same message. Despite the mistakes and misspelled words, the intended message was clear. All of the letters were dated March 21, 1981, and started:

To whom it may concern:

In accordance with the Migration Act of 1958, Frank B. Riley has been granted Permanent Residency in Australia. Mr. Riley is married to an Australian woman. Any inquiries relevant to Mr. Riley's status should be directed to Immigration Control, Canberra, Australia.

At the bottom of the text, where a signature would go, were the typed words "Robert Cotton, Consul General."

The trash had produced at least two items that were potentially significant: there were indications that Frank Burton Riley had a firearm, a felony for an ex-convict, and it appeared that he was contemplating a trip to Australia.

Then Beverly Bargamian found one more item in the plastic bag that was even more interesting, and it made her call Chuck Kupferer at Tysons Corner. It was a torn invoice and itinerary from a travel agency in Closter that showed Riley and a person listed as "H. Rabinowitz" were booked on United Airlines Flight 35 from Newark to San Francisco on May 21, 1981. The flight left at 10 A.M.

Bargamian and Alagna looked at their watches. It was almost noon.

28

TEN MINUTES LATER, THEY LEARNED THAT RILEY
had missed the flight.

Tapping the intelligence sources that give law-enforcement
agencies access to airline passenger logs, Bargamian and Alagna
discovered that Riley and a passenger named Rabinowitz had
rebooked their trip for the same day on United Flight 129, Newark
to San Francisco, which made a stop en route at Chicago. It was
scheduled to depart in less than an hour, at 1 P.M., and the passengers were at the airport. Riley had already checked in on Flight 129
and had been assigned Seat 19F. A passenger named H. Rabinowitz was in Seat 19E.

Alagna and Inspector Joe Heil jumped into a government car and
raced to Newark Airport. Still breathless from sprinting through
the tall corridors of the sprawling airport, they reached Gate 17 just
as the doors of a Boeing 747 were being shut and an airline agent
was giving final clearance for Flight 129 to leave the gate.

"Is this man on the plane?" Heil asked, showing the agent his
badge and a photograph of Riley.

The agent said he hadn't seen him, but agreed to look for him.
Over an intercom radio, he asked the stewardess to reopen the
door, and a few minutes later he returned and said the man in the
photograph was in Row 19, talking to a thin man beside him who
was in his fifties and had a high forehead.

As the plane was taxiing to a runway, Heil called Kupferer. He said that Riley and a man who appeared to be H. Rabinowitz were on Flight 129, scheduled to arrive at O'Hare International Airport in Chicago at 2:43 P.M.

The plane landed on schedule, two hours later, at O'Hare.

Riley and his companion walked out of the plane along with scores of briefcase-toting businessmen, tourists and other passengers who were getting off at Chicago. At the fringes of the crowd were two deputy U.S. marshals. They identified Riley from photographs sent by facsimile machine from Newark and followed the men to a bar. Riley and his companion had a beer and talked. A few minutes later they got back onto the 747, which left on schedule, with a predicted on-time arrival at San Francisco International Airport in four hours—at 6 P.M., San Francisco time.

"Riley's going to land in San Francisco at six on United Airlines Flight 129." Kupferer was talking to Homenick at his desk in Los Angeles. "Get somebody there as fast as you can to pick up his tail there. I've called Frisco and they'll have somebody waiting."

Homenick checked his watch. It was almost three o'clock in Los Angeles. The flight to San Francisco took an hour. He looked around and spotted Phil Sena, a big, muscular deputy who had a Black Belt in karate and a college degree in East Asian studies. He told him to reserve a seat on the next flight to San Francisco.

Sena approached him sheepishly a few moments later. The only seat available to San Francisco during the next two hours was a first-class seat, and Sena asked if it was all right to break government regulations requiring economy-class travel. Homenick gave an okay, handed him several mug shots of Riley and told him to be on his way.

While the United 747 from Newark was being towed to its gate in San Francisco, Sena and Inspector Wayne Hardage from the San Francisco office of the Marshals Service sprinted through the terminal, and were there when it docked. Sena had arrived from Los Angeles ten minutes before Flight 129.

After Flight 129 had left Newark on its transcontinental flight, Deputy Richard Callaghan in New Jersey was asked to find out what he could about the unidentified man called H. Rabinowitz. Riley's companion, he discovered quickly, was almost certainly

Henry Aloysius Rabinowitz, a fifty-nine-year-old ex-con with a criminal record stretching back to 1937 and scars from bullet wounds all over his belly that resulted from an unsuccessful effort to shoot it out with pursuing policemen in the 1940s. Rabinowitz, who had a list of arrests that filled six pages, was currently on parole for a 1968 bank-robbery conviction, and his parole officer told Callaghan that if he had left New Jersey without authorization, Rabinowitz had violated the terms of the parole and could be sent back to prison.

Frank Riley and Henry Rabinowitz hailed a taxi at San Francisco International Airport and watched darkness settle over San Francisco Bay as it headed north toward the city on the Bayshore Freeway.

In an unmarked car, Phil Sena and Wayne Hardage followed the taxi to the Hotel Stewart on Geary Street, an aging, middle-class hotel situated between swank Union Square and San Francisco's seedy Tenderloin district.

"Sit on 'em," Kupferer told Hardage and Sena when they called in to report that Riley and Rabinowitz had checked into the hotel.

There were several possibilities, Kupferer thought, that could have brought the two men to San Francisco. It could be a vacation, but given their criminal records, that was unlikely; they could be in San Francisco to plan a job, which seemed like a good possibility. Or, they could have come to San Francisco for a meeting with Boyce; or they might be planning to move on from San Francisco to meet him in Australia, South Africa or somewhere else. Kupferer decided to dispatch reinforcements from Los Angeles and San Diego, and before the day was over, eight deputies were maintaining covert twenty-four-hour surveillance of the two men.

The morning after their arrival, Riley and Rabinowitz took a stroll around Union Square, the broad, grassy plaza flanked by hotels, department stores, shops and airline offices that forms the mercantile heart of San Francisco. After an hour, they hailed a taxi, and with a team of deputies following them in a rented car, they crossed Nob Hill to Fisherman's Wharf, where they bought a ticket for an excursion boat that circled Alcatraz, the abandoned prison fortress in San Francisco Bay. Aboard the boat, two deputies eavesdropped as Riley and Rabinowitz speculated about what life must have been like for the island's inmates. They didn't give a hint as to why they had come to San Francisco.

At seven o'clock the next morning, Riley sprinted out of the hotel in a jogging suit and began loping around Union Square, then jogged into the Tenderloin district, passing derelicts still sleeping off their sweet muscatel from the night before. Phil Sena ran behind him, pretending to be taking *his* morning run. Riley returned after thirty minutes and closed the door of the hotel room he shared with Rabinowitz. This gave members of the rapidly growing surveillance team time to get organized and capitalize on a piece of luck. Executives of the St. Francis Hotel, which was across the street from the Stewart, agreed to let them use a room that looked down on the Stewart through a large picture window, and they established a command post there to wait for the next move by Riley and Rabinowitz.

In the afternoon, they saw the two men walk out the front door of the hotel and hail a taxi. Two deputies followed them back to Fisherman's Wharf, where they had lunch at a seafood restaurant and afterward wandered, with thousands of other visitors to San Francisco, along the waterfront. Several times, the deputies behind them thought they saw Riley and Rabinowitz brush hard against other people walking along the crowded sidewalks, buying souvenirs or stopping for bright red cocktails of plump Bay shrimp or Dungeness crab. But there was no expression of recognition on the faces of the strangers, or on those of Riley and Rabinowitz. After almost two hours, they took a cable car back to the hotel.

"Frog One's comin' out the front door, turning left," Deputy John Pascucci, looking down on the street from the St. Francis, said into his walkie-talkie. Dan Stolz, who was leaning against a building wall near the Stewart wearing Levi's, a dirty shirt, a seaman's watch cap and a miniature earphone, answered, "I've got him."

Across the street, his partner, Jan Axthelm, the female half of the partnership other deputies called "Jan and Dan, the Dance Team," started to move.

Riley walked north on Powell Street and crossed Union Square to Post Street, where Powell begins its ascent toward Nob Hill. Seeming to be in a hurry, he walked effortlessly up the steep hill and past the Sir Francis Drake Hotel, making it hard for the Dance Team to keep up with him. At Sutter Street, Powell Street briefly interrupts its climb up Nob Hill. Riley reached the intersection and began to cross the street. When he reached the other side, Stolz lost him. He sprinted up the hill toward the intersection; but when he got there, Frank Riley was standing there motionless and studying him curiously. Their eyes met, and Stolz leaned over to tie his shoes. Riley looked at him a few moments, turned around and resumed his walk toward Nob Hill.

Three days after they arrived in San Francisco, Riley and Rabinowitz took a cab to San Francisco International Airport and flew back to New Jersey, the purpose of their trip as much a mystery as when they had arrived.

They left only one clue behind them—a scrap of paper with several telephone numbers that the deputies found in a wastebasket in their room. The area code for two of the numbers was 213, the code for Los Angeles and most of its suburbs. The same two numbers had appeared on a list of toll calls on a phone bill that had been found in Riley's trash in Closter. Homenick had instantly recognized the exchange: it was that of Hermosa Beach, the town near Palos Verdes where he had spent a long evening waiting vainly for Chris to make arrangements for passage to South Africa and had later spent hours in a futile search for him at a white house on the Pacific Coast Highway.

He traced both telephone numbers to the same address, a large apartment complex in Hermosa Beach not far from the highway. He recognized the address, too. Less than a month after Chris's escape, deputies had gone to the apartment complex to interview a former girlfriend of Daulton Lee's who lived in one of the apartments. According to records of the General Telephone Company, one of the numbers was listed for the building manager, and the other, in Apartment 363, was in the name of Colonel Raymond Lincoln.

Homenick ran Lincoln's name and address through a data bank operated by the California Department of Motor Vehicles that contains the names and addresses of the millions of Californians who own motor vehicles or have been issued state driver's licenses. There wasn't any record of a Raymond Lincoln at the address in Hermosa Beach. Homenick decided to make a quiet inquiry of the building manager.

"We don't have anybody named Lincoln," said the middle-aged woman who managed the apartment complex with her husband. "Apartment 363 is rented to a Mr. Hudson, a retired colonel."

Homenick didn't say anything for a moment.

"Do you mean *Colonel* Hudson?"

"Yes."

"Is he an older man with glasses? A gravelly voice?"

"Yes," the woman said. "He says he's a colonel; we're not sure he really is."

Homenick couldn't believe it. He had known Paul Peter Hudson—Colonel Hudson—for almost ten years. They had met when Homenick was first assigned to booking prisoners at the Los Angeles Federal Courthouse lockup, and he had seen him many times since then over the years, usually after Colonel Hudson had been arrested for illegal possession of a machine gun or some other firearms violation.

Hudson was a tall man in his early sixties with a gaunt, cadaverous face. He was obsessed with guns and war and was forever boasting of military exploits during World War II. He'd had printed on his personal bank checks a photograph of himself in the full-dress uniform of an Army major general. A relative had once told Homenick that Colonel Hudson had never been promoted beyond major, but nobody in the family was sure. Hudson claimed to have received a battlefield promotion to general, and his family humored him about it. He entertained policemen and other prisoners with tales of service in Europe under General George S. Patton, and his stories, if embroidered with something other than the truth, were told with eloquence and color. Homenick had decided that Colonel Hudson was a wacko when he appeared in court one day wearing top hat and tails and a stiff shirt emblazoned with five rows of combat medals. "He's the kind of guy," he told Karen, "that you'd see on a *Barney Miller* show."

182

"Does he talk like this?" Homenick asked in a gravelly snarl reminiscent of Louis "Satchmo" Armstrong.

"That's him," the manager said disapprovingly.

She said that she had just initiated legal steps to evict Colonel Hudson. "He's three weeks behind in his rent, and he's giving us other problems. Some of our women tenants say that when they go into the pool he sometimes exposes himself and makes lewd remarks."

"Does the name Frank Riley mean anything to you?"

Homenick expected her to say that it didn't.

"Oh, that's the Colonel's nephew."

"What makes you say that?" She looked down at her file on Apartment 363 and pointed to a notation she had made the month before. Homenick looked at the notation carefully. It indicated someone named Frank Riley had called to inquire about Apartment 363.

"He said he was Colonel Hudson's nephew and hadn't been able to reach him on the telephone and asked me if I knew if anything was wrong. I told him he was probably in the VA hospital. And I told him the Colonel was behind in his rent and I might have to evict him. That bothered his nephew. He said he was in New Jersey but was going to be coming to San Francisco soon on his way to visit a friend in Australia, and he said he would stop and pay his back rent. I think there was something in the apartment that he said belonged to him and he wanted to get it.

"I told him the place was filthy. He asked if I knew what Colonel Hudson had left behind, and I told him I didn't know, it's such a mess in there. He said, 'Don't worry about the mess. Leave it alone; I'll get in there and clean it up.' "

Riley had called again just a few days before and asked about the Colonel's health. "He told me he would be in Los Angeles soon and could clean out the apartment and pay the rent."

What connection was there between Riley and Colonel Hudson? Could there be a connection between the Colonel and Chris? What was in the Colonel's apartment that Riley wanted?

Homenick got out the list of prisoners who had been in the cellblock with Chris at Terminal Island. Along with Frank Riley and Christopher Boyce was the name Paul Hudson.

29

FRANK RILEY, AN UNOPENED UMBRELLA IN ONE hand, locked the door of the red house in Closter, New Jersey, on June 2, looked up at a murky sky and began his run. About two hundred yards behind, Deputy U.S. Marshal Cosmo Alagna, Jr., also broke into a run. Farther back, Deputy Richard Callaghan and a detective from the Closter Police Department followed slowly in a car. Riley picked up speed, reached an intersection in the residential neighborhood and turned left. When the three men behind him reached the corner thirty seconds later, he had disappeared.

They went back to his home and took a trash bag from the curb in front of the house. There wasn't anything of interest in it. Riley was back two hours later. He still had his umbrella, unopened.

When Riley stayed home, the surveillance was easy duty for members of the task force. They could watch his house from a window of the Closter Police Department, a cup of coffee in hand. But as soon as he left the house, their work began to get harder. Suddenly, Riley began to use countersurveillance techniques, like an espionage agent who was trying to detect whether he was being watched. When he went for a walk or a run, Riley turned around periodically to survey the street behind him. When he drove, he suddenly applied the brakes to his Buick as the traffic signal turned yellow, then sped through the intersection as the light turned red. Often he pulled his car to the side of the road abruptly, forcing the deputies behind him to follow suit or drive past.

As the deputies in Closter worried about how to deal with Riley, Larry Homenick told Justice Department lawyers that he wanted badly to search Colonel Hudson's apartment. George O'Connell, an assistant U.S. attorney who was assigned to the Boyce investigation, said he would do some research on the matter.

Frank Riley was now getting personalized trash-pickup service from the Closter Department of Public Works. Each morning, a truck from the Department collected the garbage and delivered it to Boro Hall and a waiting team of investigators.

The truck made its usual pickup at seven forty-five on the morning of June 9. A few minutes later, a taxi arrived at the house and Riley got in, carrying a small suitcase. Alagna and Bargamian followed the taxi to Newark Airport, where Riley boarded United Flight 35 for San Francisco.

There was foul weather over the Midwest that delayed the departure by almost an hour. Kupferer had plenty of time to reassemble his surveillance team in San Francisco. It was waiting when the nonstop flight arrived five hours later.

Riley checked into the Stewart Hotel again, and the following day Henry Rabinowitz joined him. Across the street, most of the same U.S. marshals who had watched them on their earlier trip to San Francisco resumed their vigil through the same picture window at the St. Francis Hotel. Worried that Boyce might soon make his move, they also rented a room across the hall from Riley and took turns lying prone on the floor peeking underneath the door. The first person they saw enter the room was a young woman.

Vickie was prettier than most of the streetwalkers who trolled for customers on the frontier between the shabby Tenderloin and the expensive hotels on Union Square. She was blond, in her middle twenties, with a good figure, clothes that were too tight and a face that had not yet been hardened by the streets. She entered the hotel room with Henry Rabinowitz and left an hour later with $75.

Deputy John Pascucci was outside the Stewart in a van the following day when Riley emerged from the hotel entrance and got into a taxi. Pascucci reached out to start the engine, but the ignition key wasn't there. His partner, who had left a few minutes earlier for a visit to a rest room, had absentmindedly taken it.

Pascucci jumped out of the car and flagged a taxi. He thrust his badge toward the driver and in the lyrical tones of the Bronx said, "I'm a United States marshal. Follow that car!"

The driver, a small Chinese man, brightened. He replied, "For twenty-two years I've been waiting for someone to say that. For twenty-two years! Let's go."

Chuck Kupferer's hunch that Riley had been planning a trip to Australia was confirmed a few hours later. Pascucci followed Riley to Qantas Airlines on Union Square. After another deputy picked up the surveillance, Pascucci showed his badge to a Qantas agent, along with a mug shot of Riley, and asked if the man in the photograph had bought a ticket from her.

"He booked a seat to Sydney," she said as she looked at the picture. "He's on Flight 12 from Los Angeles to Sydney on July tenth."

It was a round-trip ticket, she added, although he hadn't made a reservation for the return flight. Pascucci asked the agent if Riley had made any small talk when he was in the office. "The only thing I remember," she said, "was that he was going to visit a friend who lived somewhere near Melbourne."

Larry Homenick drove back to the apartments in Hermosa Beach to find out more about the connection between Colonel Hudson and Frank Riley. The husband of the woman who had helped him before greeted him cordially and said he knew all about his earlier visit. Since then, they'd instituted formal eviction proceedings against Hudson. County marshals would be coming soon to remove his belongings.

"Would you mind calling me when they come, so I can look at his stuff before they take it?" Homenick asked.

"Sure," the manager said. "Would you like to peek in there now?"

"I sure would," Homenick answered.

Homenick followed him past palm trees and lush foliage through a labyrinth of garden apartments to a three-story building. Two flights up, the man waved Homenick to a stop.

"Do you smell that?" the manager asked.

Homenick smelled something rancid.

"It's coming from his apartment. I had to vacate the apartments on both sides of him because of that. You'd better stand back," he said, and he unlocked the door.

The door came open, and Homenick discovered why the manager had wanted him to stand away. A dark cloud of black gnats surged out.

"This is Colonel Hudson's apartment," the manager said.

The electricity had been turned off. It was difficult to see anything. As his eyes adjusted, Homenick began to make out the outlines of the small studio apartment. To the left there was a narrow kitchen with piles of greasy dishes on the sink and a stack of garbage that was covered by a swaying gray mantle of maggots. Beside it, what appeared to be a combination living room-bedroom was ankle-deep in newspapers, magazines and boxes. More cartons were piled on chairs, a table and a sofa. Dead plants were limp in their pots. To the right of the large room was a tiny bathroom. It smelled of human excrement. Dozens of flies hovered noisily over the toilet.

"I'll have to come back later," Homenick said. "They don't pay me enough for this."

"I didn't think you'd last long," the manager said, and closed the door.

"Frog One's going out the building, turning left," Dan Stolz said as he sat behind the picture window in the St. Francis.

"I've got him," said Bob Whisnant. He was leaning against a car near the hotel.

A bachelor, a stylist dresser, Whisnant was wearing old jeans, a torn shirt and a three-day growth of beard. "He's turning left on Post past the Saint Francis," he said into his sleeve—into the microphone of his walkie-talkie.

A middle-aged man, who must have mistaken Whisnant for one of the homosexual prostitutes who cruised the neighborhood, walked up to him with a smile and tried to start a conversation. Whisnant brushed past him and saw that Riley was walking so fast that he was almost two blocks ahead of him.

He spotted a cable car as it rattled past him on Powell Street from its terminal at Market Street. As it paused at Union Square to collect passengers, he jumped aboard.

"Police officer!" he shouted at the gripman, who had turned toward him and was about to order him to jump off.

By the time Whisnant could dig his badge out of his jeans and show it to the gripman, he realized it had been a mistake to get on the cable car. Once it left Union Square, it accelerated up the hill. He was overtaking Riley.

Whisnant dived to the floor of the car and flattened himself beside the shoes of several dozen curious tourists. Holding his badge over his head, he whispered that he was following a man on the sidewalk. Before long, most of the passengers had enlisted in the adventure.

"He's going straight," one whispered.

"He looks like he's going to turn the corner," another said.

Whisnant waited a few moments and then leaped off and ran back down the hill to intercept Riley, but he had already turned the corner.

As he ran down the hill, a passenger on the cable car waved wildly at him, and then another, and soon there were half a dozen waving at him silently, as if to say *"Go back."*

Whisnant stopped in his tracks, looked around and saw a garage a few feet away. The door was open. He ducked inside, closed the door and peeked out through a crack. A moment later, Riley walked past. He had doubled back, checking to see if he had been followed.

As the surveillance continued, the deputies watching Riley realized that he had developed an interest in Vickie, the Tenderloin hooker. When he went for a walk he began to make a detour through the Tenderloin and bring her back to his room. Soon he was buying flowers for her at the open-air kiosks around Union Square and inviting her to lunch and then dinner at expensive restaurants. The deputies began to suspect that Frank Riley was becoming sweet on Vickie.

After almost a week of around-the-clock surveillance, the deputies were exhausted. The early camaraderie often turned into bitter clashes over strategy and assignments. They still had no idea why Riley was in San Francisco. The only thing the surveillance had yielded so far was that he had reserved an airline seat to fly to Australia on July 10.

Kupferer told Pascucci to make reservations on the same flight for himself and Larry Homenick.

Riley's life in San Francisco had settled into more of a routine. Most mornings, he jogged twenty minutes or so around the center of the city, then took a cab to Fisherman's Wharf. The tide of summer tourists jamming the narrow streets and sidewalks along the waterfront was growing bigger by the day, and keeping up with Riley was becoming more difficult. His predictable meanderings suggested that he was looking for someone in the crowd to make a contact. But the only people he spoke to were vendors or shop clerks or the waiters who served him lunch. The deputies shadowed him each outing he took, but lost him in the crowd enough times to be nagged by the possibility that he might already have made contact with Boyce.

Riley's evening routine was also predictable. When he returned to the hotel, he changed his clothes, jogged about a mile, walked a mile and repeated the cycle before returning to the hotel. He never spoke to strangers, but when he ran he usually kept his head high— not in the head-down attitude common to joggers. It was very much indeed as if Riley were looking for something, or someone. Afterward, he returned to the Stewart and then went out to dinner, sometimes with Rabinowitz, more often with Vickie.

On June 14, Riley checked out of the Stewart Hotel and moved into a hotel near the San Francisco International Airport. The next day he flew back to Newark.

30

LARRY HOMENICK SENT TWO DEPUTIES AHEAD OF
him for the assault on Colonel Hudson's apartment. Cocking their
arms as if they were lobbing hand grenades at an enemy, Deputies
Bob Whisnant and Steve Schaffer each hurled an insecticide bomb
through the open door of the apartment. Then they closed the door
and went away to wait for the poison to work.

Homenick had confirmed that Colonel Hudson was in a Veterans Administration hospital. Justice Department lawyers had decided that if the manager gave his consent, it was lawful for him to
search the Colonel's apartment without a court-authorized search
warrant, on the ground that his property had been abandoned. Kupferer told Homenick to move in before Riley decided to go after
whatever it was that interested him in the apartment.

Two hours after the cans of insecticide had been thrown in,
Homenick and Schaffer entered the apartment, wearing surgical
masks and gloves. The bugs were gone, but not the stench. By the
light of their flashlights and a few shafts of sunlight filtered
through a filthy sliding glass door, they saw the same chaos that
Homenick had seen on his first visit, although the flashlight spotted
something he hadn't noticed before: From opposite walls of the
apartment, identical poster-size photographs of the mustachioed
Colonel Hudson, his general's uniform neatly pressed, looked
down on them.

They divided the main room in half and began sifting through the chaos. After an hour, it was so hot that they had to take off the surgical masks.

Operating manuals for every machine gun that Homenick had ever heard about were stacked around the room. There were hundreds of ancient magazines reeking with the musty smell of mildew, boxes of ammunition, books, letters, cancelled checks with the Colonel's picture on them and stacks of newspaper clippings, including a lot of articles about the CIA and spying. After ninety minutes, Homenick finally unearthed something that made his heart beat faster: a clipping about the escape of Christopher John Boyce. A tenuous connection, but encouraging.

After another hour, afternoon shadows were darkening the room and it had become all but impossible to see in the gloomy apartment.

"Bingo!" Schaffer shouted.

He was holding up a typewritten letter dated December 2, 1977. "Terminal Island, California" was typed at the right-hand corner.

It began "Dear Colonel" and was signed "Your Rhodesian friend, *Frank Riley.*" It appeared to contain mostly reminiscences about prison life written by Riley to Colonel Hudson after Hudson had been released from Terminal Island. But along with the reminiscences was the passage that had caught Schaffer's attention: *"Chris just let me read the brief note you wrote to him. . . ."*

A few sentences later, Riley wrote: "Boyce is in the population and he seems to be doing real well. He's an orderly here in 'C' Dorm and he has his own room. . . ."

"Let's keep going," Homenick said, trying not to sound excited, and they plowed deeper into the mess.

Schaffer moved to a small white cabinet with a single drawer. It was stuffed with faded old bills and letters.

"Larry," he said a few minutes later. "Here's an envelope addressed to Colonel Hudson with a return address for Frank Riley in New Jersey."

"Let me see," Homenick said.

He opened the envelope and began to read the letter.

Suddenly his heart was pounding.

191

November 7, 1980

Dear Colonel

Two marshals interviewed me yesterday about our escaped friend. Somehow they've discovered that I helped get him into South Africa. In fact, they have even managed to pinpoint the exact geographical area in RSA, the Orange Free State. I suspect an informer has been at work.

If the feds contact you say nothing. Don't mention that I contacted you. Be your usual obnoxious self. If necessary phone me at the number I sent you previously.

F.R.

Homenick knocked a pile of magazines off a chair and sat down and looked at the letter again.

He *had* to sit down. It was incredible. He looked up at Schaffer and said, "This is what I've been looking for for a year and a *half.*"

The letter was evidence that showed not only where Boyce had gone following his escape but how he had gotten there.

The letters to the embassy in Pretoria, the mysterious phone call from the lieutenant colonel in South Africa, the inmates who had said Chris might flee to South Africa . . . the whole case came together with that letter in the dusty cabinet.

Five minutes later, they found another letter from Riley to Colonel Hudson. Dated November 24, 1981, it was apparently a response to the Colonel from Riley after Hudson had replied to the previous letter. Riley again mentioned the visit by the marshals:

There's a big push on for Boyce. I told the bums nothing. However, they seemed very suspicious, asking me about my recent trip to South Africa . . .

Take care, Colonel, and feel free to phone me any time. And if the feds question you about Chris please don't mention me or letters you've received from me.

Frank Riley

"You keep looking. I'm going to call Chuck Kupferer," Homenick said.

It was 7:30 P.M. in Washington, and there was no answer in
Kupferer's office or at his home. Homenick called the duty officer
at Tysons Corner, who found Kupferer working in another part of
the building.

"Have the bugs got you yet?" Kupferer asked when he came
onto the line. He knew that Homenick had been planning to enter
Colonel Hudson's apartment that afternoon.

"Chuck, I hope you're sitting down."

"Why?"

"You're not going to believe this, Chuck, but do you know what
I've got in my hands?" Homenick's voice was tense. He paused a
moment. "I've got two letters signed by Frank Burton Riley to
Colonel Hudson in which he *admits* everything we think he's
done."

There was silence at the other end of the transcontinental telephone line.

"Wait a second," Kupferer said. "Let me get my tape recorder
set up; then read them to me."

He switched on the recorder and listened while Homenick read
the letters slowly.

"I don't believe it," Kupferer said, and then he let out a whoop.

"Hell, that's it, buddy!" he said. "Call George O'Connell; tell
him what you've got. I'll tell Safir."

Howard Safir's response when he heard the news was "Incredible." But Safir was a skeptic, and he still had some doubts that
Frank Riley would lead them to Boyce.

The clerk at Qantas Airlines had agreed to notify John Pascucci
if Frank Riley changed his reservations for the July 10 trip to
Sydney, and on June 20—two days after the letters were discovered
in Hermosa Beach—Qantas notified him that Riley had cancelled
his seat on the flight.

The following day, however, deputies in New Jersey followed
Riley to a travel agency in Tenafly where he exchanged his excursion ticket for a regular economy-class ticket to Sydney. It had an

open departure date; he could leave for Australia on any flight with an available seat.

The deputies watching him in New Jersey were convinced that Riley was escalating the tempo of his campaign to evade them. Both on foot and in his car, he routinely used ruses to lose them. Two mornings after returning from his second trip to San Francisco, he left home for his usual morning jog wearing jeans and a gray sweat shirt. Suddenly he accelerated his pace and broke into a dead run, and as he seemed capable of doing at will, he lost his tail by ducking between two houses. An hour later, deputies spotted him in a crowd of shoppers in Closter. He was wearing dark glasses and a dark green shirt that he had apparently been wearing beneath the sweat shirt, which was now nowhere to be seen.

On the highway, Riley drove alternately at high speeds and very slowly; he would pull over to the side of the road often and make sudden U-turns and other evasive maneuvers and look back to discover if he was being followed. Kupferer assumed that Riley knew he was under surveillance and was testing the people following him before choosing the time to flee.

On June 20, Michael Adams, the chief deputy in the Newark office of the Marshals Service, made a secret appearance before a U.S. magistrate in Newark. In a sealed petition, he disclosed the contents of the letters that had been found in California and outlined Riley's evasive tactics. The chances were high, he told the magistrate, that Riley would soon make a break for it; he asked for authority to attach a clandestine radio transmitter to Riley's car. Permission was granted. That night, a deputy U.S. marshal slipped beneath Riley's 1979 Buick and attached a magnetized transponder to its undercarriage. Henceforth, whenever Riley drove away from his house in Closter, deputies followed him at a comfortable distance of several blocks, guided by the beeping signals of what they called their "Bird Dog."

The magistrate's order allowed the transponder to be used for twenty days, until July 10. All they could do now was wait for the Bird Dog to lead them to Boyce.

By July 9, Riley had still not made his move. His Buick had led the deputies over much of northern New Jersey, but they believed he still had not made contact with Boyce. Adams went back to the magistrate and submitted another sealed petition to him:

> I have probable cause to believe that Riley continues to ac-
> tively concern himself with possible surveillance by interested
> agencies, and, more importantly, continues to make active
> plans involving international travel, which travel, it is be-
> lieved, will place him in proximity with the fugitive, Christo-
> pher Boyce. I therefore request that the Court grant a limited
> extension of twenty days to the order originally signed by the
> Court on June 21, 1981. The use of the beacon will permit the
> U.S. Marshals Service to follow the movements of Frank Ri-
> ley as he prepares for his upcoming trip out of the country.

The magistrate granted an extension for twenty days.

Chuck Kupferer had flown to Glencoe, Georgia, along with Homenick and Duke Smith, to teach at a long-planned Marshals Service seminar and training program on fugitive hunting. He knew that time was running out on the surveillance of Riley in other ways, too. There were rumors circulating in the agency that Howard Safir was so unhappy with Kupferer's failure to find Boyce that he was contemplating replacing him as chief inspector. Kupferer wasn't worried about the rumors. But the cost of main-taining Riley's twenty-four-hour-a-day surveillance was gutting the agency's budget.

Kupferer led Homenick and Duke Smith into a classroom at the training academy. On a large tablet that was mounted on an easel he made two columns listing the status of the case.

They could never get an indictment, Kupferer said, solely on the basis of the letters. But they did have the goods to arrest him now if they wanted to. The holster case found in Riley's trash bag had led them to a New Jersey gun shop where a clerk had told them Riley owned two handguns. That was enough to put an ex-convict in jail. And, Kupferer continued, it might provide the leverage they needed to squeeze Riley for information about Boyce. Safir tentatively favored this option. But Kupferer said he was afraid that a judge might set Riley's bail so low that he would spend one night in jail and then disappear. They could continue to lie back and wait for him to make a move. But that was also risky. Riley might slip the surveillance and disappear, or he might do nothing and they would watch him forever. The end of the Federal Government's fiscal year was approaching, and the Marshals Service was running out of money. It hadn't received enough funds to finance the fugitive program to begin with. An open-ended surveillance, with four people a shift, three shifts a day, was out of the question. Riley could afford to wait. He was living off a family trust fund of almost $400,000.

"Look, Boyce is the most-wanted man in the country and we're getting nowhere," Kupferer said, rebuking himself as well as Homenick and Smith. "We have to do *something*. The worst thing is to do nothing."

He called Howard Safir, and they decided to look for Boyce in South Africa.

31

DUKE SMITH WAS MET BY TWO SENIOR OFFICERS of the South African Police, Special Branch, when he landed at Johannesburg's Jan Smuts Airport on July 19. He had scheduled a vacation with his wife in Northern California's wine country for late July, but had postponed the trip gladly—not only because he felt that the cord was tightening around Christopher John Boyce, but because he had a lifelong fascination with Africa.

Looking down at the endless expanse of South African veld as they had approached the city, and later at the tall skyscrapers of central Jo'burg, Smith pondered the odds against finding anyone in a country as large as Germany, France and Portugal combined.

As they drove into the city, the South African policemen agreed that it would not be easy to find Boyce. But they discouraged Smith's needle-in-a-haystack outlook. Fewer than 20 percent of South Africa's twenty-four million people, they said, were white, which improved the odds considerably. They said they weren't surprised that Boyce was suspected of being in South Africa. Soviet spies and Moscow-trained surrogate agents, some of them based in neighboring Mozambique, were busy throughout Africa trying to stoke up black nationalism. If Boyce was in the country, that was probably his mission, they said.

After he checked into his hotel, Smith called Kupferer in Tysons Corner. "If he's here," he said in his soft Florida drawl, "I think we've got a good chance of finding him. I think these guys want him as much as we do.''

The South Africans produced immigration documents that Riley had signed during the two trips he was known to have made to their country. On the first visit, in February 1980, Riley had told immigration agents that he planned to stay at the Golden City Hotel in Johannesburg and later at the President Hotel in Bloemfontein, the capital of one of South Africa's four provinces, the Orange Free State. When he returned, in January 1981, Riley had indicated that his itinerary would include Johannesburg, Durban, Krugersdorp and Bloemfontein. The first night, he said, he would stay at the Rand International Hotel on Bree Street in Johannesburg. Later, he planned to visit a friend, Babette Bekker, who lived in Krugersdorp, a suburb of Johannesburg.

No address for the woman was given on his immigration declaration, and no such name was listed in telephone directories anywhere in the country. The police had ordered a search for her which, so far, had been unsuccessful. Until they could locate Miss Bekker, the two senior South African police officials suggested that Smith join them in retracing Riley's steps in South Africa.

Smith was in the country less than twenty-four hours before he and the South Africans got their first piece of encouragement. The Rand International Hotel confirmed that Riley had stayed there on February 1, 1981, and Room Service records showed that he had charged breakfasts for two in his room the next morning. No record could be found of the Golden City Hotel, the second hotel where he had said he intended to stay in 1980. It appeared not to exist. The investigators found a Golden Hotel, but it had not accepted whites since 1978.

Many things about police work were different in South Africa from the way they were in the United States, Smith noticed before he had been there long. In America, when a cop asked questions of a stranger, the response was often a look of hostility and frequently a demand for a ''Miranda warning''—the admonition ordered by the U.S. Supreme Court giving every person the right to remain silent when confronted by police. But in South Africa, he discovered, when the cops asked questions, people tended to grow rigid and stand at attention, and not a few trembled.

Despite the promising beginning in Johannesburg, their leads in the city were soon exhausted, and the two police officials assigned to help Smith suggested that they drive 140 miles or so to Sun City, where, according to one of the anonymous letters that had been sent to the U.S. Embassy, Boyce had taken work in a hotel.

Sun City had been called "Sin City" from many pulpits in South Africa. It was the nearest thing South Africa had to compare with Las Vegas. Situated in the all-black enclave of Bophuthatswana, which critics of the nation's *apartheid* policies regarded as a sham, a puppet state of the white-supremacist government, Sun City was a neon-lit resort of hotels, roulette wheels, swimming pools, nightclubs and bare skin that were in gaudy contrast with the morally stern climate of the rest of South Africa. Like Las Vegas, it was set incongruously in an otherwise arid wasteland.

In Sun City, Duke Smith and the South African detectives began the universal trench work of police life. They visited hotels, gambling casinos, bars, restaurants and stores and showed photographs of Christopher Boyce and Frank Riley to employees, asked questions and studied reactions. But after two days, they had uncovered no one who knew—or admitted knowing—Boyce or Riley.

From Bophuthatswana, they drove south to Bloemfontein, a small town of pastel shades set in the veld 260 miles south of Johannesburg and flanked by sandstone buttes, wheat fields and cattle ranches that stretched far into the horizon. They came up empty-handed in Bloemfontein too.

The manager of the President Hotel dug out records confirming that a man named Frank Riley had stayed at the hotel for two days in 1980. The hotel's records showed that he was traveling alone and that he had listed his citizenship and residence as Rhodesian. No record could be found of a guest named Schmeiser, Hollenbeck or Boyce.

They had now talked to scores of people. After each day of the odyssey, Smith called Kupferer to report on his progress. It resembled a travelogue more than the report of a manhunt. Evidence was as scarce that Boyce was in South Africa as it had been in Costa Rica, and Smith was becoming discouraged.

Six days after Smith landed in Johannesburg, there was at last some good news: the South African police had found Babette Bekker. She was working as a secretary for an automobile import company in a suburb of the city. Detectives had knocked on more than four hundred doors in Johannesburg and its environs before finding her, Smith's colleagues informed him, not trying to conceal their pride in the triumph.

Smith broke the news to Kupferer and said that she would be interviewed in the morning. He went to bed but couldn't sleep.

What had brought her together with Frank Riley, Babette Bekker admitted eventually, was dirty pictures. But not at first.

The interrogator from Special Branch began the interview:

"Have you been visited by someone from abroad in the past year?"

She did not hesitate more than a few seconds.

"Is it Fraank Rilee?" She said it quickly, in a hard Afrikaans accent. "Is that who you mean?"

"Yes. We'd like to know what you know about him."

"I figured it would be him when you walked in here."

"Why?"

"I knew he was in trouble."

"Why?"

"You probably want to know about the letters."

"What letters?"

"The ones about the falcons and the American."

Babette Bekker was in her late twenties. Her dark blond hair framed an oval, coltish face that was not especially pretty, Smith thought. But she had a haughty look that he imagined probably drew second glances from men she passed on the street. The daughter of a physician, she was an Afrikaner, a descendant of the Dutch settlers who had colonized South Africa in the seventeenth century. As with more than half of South Africa's whites, her natural tongue was Afrikaans, but she spoke English fluently.

If she had been an American, Smith decided, Babette would probably have been running with a motorcycle gang. In South Africa, she was called a "free spirit." This was the description used by the policemen, and it was not a complimentary one. In a country where much of life was as rigidly controlled as it had been in Nazi Germany, she was a rebel against the conservative social order and a closet rebel against

200

the political order, who might do anything to prove it. She smoked *dagga,* the forbidden leaves of the cannabis plant, and lived as much of a bohemian existence as was permitted in South Africa.

Nevertheless, from all appearances, Smith thought, she was not immunized against the paranoia that appeared to seize South Africans, black or white, when they were brought to the offices of the national police force in Pretoria.

Her hands shook as she began to tell her story.

Early in 1979 she had traveled to the independent province of Swaziland and purchased a copy of *Easy Rider,* an American magazine that catered largely to aficionados of large motorcycles and sometimes contained photographs of partially nude young women. It was a circumstance that automatically made the magazine contraband.

She admitted that she had smuggled the magazine into South Africa and looked sheepishly at the policeman who was interrogating her.

"You're not going to get me on a porn rap, are you?" she asked.

It was a question of more than small importance to her: conviction for possessing the magazine might mean two years in prison.

"Go on," the policeman said.

The magazine, she continued, contained a page of classified ads listing people who were looking for pen pals, and she had responded to an ad placed by an American named Frank Riley. Later, she learned that he was an inmate at a prison in the state of Maine, but that didn't discourage her from continuing a correspondence with him.

She looked up at the two South Africans and, staring into their eyes, said, "I like to correspond with anyone who's pro–South African."

Over a period of several months, she continued, a friendship had developed at long distance. Not long after his release from prison—"I think it was February of 1980"—he had flown to Johannesburg. They had met for dinner, and after his return, a few days later, to America they had continued to exchange letters. Later that year, probably in August or September, she had received a letter from him that contained a sealed envelope addressed to someone in Australia, and at his request, she had mailed it to Australia from Johannesburg.

A few months after that, she had received a note from Riley in which he asked her to copy a short message in her handwriting and send it to him.

"He said to sign it with any woman's name except my own," she said.

Babette could not remember the substance of the message, but remembered that it began "Dear Frank" and included these phrases: "Chris is somewhere in Natal. I don't know where he is. . . . He misses America. You know how he misses his goddamn falcons."

She had forgotten about the request for a month, until Riley wrote to complain that she hadn't done what he asked.

"So I copied the message and sent it to him and signed it 'Susan,' " she said.

In February 1981, Riley returned to Jo'burg, and they decided to get married—but, she added quickly, nothing ever came of the plan. It was to have been a marriage of convenience, allowing her to immigrate to the United States as the wife of an American. They had never slept together; their relationship, she claimed, had always been platonic.

After Riley made his marriage proposal over dinner at the hotel in Johannesburg, they had made a date for him to meet her parents in the morning. But he hadn't shown up and had later called to apologize with an explanation that an emergency had come up and he had to leave South Africa in a hurry. A few months later—"probably around May 1981"—Riley had sent a letter from the States with another sealed envelope with another sealed envelope inside and asked her to mail it to an address somewhere in South Africa. Although she had done what he asked, she couldn't remember who was to receive the letter. Since then, she had lost contact with Frank Riley.

She had never heard of Christopher John Boyce, she said.

While Babette Bekker was being interviewed, her apartment was searched by detectives. After they found *dagga* there, any doubt that she would cooperate in a scheme that was being planned several thousand miles away in Tysons Corner evaporated.

The night before it was to be executed, Duke Smith took Babette out for dinner. They had cocktails and *escargots de Bourgogne*, followed by steaks and a bottle of South African wine. Smith urged her to drink a lot of wine. He said that it would help her get some rest for the task she was going to face in the morning.

32

A DOZEN MEN AND WOMEN WEARING BULLET-
proof vests and carrying automatic rifles surrounded the red house
on High Street in Closter, New Jersey, at three o'clock the following morning. An airplane carrying more federal agents circled in
the darkness overhead. Inside Boro Hall, Chief Inspector Thomas
C. Kupferer, Jr., was on an open telephone line to Duke Smith in
South Africa.

It was 9 A.M. in Pretoria, and it was Duke Smith's birthday. Babette Bekker sat at a desk with a telephone and a blackboard in
front of her. Smith and a South African Special Branch police inspector, earphones clamped over their heads, sat nearby.

The telephone number in New Jersey was dialed and they waited
to hear Riley's voice. Seconds passed, and then minutes. There
was no answer. They dialed again and waited.

No answer, Smith reported to Kupferer.

"Why doesn't he pick up the phone?" Kupferer asked Bob
Dighera, who was standing next to him in Boro Hall.

The night before, they had watched Riley return to the house after going out to dinner. The lights had gone out a few minutes before midnight. Since then the house had been under constant
surveillance. He couldn't have gone anywhere.

Kupferer had scheduled the call in the dead of night intention-
ally, so that he could roust Riley out of bed before he had his wits
about him.

"Try again," he told Smith.

They dialed the number in New Jersey again. No answer.

"Keep trying every fifteen minutes," Kupferer said.

"Are you sure we've got the right number?" Smith asked.

"Yeah," Kupferer said. "I don't know what the fuck's going on."

"Maybe he's got his phone unplugged," Dighera suggested.

"The son-of-a-bitch probably has his phone unplugged," Kupferer told Smith.

Two hours later, there was still no response to the telephone at Riley's home. It was almost noon in South Africa. Duke Smith had gotten up before dawn, and he was hungry.

"Chuck, we're going to get something to eat," he said.

He took Babette and his two South African colleagues to a restaurant near the police barracks in Pretoria for a relaxed, if fast, lunch.

Kupferer decided to call the house across the street himself.

He dialed Riley's number at five thirty. No answer. He tried again at six and at seven o'clock. Still no answer.

At seven thirty, Riley answered the phone.

"Hello," he said sleepily.

Kupferer hung up and called Pretoria.

"I'm sorry, sir," said a man in a melodious South African accent, "Inspector Smith has gone to lunch."

"Corporal," Kupferer replied, "I don't want you to get excited, but if you have to empty your entire barracks, would you please send teams to every restaurant in the city to find Inspector Smith?"

Fifteen minutes later, Frank Riley picked up the telephone again.

"Fraank, it's Babette here."

"Who?"

"*Babette.*"

Babette Bekker?"

Riley's words came out rapidly, so fast that if you weren't listening carefully they could have been gone before you realized it.

"Yes."

204

"What the heck are you calling for, Babette? I can't believe this."

"Fraank, there's hassles."

"Sorry?"

"Fraank, the police came to see me. They questioned me about somebody I was writing in the States, and you are the first person I thought of."

"I just sent you a magazine. Did you get it?"

"It's not the magazine, Fraank. You remember that letter you asked me to write . . . you know—the one from Natal; you know—about the guy with the falcons; what was his name again?"

"Boyce?"

"Well, they were questioning me about—"

"Nobody knows about that."

"Look, I denied all knowledge. I told them I don't know nothing, but listen, who is this guy? What's going on?"

"Nothing. He's an escaped spy. I knew him in prison. . . . Did they ask about me?"

There was more tension in Riley's voice.

"No. . . . You see, Fraank, they've taken my prints; they searched my house; they found grass in my house. . . ."

"Let's start at the beginning, Fraank. Why did you want that letter written? Let me try and work out what's going on so I know where I stand."

Like a football coach sketching plays for his team, Duke Smith scrawled notes to Babette on the blackboard, suggesting questions to her.

"Ba-bette!" Riley said rapidly, landing on the second syllable as if he were using an ax. There was a pause, as if he were trying to get himself under control. "Can you get to Canada?"

He repeated that he could not understand how the South African police could have seen the letter, but if Babette was in trouble she should escape as quickly as she could to Canada or another country.

"Tell her to get back to Boyce," Kupferer, who was listening in on the conversation in Closter, told Smith.

He could see a disaster coming; he was worried the fish would get off the hook.

"What is his connection to Boyce?" Smith wrote on the blackboard.

"Fraank," she appealed. "Listen, what is actually your connection to this Boyce? You know, besides being a friend in prison?"

There was a genuine nervousness in her voice. Smith saw that her hands were shaking. It made her sound more convincing.

"That's it; that's it," Riley said. There was a low, guttural sound at his end of the line. "I helped him to a degree in the United States, that's all," he said.

"Listen, Fraank, I caan't take it anymore, man. I can't take it."

"Ba-bette, I'm really sorry. I don't know what happened."

Ten minutes had now passed and they had nothing. Kupferer decided to regroup and try again. He told Smith to have Babette hang up and tell Riley that she would call him back later.

The second phone call an hour later, after Duke Smith had coached her, was more successful.

"Babette, I don't know. Maybe they were watching the *Easy Riders*. I, I can't—"

"Yeah, well back to this guy Boyce again. . . . Have you seen this guy since you left prison? Because you say you, you helped him, or you got to know him, or what?"

"Babette. I don't like to say too much about this on the phone. All I can say is that he is no longer in South Africa."

Kupferer looked at Dighera and his face tightened.

"Yeah," Babette replied.

"He's no longer there, so that can't hurt anyone. He was in Pietermaritzburg . . . and I helped him there, and I . . . he's no longer there. That's all. He's no longer in South Africa. I helped him get in there and he's no longer there. He's no longer in South Africa, so nothing can be done. Naturally I'm not going to say where he is now. Because I'm not even sure. . . ."

They talked for three or four minutes more. Babette said that she would call again later, they said good-bye and the line went dead.

"Duke, you did it!" Kupferer said.

Thirty seconds after he hung up the phone, Riley, shirtless and in his running shorts, ran into his backyard and began lifting a set of weights.

"United States Marshals! You're under arrest," Bob Dighera, his gun in hand, shouted.

Carrying their automatic weapons, other deputies and Closter policemen emerged from hiding places behind bushes and trees around the house and surrounded Riley. Overhead, the government plane was still waiting for Riley to make a run for it. But he never had a chance.

"Put your hands up," Dighera demanded.

Riley, dumbfounded by the massive armed invasion of his backyard, began to lower the weights to the ground; but as he did, he dropped the barbells and lost his footing at the same time and tumbled into the dirt.

"That bitch!" he said.

When they searched the red house, the deputies found a .38-caliber pistol and a 9mm semiautomatic. At the Federal Courthouse in Newark, Riley was booked for illegal possession of firearms and grilled by Kupferer and Dighera.

"Boyce. Boyce? I don't know who you're talking about."

Then Kupferer read from the notes he had made during the phone call:

"He was in Pietermaritzburg . . . and I helped him there."

"You're up to your ears in shit," Kupferer said. "You're not only a felon in possession of firearms, but you helped one of the most-wanted men in the world get out of the country."

Riley seemed dazed by the events. He refused to talk to anyone and demanded the deputies' departure. They left him alone to think. In less than an hour he sent word that he wanted to make a deal: if Kupferer made sure that he did not go to prison, Riley said, he would talk.

"I can't do that, Frank," Kupferer said.

But, he added, if Riley really helped find Christopher Boyce, "that will be taken into consideration."

Kupferer had little interest in Frank Riley; he wanted Boyce.

"Okay," Riley said. "I'll tell you everything I know.

"I helped him get into South Africa, but I don't know where he is now. I tell you, I really don't. I don't know how you found out, but I'll tell you what I know."

In the rapid, machine-gun style of speech that he seemed to adopt when he was nervous, Riley confessed that he had met Boyce in San Francisco and helped arrange his flight out of the country within three weeks of his escape.

"I knew Chris at Terminal Island. He was a nice kid, really inexperienced in prison. A few days after his escape, sometime in late January, I think, he called me at the home of my parents in New Jersey and told me he had just broken out of Lompoc. I couldn't believe it. That's a maximum-security prison. He reminded me that when we were in Terminal Island I'd promised to help him get into South Africa if he ever got out. I remembered he was always talking about escaping, but I never thought he'd be able to do it.

"He told me he was calling from someplace in California, a place called Carmel, near Monterey, staying with someone he had known in prison.

"But he said he didn't trust this guy, whoever he was, very much. He said people were hunting for him in the woods and asked me if I could help him get a passport. How'd you find out about this?"

Kupferer and Dighera ignored the question, and Riley continued.

He explained that he had felt he had an obligation to Boyce because of his promise at Terminal Island. As soon as he got the call, he had telephoned a friend, a printer named Henry Rabinowitz—"a guy who's a Michelangelo of forgery"—who had agreed to make a passport for Boyce under an alias he suggested.

"What name?" Kupferer asked.

"Richard Hollenbeck."

Riley said that after he picked up the passport from Rabinowitz, he had flown to San Francisco and met Boyce in early February at the St. Francis Hotel. They had gone to a camera shop near Union Square and had a passport photo taken of Boyce. Following directions from Rabinowitz, they had attached it to the passport and stamped a counterfeit Department of State seal over it so that it looked authentic. Boyce had taken the passport and $2,000 from Riley and returned to wherever it was that he had been hiding in the San Francisco Bay Area. Then, Riley said, he had flown to Johannesburg via New York to make arrangements for Boyce.

The fugitive had arrived in South Africa a few days later. Riley said that he couldn't remember the date, but that it was probably about February 10. In Johannesburg, he said, he had seen Boyce only briefly, but had introduced him to a woman he knew who lived there, a wealthy Afrikaner with a rebellious streak—the woman who had called him that morning: Babette Bekker. She had volunteered to help Boyce, Riley said, because she didn't like the totalitarianism of the South African government.

"Now, remember, I've helped you; don't forget. You promised to help me."

Kupferer felt enormous relief. After almost nineteen months, they had at last discovered Boyce's escape route and at least part of his support system. It was as if he were nearing the end of a long and unpleasant voyage. But his next thought returned him to reality. There was one heartbreaking void in the story: Riley claimed that he hadn't seen Boyce in more than a year. He claimed that he knew nothing that would lead them to Boyce right now. He said that Babette had met Boyce, but Duke Smith had said he was inclined to believe her story that she hadn't.

Kupferer was convinced that Riley knew a lot more than he had told them.

"Why did you tell Babette on the phone this morning that you knew Boyce had left South Africa when you claim you had lost touch right after he got there?"

"I had an idea when I was on the phone that South African intelligence was listening, so I said 'he's left the country'; I wanted to throw them off."

In truth, he repeated, he did not know what had happened to Boyce after they parted. Kupferer asked him why he was planning a trip to Australia. Riley claimed that the trip had nothing to do with Christopher Boyce.

"Sure, I was going to Australia, but on a vacation, and I thought I might immigrate there. I like their racial policies."

Kupferer had interviewed many men who broke down and turned against a partner when the choice was between loyalty and a prison cell. He saw a look in Riley's eyes that he had seen many times before. But was Riley lying? Was he bargaining with all his chips, or only a few of them and concealing the most important thing he knew—the whereabouts of Boyce?

"He's platinum, but he's holding back," Kupferer told Homenick in a phone call to Los Angeles. He said that Riley was being moved to a safe house in the New York suburbs for further questioning. Homenick knew the case better than anyone else. He was to get on the next flight and take over the interrogation. Meanwhile, Kupferer said, Duke Smith would stay in South Africa to check out Riley's story there. He and Dighera, after seventy-two hours without sleep, were going to Washington for some rest.

Homenick scanned the top of his desk to see if there was anything urgent. There was another report from a psychic who claimed that Chris was living along the California coast near the town of Newport. There were reports to be checked of purported sightings in California; a message from Inspector Dave Neff in the Denver office saying that he was following up a request from Homenick to interview an informant who claimed to know something about Boyce; a report that Chris had been seen sunbathing on Waikiki Beach in Honolulu. He pushed aside most of the papers, met briefly with Assistant U.S. Attorney George O'Connell, the prosecutor on the case, and asked Deputy Jim Sullivan to take him to Los Angeles International Airport.

At the airport, he discovered that he had forgotten a list of questions for Riley prepared by O'Connell. From a pay phone he called the courthouse and asked Sullivan to telex the questions to him in New York the next day.

"Don't worry. Stay put," Sullivan said; "I'll get 'em to you."

"The plane leaves in less than twenty minutes," Homenick said.

"Don't worry," the other deputy said, and somehow Sullivan, who had once worked as a Boston fireman, made the twenty-five-minute trip to the airport in twelve minutes. When Homenick heard someone pounding on the door of the plane after all the passengers had buckled their seat belts, he figured that it was Sullivan, and he was right.

As the jet took off, he looked down on the lights of the Palos Verdes Peninsula where it juts into the Pacific, and then down at the papers handed him by Sullivan. He decided that the trip to New Jersey had gotten off to a good start.

33

CHIEF INSPECTOR KUPFERER LOOKED AT THE newspaper headline and was livid:

SUSPECT SEIZED IN SPY'S ESCAPE; MAY HAVE
AIDED BOYCE IN FLIGHT TO SOUTH AFRICA

Someone who worked at the Federal Courthouse in Newark had neglected to keep a seal on the affidavits submitted by the Justice Department with its applications for the Bird Dog on Riley's car and a search warrant at his house. A reporter for the Newark *Star-Ledger* had uncovered the story, and newspapers around the world were reporting that Christopher John Boyce had escaped to South Africa with help from an American ex-convict who was in federal custody.

"Jesus Christ," Kupferer said in Tysons Corner. "If Boyce reads this, he'll be out of the country in twenty-four hours."

At a motel in Hempstead, Long Island, Frank Riley was also outraged. The papers and television stations were reporting that he was cooperating secretly with federal agents who were pursuing the missing spy. "If I go to the penitentiary now," he told Larry Homenick, "everybody knows I'm a snitch; I'm a dead man."

Homenick calmed him down and began asking questions. Riley

repeated the story of his meeting with Boyce in San Francisco and the arrangements he had made for his flight to South Africa, but said again that he did not know where Boyce was, although he said he suspected that he might have gone underground in Pietermaritzburg, in the province of Natal. It was mostly the same story that he had told Kupferer and Dighera, but he added an important new detail: in October 1980, about eight months after he had helped get Chris to South Africa, Boyce had called him at his parents' home in New Jersey—from someplace in the United States, he thought—and had asked him to deliver a load of documents to Soviet agents in either Chile or Brazil.

It was a friendly call in which Boyce didn't volunteer where he was and Riley didn't ask. Riley claimed that he had told Boyce he didn't want to get involved in espionage and had turned him down. "I don't know if he got somebody else to take the documents or not," he said. "I never heard from him again."

At midnight, Homenick said it was time for both of them to get some sleep. At eight the next morning, he returned to Riley's room to resume the questioning. When he walked in, a deputy from the Witness Security (WitSec) unit who had been assigned to guard Riley called him aside.

"This guy's awfully strange," he said. "Last night, he went into the bathroom and started talking to himself. We could hear him through the wall. He stood in front of the mirror and said, *'Mein Führer,* they don't believe me.' Then he answered back as if he were a different person and said, 'But you're being true to the Third Reich,' and he started talking about the glory of Hitler and the Reich and the supremacy of the white race."

A few minutes later, Homenick and Deputies Beverly Bargamian and Tony Odom ordered Riley to repeat the story of his meeting with Boyce and his flight to South Africa, so that they could look for inconsistencies or details he'd overlooked. Seven hours later, they knew little more than they had known the day before. Riley, insisting that he was telling them everything he knew, told the story again and again, but added little to flesh it out. As before, the story ended when he said good-bye to Boyce on a Johannesburg street. He claimed to have forgotten numerous details about his dealings with Boyce. His memory was hazy, for example, about the location of the camera shop in San Francisco; he couldn't remember the location where he had first met Boyce in Johannesburg; he couldn't give Homenick the name of anyone else who was present during the meetings with Boyce.

"Frank, you were dealing with a major international spy," Homenick said. "I just can't believe you don't remember more details."

"To me, he was just another convict. I'm used to dealing with people like that."

Tony Odom opened the third day of interrogation the following morning: "Frank, we've gone over everything you've said and haven't been able to corroborate one iota of it."

"We've had an American investigator and the South African police checking out your story," Homenick interjected. "They haven't found one piece of evidence that shows Boyce was in South Africa."

"Well, that shows I did a pretty good job, doesn't it?" Riley said.

His eyes darted quickly from Homenick to Odom to Bargamian.

"True," Odom answered.

Riley had a knack for putting his interrogators on the defensive.

As the third day of questioning neared an end, there was eagerness in the voices of the investigators. They wanted to believe what Riley was telling them. They desperately wanted the manhunt to be over. But there was also a growing sense of uneasiness in their voices.

"Frank, why did you make those two trips to San Francisco just a few weeks ago?" Homenick asked.

"I told you. I just wanted to go there with Rabinowitz for a vacation."

He was lying, Homenick thought. It didn't make sense for two ex-cons with their backgrounds to fly twice to San Francisco and do nothing more than loiter around places like Fisherman's Wharf.

"Was Chris going to meet you there again? Is that why you went there—to make a contact with him?"

"No, I told you. No. You do believe me, don't you? You do believe I'm telling the truth?"

"Yes, we believe you, Frank," Homenick said. "But we don't want you holding back anything."

"I'm trying to remember, I'm trying to remember. Believe me. I'm telling you all I know."

The words came out like machine-gun bullets.

Babette Bekker, he said, was the person to talk to. She knew everything about Boyce's travels in South Africa, but was probably denying it because she was afraid she'd be sent to prison for helping a Soviet agent.

Babette, Homenick said, had taken a lie-detector test the previous day in South Africa. She had denied helping or knowing Boyce and had passed the test.

"You don't believe in those things, do you?" Riley demanded, his face flushed. "You know what they say about polygraphs; they're not always right."

In the morning, Homenick told him, Riley would have his chance to prove that he was telling the truth.

Just after dawn they left the motel on Long Island and drove to the gray marble Federal Courthouse on Foley Square in lower Manhattan. A polygraph examiner had been borrowed from a New Jersey police department. As he set up his equipment, Riley asked Homenick if he could go to the bathroom. He was nervous, he said. Homenick said that he had no objection and led him to a rest room.

Riley objected: "Larry, I can't go to the bathroom when someone is watching me."

"Frank, I don't want to watch you, believe me; go by yourself."

The rest-room door closed behind Riley. Homenick, taking a routine precaution against escape or a suicide attempt, cracked it open an inch and looked in. In a mirror that ran the length of the wall, he saw a reflection of Riley standing in front of a basin and holding a conversation with himself.

"Frank, you're going to have to try harder; they don't believe you."

215

He was standing at attention and speaking in a German accent.

Riley switched abruptly to a clipped South African accent that reminded Homenick of the voice of Babette Bekker tape-recorded during her telephone calls with Riley.

"But . . . but . . . they have to. I'm telling the truth. *You* believe me, don't you?"

"Yes," Riley answered in his German accent. *"But Frank, you know what they say about polygraph tests; they don't prove anything."*

"But I'm telling the truth; I'll show them."

It is the custom of polygraphers to disclose to their subject the questions they plan to ask during a lie-detector test before the test actually begins—largely to plant a sense of fear in those who intend to lie.

Riley listened calmly to the list of questions that he was to be asked: Did you help Christopher Boyce escape? Did you help him get into South Africa? Did he ever ask you to pass documents for him?

Riley nodded, signaling that he understood the questions. He asked if Beverly Bargamian could be with him in the examination room, and the examiner said he had no objection. The door to the room was closed, and Homenick waited outside.

Almost three hours later, the examiner bolted out of the room into an adjoining hall and told Homenick, "I can't test him. I can't test him."

"Larry, you'd better come in here," Beverly Bargamian said through the open door.

Riley was pacing the floor. His face was red and he was breathing hard, almost as if he were hyperventilating.

"Larry, Larry, do you know what they tried to do to me?"

His machine-gun-style speech had become a sorrowful whine. "He asked me if I met with a one-armed Russian named Victor Laslov. Larry, I don't know any Russians! What are they trying to set me up for? You promised they wouldn't do it."

Homenick led the examiner aside and asked him to explain.

"I know he doesn't know any Russians," the New Jersey policeman said. "But I was having so much trouble examining him

216

that I was experimenting. I had to establish a benchmark for his responses.''

''I was telling the truth,'' Riley said. He was almost in tears. ''He tried to trick me and make it seem that I was lying and working with the *Russians*. I don't know anything about a one-armed Russian.''

His eyes darted between the two marshals. ''*You* believe me, don't you? I'm not going to answer any more questions. He's out to get me.''

Homenick was furious with the examiner. It had taken two days to talk Riley into sitting for the polygraph test. Now it had blown up in his face. They returned to the motel on Long Island that was serving as their safe house.

At Tysons Corner, Howard Safir was suffering from an increasingly queasy feeling about the man described by virtually every investigator on the case as ''platinum.'' To resolve the matter, he called a friend in the New York Police Department, which had a waiting list of two weeks for polygraph examinations, and asked him to lend the Marshals Service a first-rate polygrapher on a priority basis.

The friend agreed, and with that, the South African connection began to come unraveled.

''This guy is full of bullshit, and if you ask me, he has a death wish,'' the police polygrapher told Larry Homenick the next day after being closeted with Frank Riley at the NYPD Police Academy for two hours.

''He failed every question. He made up the whole thing: he never got a phone call from Boyce; he never saw Boyce; he never got him a passport; he never helped him get to South Africa.''

The revelation hit Homenick with a force that felt like a fist in his stomach. All of it had been a deception: the anonymous letter placing Boyce in South Africa that was sent to the warden at Lompoc after the escape; the letter to the embassy in Pretoria; the letters from Riley to Colonel Hudson; the letters to Babette Bekker; the phone call that Chris was going to surrender in Cape Town; the countersurveillance maneuvers; perhaps even the trips to San Francisco. They were all a charade by a rich gun freak with a contorted mind who wanted to set up a false trail that would make it appear that Boyce had gone to South Africa. It was so elaborate, it had gone on for so long, and the people chasing Chris wanted so much to believe it that they had been fooled.

Homenick went into the examination room, where Riley was still sitting at a desk attached to the wires and tubing of the lie box.

"Frank, I'm done with you. You've lied long enough. You're going to prison," Homenick said.

"But Larry . . . but Larry, I'm telling the truth. I'm telling the truth. You've got to believe me. . . ."

Homenick turned to the two WitSec deputies who were guarding Riley and said, "Get him out of here. I don't want to see him again."

The next morning, Homenick boarded a train for Washington and a meeting with Chuck Kupferer to plan their next move. As the Metroliner pulled out of Pennsylvania Station, he looked out the window and tried to remember what loose ends he had left behind in Los Angeles when he departed for New Jersey in such a hurry. There had been another report from a psychic, half a dozen reports of purported sightings in California and three or four of sightings in other states. He wondered if the informant he had passed on to Dave Neff in Denver had amounted to anything.

And then he sat back in his seat and wondered where Chris Boyce was. He had never been so depressed.

II

Where every day
is Sunday

1

SOMEONE IN ANOTHER ROOM, PROBABLY DOWN the hall, turned on a switch, and suddenly the chapel was filled with organ music and, rising above it, a woman's voice. It was piped through a loudspeaker concealed in the wall.

"Fast falls the eventide," the woman sang slowly and with tenderness. *"The darkness deepens; Lord with me abide.*

"When other helpers fail and comforts flee, Help of the helpless, oh abide with me."

The room was scented with the sweet aroma of gardenias and carnations, and in the dim light, several people cried as the Reverend Ernest Pihl read from Romans 8:

"What then shall we say to this? If God is for us, who is against us? He who did not spare his own Son but gave him up for us all, will he not also give us all things with him?"

The man in the coffin had never had a chance, said his friends, who looked today not only sad but uncomfortable in seldom-worn suits. In more than fifteen years as an ironworker, they said, he had never had even a minor accident. But one morning—maybe he had had too much to drink the night before—he had gone to work and climbed up the rigging, and not fifteen minutes into the day, his feet had slipped out from under him. He had slid down a roof, hit the scaffolding and landed on his head, fracturing his cervical vertebrae, his jaw and his left hand.

The minister turned from Romans 8 to 1 Corinthians 15:

"Now if Christ is preached as raised from the dead, how can some of you say that there is no resurrection of the dead? But if there is no resurrection of the dead, then Christ has not been raised. . . .

"But some one will ask, How are the dead raised? With what kind of body do they come? You foolish man! What you sow does not come to life unless it dies. And what you sow is not the body which is to be, but a bare kernel . . ."

When he had finished, someone in the other room turned on the tape player again, and the woman sang "How Great Thou Art."

The ceremony was brief and tasteful, and after it was over, Jim Namcheck was buried near the water at Riverside Memorial Park in Spokane, Washington, on February 23, 1980.

The Kid was in again, flashing one-hundred-dollar bills and ordering Kahlúa as usual. So were Dirty Dan and Fat Jack. Some of their friends from the mountain were there too, guns strapped to their waists.

Most of the regulars were lined up at the bar on their regular stools. As usual, the TV set was on. In the final weeks of summer in 1980, there was a lot of news on television about Jimmy Carter and Ronald Reagan. But it was a news item about someone else that brought a brief stillness to the room that night.

. . . Justice Department sources said today that Christopher John Boyce, the Soviet spy who disappeared from a California prison almost a year ago, is believed to be living in Mexico and smuggling drugs into Southern California. One investigator said, "We are just one campfire behind him. . . ."

For a moment, the place grew silent, and a few eyes looked toward the man at the end of the bar. Then there were cheers, and several of the regulars raised their glasses in a toast to the man they called Jackass Jim.

Jim Namcheck raised his beer and, with a smile, returned the salute.

2

NO MATTER HOW FAST HE RAN, THE DOGS RAN faster.

From the day they locked him up, he had dreamed and disciplined himself for this moment. The weight lifting, ten miles a day around the prison yard, even yoga to prepare his mind—everything had been for this moment. And now it was jeopardized by a pack of friendly, yapping dogs who could run faster than he could.

The winter of 1980 was one of the wettest in Central California in years. During the previous two years the state had been parched by a drought that forced some communities to ration water. But in 1980, nature made up for its miserliness with a deluge that lasted most of the winter.

The horizon was gray and sodden, and his clothes were soaked and caked with mud; as he sprinted over the brown foothills of the coastals in the twilight, he knew that any pilot who would attempt to fly in this weather would be crazy, and that comforted him. Twice—when the high-winged plane skimmed the treetops as he relaxed in a yoga exercise and, on the first morning, when the helicopter flew by and he had to throw himself beneath a prickly bush—they had seemed close enough to snatch him up and take him away like a kestrel diving on a rabbit for breakfast. He burrowed into a thicket and flattened himself on the ground and didn't move a muscle until dusk, and he listened to the voices of the marshals and trackers as they walked past him.

They missed him, and so had the military policemen in jeeps from Vandenberg Air Force Base who passed by him as he crouched in the bushes, his toes aching with frostbite. Now there were the dogs.

At first the barking was far away, reminding him of the sounds of his neighborhood late at night when he was in grade school. But before long the dogs were running right beside him, jumping and howling and trying to be friendly. "Go away," he said, waving his hands; but they were enjoying the run and matching his pace, and when he tried to outrun them, they just ran faster. His feet were wet, and so cold from running through the muddy slush that his toes seemed ready to fall away. He stopped and kicked at the dogs, but they only thought it was part of the game and jumped higher. Then he saw several men silhouetted against the horizon, and it propelled him faster through the mud. He knew he could outrun the men, whoever they were; but he didn't know if he could outlast the dogs.

As he ran deeper into the mountains, the last rays of daylight were falling over the coastals. The silhouettes of the men were receding in the distance and the shadows; but the dogs were still with him. Several miles later, they were still there.

He reached the top of a ridge dominated by a stand of oaks, and suddenly part of the ridge vanished, as if it had been sliced away by a cleaver; below him, barely visible in the moonlight, there was a river. He looked down at it and then at the dogs and he thought of the men somewhere behind him, and he groped for air.

He thought of the prison and he thought of his mother and he thought of the wretchedness of the world he had just left and was certain he wanted never to return to it. He filled his lungs, took a few steps backward, ran toward the cliff and jumped.

Before he hit the water and then the rocks, he could still hear the yapping of the dogs. But as his head went under, he knew that he wouldn't have to worry about them anymore: they were too smart to jump in after him.

How long he lay in the shallow river, dazed, he never knew. The cold water revived him, and he staggered to the other side of the river and slipped in the mud. He fell on his face and began to cry.

He let himself sob and pounded his fists into the mud, and then he started to run again.

His lawyers had told him that the average length of the prison sentences given to Americans convicted of espionage since the 1950s had been fifteen to twenty years. That meant five to eight years if you behaved yourself. The forty-year sentence from Judge Kelleher had stunned him as well as his lawyers. The judge, the lawyers said, wanted to make an example of him. Espionage, he had said, is a "game you do not play." Just a month ago he had sent a letter to Judge Kelleher asking for a reduction of his sentence; the law gave him one chance to ask the judge to modify it. His lawyers had urged him to express his remorse for his act of betrayal. He had refused, but had made a kind of concession when he wrote to Judge Kelleher:

When I was twenty-one and not so very wise, I considered American society and government degenerate and, being disillusioned, I committed a nonconstructive act. "Obey little. Resist much," I read of Walt Whitman and took it to heart. I had no comprehension of the extent to which that quote would infuriate the established order. I would be misrepresenting myself were I not to state that my disillusionment now is greater than ever.

It was never my intention to serve the interests of the Soviet Union and if, in fact, those interests were ever materially served, which I have always doubted, then I regret that consequence of my act. My purpose was consummated in having committed an act of defiance, but that completed I was left with a millstone. I found that I had locked myself into an impossible position and having discarded all nationalistic sympathies, I then sought only to survive.

I realized early on that plots in the middle of the night are dishonorable folly and better left to agents of the United States. I am now finished with angry gestures. The difference between the Christopher Boyce who at twenty-one took matters into his own hands and the Christopher Boyce who composes this letter is that I have discovered a powerful constructive vehicle to convey my criticism. I have received professional encouragement that I will be published and I concentrate daily my efforts toward that purpose. I look about me in this penitentiary and I am surrounded by a debased concentration of many evils. In three years I have matured and I have realized that my government possessed the malevolent ability to dispense domestic misfortune to a far greater extent than I ever thought possible. . . . I am a student of history. You cannot expect me to accept that the United States is any more righteous to its adherents than any other great national state. She was bred and birthed in war, she matured in wars and as all other political entities have down through the ages, she will destruct in war.

There was a hearing before Judge Kelleher in December, but he had known from the beginning that there was as much chance the judge would reduce his sentence as there was that he would acknowledge from the bench that it had been wrong for the CIA to meddle in the domestic politics of Chile or for the United States to bomb Cambodia or for it to squander the lives of fifty thousand Americans in Vietnam. Still, he could not leave until the judge had made his decision, because of the slim possibility he might be wrong. When Judge Kelleher turned him down in early December, he had made his final decision to leave. *Forty years was forever.*

A week before he went over the fence, a member of the Aryan Brotherhood—a biker with tattoos, long hair and contempt on his face—had confronted him in a corridor, tossed a shank on the floor, brandished his own knife and said, "Pick it up, motherfucker."

Chris had turned and walked the other way.

Even in high school, when it had been fashionable, he had never thought of himself as a tough guy, and he couldn't start being one now.

But it had reaffirmed his decision to leave. He had been sent to prison with a forty-year sentence, not a death sentence. Unless he escaped, he told his friends, he would be dead in six months. He was a convicted spy, ripe for redneck revenge. He had broken the code of the convict which was to know your place. A book about his life and his espionage activities had been published. Other inmates hadn't liked the notoriety he'd received, especially when he told the inmate bosses that he hadn't received any income from the book, which meant there was no money for them to extort. Producers from television's *60 Minutes* and other reporters had been to see him after publication of the book, and he was getting letters from young women who had read about him and compared him to James Dean. Some people had even begun to regard him as a kind of American folk hero—an antihero—despite the claims at his trial that he had sold out his country for a few thousand dollars. Neither the inmates nor the guards nor the prison administrators liked his notoriety. He did not know his place.

His experience in the prison system, he claimed in letters to friends, had confirmed everything that he had felt about the corruptness of American ideals since he was sixteen. These were not the prisons of a civilized society. There was no rehabilitation in them, no hope offered their inmates for the future. They were warehouses and madhouses, as devoid of morality as a country that espoused democracy for its own people while propping up Latin American dictators who tortured, oppressed and robbed as long as they pledged support to Washington. "There are so many bruised minds here," he wrote one friend. "You should see the difference in these young people around me after only one month. These places are mere Band-Aids for cancer. What really galls me is that they are building more of them. To my scrutiny it is our society as a whole that is afflicted. The debasement I see around me is the ravages of a general canker."

The administration and the guards did not run the prisons. They only controlled the walls. Inside the walls, inmates ran things; organized in gangs that exploited the weak; murdered, raped and maimed; and they were let alone to run the prison as long as they kept the peace inside the walls. If someone tried to challenge the system, and normal prison discipline did not keep him in place, the hacks knew how to silence him. They passed the word around the yard that he was a snitch and waited for prison justice to take its course.

* * *

227

If it lands on me, I'll eat it; if it's on the ground, I won't.

Insects, he had read, contained concentrated amounts of protein. All he really needed was something in his stomach to go with the vitamins. As long as they lasted, the vitamins he had carried over the fence would help him survive until he got within range of real food. Flying insects, wild grass and berries would make up his diet for a while.

There was only one person he knew who lived close enough to the prison who might help. Mike Adams, one of his best friends from childhood, was working as a carpenter and living in Goleta, a town about sixty miles south of Lompoc.

He traveled at night, hiding out in the wilderness by day. He made his way south toward Goleta, picking up a new set of clothes from a clothesline along the way and a sleeping bag and a tent from an untended campsite.

"Pardon me," he asked the woman, "do you know where Mike Adams moved to? He used to live here."

She looked at him quizzically. Even by the standards of Goleta, a suburb of Santa Barbara with a college-town atmosphere, where many students and hangers-on at the local campus of the University of California dressed and acted as if the youth revolt of the 1960s were still in full bloom, he looked strange. He needed a shave, looked dirty and was wearing designer jeans cut for a woman.

The tenant at the apartment house said she was not sure where Mike Adams had moved to, but had heard he might have moved to San Luis Obispo, which was about a hundred miles north of Goleta. He thought of asking other neighbors about Adams, but he hadn't liked the look on the woman's face and left the neighborhood. After walking a block, he looked back and saw two police cars pull up to the apartment building.

As he left Goleta, the man who was rapidly becoming the most-wanted fugitive in America visited a store and shoplifted cigarettes, candy, a package of bologna and other food.

Christopher Boyce, his mother had told investigators, enjoyed taking risks.

He hiked back into the wilderness and headed north toward San Luis Obispo through the mountainous Los Padres National Forest. He resumed his diet of insects and wild berries and diversified it with food he found in the cars of campers and picnickers and garbage cans in campgrounds.

On one of his scavenging missions, he picked an old newspaper out of a garbage can and spotted his name in a headline on the front page. It headed a report that federal agents looking for him had staked out an apartment in San Luis Obispo where one of his friends lived. The friend, Mike Adams, had told a reporter about seeing a van parked outside his home on which was a periscope that followed him as he walked.

Christopher Boyce dropped the newspaper back into the garbage can and concluded that he would have to make alternative plans.

In Danish, Solvang means "sunny valley." Considering its setting at the edge of the beautiful Santa Ynez Valley some forty-five miles north of Santa Barbara and about thirty miles east of Lompoc, the name was appropriate, although historically incongruous. It was on the King's Highway, El Camino Real—the road built by a band of Spanish padres under Father Junípero Serra who had come north from Mexico in the eighteenth century to convert California Indians to Roman Catholicism. They had built a five-hundred-mile chain of religious missions from San Diego to Sonoma, creating a spine of civilization from which the modern state of California grew. Some of the most beautiful of the missions were built in and around the Santa Ynez Valley. But this did not discourage a group of Danish Lutherans who came a century later and established Solvang as a community for displaced Danes. Later, other Danes saw commercial possibilities in the heritage and established restaurants that offered Danish cuisine in half-timbered buildings with steep-pitched roofs. They created an ambiance reminiscent of a small town in Denmark, and Solvang evolved into a popular, if commercialized, tourist attraction for travelers a short distance from Highway 101, one of the main routes between Los Angeles and San Francisco.

From a hillside where, almost two centuries earlier, Spanish padres had grazed their cattle, Boyce looked down on Solvang, watching the tourists. He was naked, waiting for his clothing, which was sodden from another storm and hanging over a bush, to dry.

As a reflection, perhaps, of its religious roots, Solvang shut down early. By seven in the evening most of the tourists were gone, and by ten o'clock the town was silent. No different from any other hungry animal stalking its next meal, he waited several hours on the hillside after almost all the lights had been turned out, then ventured slowly to the edge of town. He moved through the darkened town from house to house, looking for garbage cans, dumpsters or other likely sources of food—and of course, for the black-and-white patrol cars of the Santa Barbara County Sheriff's Department which he had spotted from his hill. *One mistake and it was over.* It would take only one shot from the pistol of a rookie cop intent on making a name for himself; or a blast from the shotgun of a redneck deputy sheriff who couldn't have been more pleased than by the chance to execute a Soviet spy; or any policeman, for that matter, who saw a man in his headlights, ordered him to stop and fired when he kept on running.

From now on, this was his life.

Behind a steep-roofed building—a restaurant, perhaps—he thought he saw a large refrigerator and ran to it. Eagerly, he pulled the handle. It was unlocked. It opened to a treasure. It was stuffed with sausages and fresh loaves of bread, and he scooped up as many as he could carry; he ran back to his campsite and gorged himself. Two days later, when the food was gone, he returned and had another feast.

After another day, he was hungry again. Darkness had fallen over Solvang several hours earlier, and he entered the town a third time. He grabbed more pumpernickel bread and returned to his lair.

He enjoyed another satisfying dinner; but within an hour, an unpleasant feeling began to stir in his stomach. At first it was a rumbling turbulence and a sense of foreboding. Then, quickly, his stomach was afire. He vomited again and again, but the pain got worse. He doubled up with the worst diarrhea of his life.

Someone had laced the bread with poison.

As he passed out, he suspected that somewhere down the hill someone was probably having a laugh at his expense.

3

MOST POLICEMEN DO NOT PUT MUCH STOCK IN the visions of psychics or soothsayers. They would rather get their tips from an informant motivated by greed or self-interest than from one who has visions and dreams. Yet they know that whenever they investigate a case that attracts an extraordinary amount of publicity, their phones will be kept busy by psychics claiming they can find a murderer or a missing child or solve a mystery. It goes with the territory. Most policemen humor them briefly and then hang up, convinced that all psychics are crazy. Because of his skepticism, the people who were unable to find Christopher Boyce in the spring of 1980 would dismiss the tip from Marilyn Mitchell, the psychic who had called Larry Homenick from a pay phone in Santa Barbara, as a fantasy.

"I saw him in a cabin along the ocean. There were boats. I think there were three people in the cabin. . . . I can see a woman picking him up in a car," she said.

"Do you remember the address of the cabin?" Homenick asked, and she'd said, "No, but I think it's somewhere near Monterey."

On Marsh 23, 1980, two days after Homenick had his conversation with Marilyn Mitchell, the telephone rang in Apartment 24 of the Riviera Motel in Santa Cruz, California, a sunny resort town a few miles up the coast from the city of Monterey.

It was answered by a man who towered over the woman in the

room. Cameron Johnson hung up and told his wife, Estelle, that they would be having a guest.

The first thing people noticed about Cameron Johnson was his size. ''Five foot, eighteen'' was his usual response when new acquaintances, as they almost always did, asked him how tall he was. But it was not only his height that attracted attention. He weighed almost 270 pounds, and he was so strong that if he had not decided early in life that he liked money too much not to steal it, he could probably have found work as a strong man in a traveling carnival. His red hair was starting to thin, and at thirty-eight he had a bit of a paunch, but Cameron Johnson was a handsome man who was highly attractive to women. Indeed, his attractiveness created a problem for him because he often had difficulty making choices. More than once he had found himself so torn between his affection for two different women that the only way he could resolve his dilemma was to live with both of them and move back and forth from one household to the other. This elicited jokes from envious friends that Cameron Johnson was a man big enough to satisfy two women, although the cost of supporting two households sometimes caused him serious cash-flow problems.

Johnson was born into a poor blue-collar family that had emigrated from Oklahoma to the bountiful wine-producing Napa Valley north of San Francisco. His father died when he was young, adding to the family's financial problems. But his mother subsequently had a stroke of luck. She had befriended an elderly man of considerable affluence and nursed him for many years, and when he died, she became his heir and, some people suspected, a millionaire. But when Cameron was growing up, the family did not have much income, and he found himself unable, or unwilling, to resist taking other people's money; his first arrest, for petty theft, occurred when he was eighteen. He had a high I.Q. and a passion for reading. These qualities were insufficient to keep him out of more prisons, and during the next twenty years he would be arrested many times for burglary, forgery, counterfeiting and other transgressions. By the time he was thirty-five, when Christopher Boyce met him at Terminal Island prison, he had spent more than one-third of his life behind bars.

Despite his imposing size and chronic inability to obey the law, Cameron Johnson was not a violent man. Indeed, there was a gentleness and sensitivity in him, as well as a savvy about prison life, that had attracted Boyce to him when they met, and later when they were both at Lompoc, where they became close friends. In an environment where sensitivity to world affairs and issues of political morality usually runs no deeper than the moisture that condenses nightly on the cellblock walls, Johnson was charmed by the soft-spoken, unusual prisoner who was well informed on world affairs and history and condemned what he saw as flaws in American foreign policy. In a hostile world populated by killers and thieves, Johnson was charmed by Chris's naiveté and decided to look out for him in the prison.

On the day after Christopher Boyce escaped from Lompoc, Cameron Johnson had been the first person his pursuers went looking for. An FBI agent found him in a prison halfway house in Oakland where he was living before his formal release from custody. Johnson told the agent that he knew nothing about the escape and passed off his friendship with Boyce as no more than a "jailhouse acquaintance." He had promised, if Boyce ever approached him, to tell him to "get the hell out of my life." When U.S. marshals learned the same day that Johnson had already been interviewed by the FBI agent, they turned to other things and never came back to him, even after the special task force to find Boyce was established, in October 1980, with the slogan, coined by Tony Perez: *No Hay Piedra sin Vira.* No Stone Unturned.

Exactly what happened in Santa Cruz during the final days of March 1980, after the telephone rang in Apartment 24 of the Riviera Motel, was never proved in court, and Cameron and Estelle Johnson later gave differing accounts of what had occurred. Cameron Johnson said that he had given no help to Christopher Boyce, while his wife gave the following account of what happened:

As usual for a late Sunday afternoon, the traffic was heavy in Santa Cruz on March 23 as visitors began returning home to San Jose and other nearby cities following a day on the beach.

Cameron Johnson eased his Buick Skylark into the flow of traffic, and it took him several minutes to cover the few blocks between the motel and Monterey Bay, where boats were rolling softly under a light wind and a few bathers were still on the sand.

He drove slowly along the edge of the harbor, his wife beside him, then stopped abruptly. Estelle Johnson saw a bearded man laden with a heavy backpack emerge from a row of bushes and walk toward the car. He smiled but didn't say anything, and her husband opened the door for him. Estelle noticed that the man was wearing women's designer jeans.

The two men were silent until they reached the motel. Inside the Johnsons' small apartment, they had a celebration. They hugged each other, and Johnson congratulated his friend on having pulled off the escape. Estelle Johnson, however, was not in a celebratory mood. When she discovered that their guest was an escapee from a federal prison, she reminded Cameron that he had promised to go straight. By even talking to this man, she said, he was jeopardizing his parole.

But Johnson ran things in his household, and as he often did, he ignored Estelle.

Johnson decided that the owner of the restaurant in Solvang had filled his pumpernickel bread with rat poison or a huge dose of laxative. Boyce was now able to laugh about it, but it had nearly killed him, he said.

"I was so weak I thought I was going to die," he said. "I was sure it had ripped out the lining of my stomach."

He said he had regained his strength after several days and had hitchhiked to Santa Cruz, which was about 250 miles north of the prison.

"What are you going to do now?" Estelle asked. She was eager for him to leave their apartment for any place.

"I'm going to Canada and write a book about the prison system and other things."

Estelle won a minor victory. She persuaded Cameron that it was taking too big a risk for Boyce to remain overnight in the apartment, and they dropped him off beneath a stand of redwood trees in a wilderness park near Santa Cruz. For almost a week, Boyce camped out there by night while preparing for his new life by day.

At a Goodwill Industries thrift store in Santa Cruz, he bought a new set of clothes and got rid of his jeans, and at a public library, he buried his identity as Christopher John Boyce with a few keystrokes on a typewriter. He borrowed the hospital birth certificate that had been issued to one of Cameron Johnson's teenage sons and, for 10 cents, made a copy of it on a Xerox machine at the library. Using a product called Wite-Out, he blotted out the name of the son, the identities of his parents and the date of his birth and made a Xerox copy of the copy. He typed a few words into the blanks, revisited the Xerox machine and made a copy of the now reconstituted document. His alterations were nearly impossible to detect.

When he had finished, Christopher Boyce had a new birth certificate and a new name. He was *Jim Namcheck*—a friend of Cameron Johnson's who had died the month before in a tragic fall from a building.

In prison, Cameron Johnson had told Chris about a kind of Shangri-la, hidden away in the mountains, where someday he might want to hide out if he ever escaped. In Santa Cruz, Johnson gave him the name of a friend who lived there. Chris, he suggested, might want to spend a few weeks there before heading into Canada.

On Thursday morning, after Johnson picked up his weekly paycheck, they went to the Greyhound depot and Johnson gave him $101 to buy a bus ticket.

That night, Cameron and Estelle Johnson had one of the worst rows of a turbulent marriage.

"You can't do that to Gloria," she said. "She's got enough problems already. At least, give her a choice. Tell her who he is."

"If *he* wants to tell her, that's up to him."

They argued long into the night; but as usual, Cameron won the argument.

The next day, the Johnsons dropped their guest at the bus station. Cameron gave him $20 for pocket money and they both hugged him.

"How are you going to live and support yourself up there?" Estelle asked.

235

"I've got some ideas," said Chris, smiling. "I didn't waste all my time in prison."

The air brakes of the bus hissed softly as it left Interstate Highway 90 and came to a stop. An arrow to the right pointed to the town of Moscow; an arrow to the left pointed to "SANDPOINT AND CANADA." The bus turned left, passing a sign that read "U.S. OUT OF THE UNITED NATIONS!" and headed north.

4

BOUNDARY COUNTY OCCUPIES THE NORTHERN TIP
of Idaho. It is part of the Idaho Panhandle, a narrow, rectangular
peninsula squeezed between Washington, Montana and British Columbia that was created by Congress in 1864 when the Idaho Territory was cut up into what became the state of Idaho and parts of
Montana and Wyoming. In choosing the Bitterroot Mountains as
the eastern boundary of Idaho, Congress created an oddly shaped
state which measures more than three hundred miles across its
southern edge and less than fifty miles across its northern edge.
The Panhandle, at the top of the wedge-shaped state, is a
wilderness of lakes, mountains and alpine valleys that for most of
its existence has been isolated from the rest of Idaho, not to mention the rest of America. Even Lewis and Clark, who traversed
Idaho on their way to the Pacific Coast in 1805, bypassed the Panhandle for less intimidating terrain to the south. Three years later, a
party of Welsh mountain men penetrated the area, and finding its
rivers and streams rich with beaver, they established a trading post
and a tradition of rugged individualism that survived into the twentieth century. Dependent entirely upon themselves for survival,
they founded a small settlement on the Kootenai River, named for
the local Indian tribe, about twenty miles south of what would become the U.S.-Canadian border. The settlement grew and mod-
estly prospered, and after an entrepreneur named Edwin L. Bonner
opened a ferry across the river in 1864 to accommodate miners

who were racing to a gold strike in British Columbia, it became known as Bonners Ferry.

The beaver hat, however, was doomed soon to fall out of fashion, forcing the town to look elsewhere for its sustenance. Gold and silver strikes brought transient prosperity to the north and south of it, but Boundary County was not as richly endowed with minerals as were some parts of Idaho and neighboring Canada, and ultimately it had to turn for its economic survival to the stands of cedar and white and lodgepole pine that rolled toward the horizon in all directions in a feathery green mantle.

Another of its resources, for those who wanted it, was isolation. In the latter years of the nineteenth century, it became one of several legendary hiding places for outlaws of the Old West. From their sanctuaries, bandits ventured out of the hills to rob banks, trains of the Northern Pacific and Great Northern railroads and stages carrying gold and silver from the mines.

A century later, much of Boundary County still had the primitive atmosphere of a frontier; and as the events that unfolded in 1980 would demonstrate, it had not changed in other ways as well.

In mountain ranges not many miles from Bonners Ferry, there were slopes on which only Indians had walked. Black bears roamed the back-country, sharing it with wolves, elk, deer, caribou, moose, cougars and buffalo. When rangers in Glacier National Park, eighty miles to the east, had a nasty grizzly bear to get rid of, they brought it to one of the nearby mountains. It was a place where people made new starts too. There was a sense of frontier independence in Bonners Ferry. Men walked with guns strapped to their waists to protect themselves from the wildlife in the logging country. Some people survived by poaching elk and deer and making whiskey and growing marijuana in the mountains. Families cut their own firewood, and many found all the happiness they ever wanted around a fiery metal stove in a log cabin built with their own hands. The people of Boundary County were, by and large, hardworking. There was a willingness to accept strangers with no questions asked, and, among many, a wariness of the law. Over the years, its forests and sawmills helped meet a capricious demand for lumber, and there were occasional booms. But in the early 1980s, it was chronically depressed economically, a kind of northern Appalachia.

In April 1980, U.S. marshals in California interviewed more than two dozen former associates of Christopher Boyce's and investigated tips that he had been seen in Mississippi, Canada, Mexico, Italy and the Philippine Islands. In Tysons Corner, Virginia, Thomas C. Kupferer, Jr., the newly appointed chief inspector of the Marshals Service, was ordered by his boss, Howard Safir, to come up with a plan that would track down Boyce and subdue the growing pressure from Congress. And in the Idaho Panhandle, a bearded young man arrived with a pack on his back.

He asked a stranger for directions and began walking.

The rain was falling heavily as Lee Rogers drove a dented red Datsun pickup truck through Paradise Valley, a grassy plain flanked on one side by a range of jagged mountains and on the other by the Kootenai River, flowing north into Canada. It was raining so hard that the lumberjack figured he couldn't see more than thirty yards in front of him, and eased up on the accelerator pedal. As he did, he saw a man walking along the edge of Cow Creek Road. The stranger was drenched, and Rogers stopped to offer him a ride. He opened the door of the Datsun and looked into blue eyes that seemed at once friendly and wary.

"Where you goin'?"

Christopher Boyce said that he was looking for the home of Gloria White.

The logger informed him that he was a neighbor of Gloria's and could take him to her doorstep. Gloria, he knew, wasn't home; she was at her other home in Oregon, and he was helping look after her livestock. But he didn't say anything. It wasn't his nature. Strangers, most of whom didn't want to say much about themselves, were always dropping in at Gloria's, and that reinforced his natural tendency not to ask questions. This stranger, however, volunteered that he knew Gloria was gone. He said he'd been told that he could stay there a few weeks until she got back. Rogers introduced himself, and Chris took his hand and introduced himself as Jim Namcheck.

The pickup truck turned off Cow Creek Road and started ascending a narrow dirt road bulldozed through a forest of cedar. The truck made a turn onto a side road, and a few minutes later, Chris saw a huge rustic wooden house dominating a bluff that a century ago might have been built by a frontiersman who had struck it rich in cattle or wheat.

"Gloria built it herself," Rogers said. "Took her three years, by hand—some of it when it was twenty below."

The house was three stories high and made of logs and a corrugated-tin roof. On the unfinished top floor, timbers were exposed and sheets of plastic covered the windows. The imposing log cabin was set on a plateau overlooking a broad valley where the Kootenai made its way into Canada. Fifty yards from the house, at the edge of a cliff, there was a cedar hot tub, and behind the house, rising thousands of feet high, was the green face of Katka Mountain.

Inside, Boyce discovered a dark labyrinth of rooms. There wasn't any plumbing, electricity or telephone; but there were candles, two huge wood-burning stoves and lots of wood stacked nearby. He started a fire and made himself at home.

Lee Rogers took to the newcomer, whose looks and intelligence made him think of a college student, and when the stranger said that he had come to Katka Mountain to write a book, it did not surprise him. He left him in the cabin, but dropped in when he came each day to feed the chickens and horses. There was one thing that puzzled Rogers about Jim Namcheck: although there was lots of canned food in the house, the only thing Namcheck ever seemed to eat was eggs he collected from the hens outside. When Rogers asked him if he was getting tired of eggs, Namcheck replied that he was having problems with his stomach and liked eggs because they were easy to digest.

At night, in the big house, Chris had begun to dream a lot, often the same dream: he saw himself being chased, and as he ran, his pursuers kept gaining on him; they got closer and closer, and he tried to hide, but they always caught him, and he was led away in handcuffs. Then he woke up in a cold sweat.

In the morning, he usually went outside for a walk, enjoying his freedom and looking for birds that he recognized. He had never felt better in his life.

After spending ten days in the cabin, he packed up his tent and sleeping bag for an expedition to explore the region and think over what he should do next, where he would go next. As long as he was in the woods, he felt safe. Cameron Johnson had been right about the beauty of the country. It *was* a Shangri-la, as primitively beautiful as any country he had ever seen. Inhaling the aroma of pine and cedar, Boyce made his own path much of the way. As he walked, he spotted elk and black bears and kestrel hawks, and he felt at peace. In time he would wish that he had stayed there forever.

He hiked over the peak of Katka Mountain and explored an old mining town on the Idaho-Montana border, then turned north and followed the Kootenai River, and then the Moyie River, which led him into Canada.

Three months had passed since his escape on January 21. He had survived. He had reached his goal. He was out of the country.

It was a junction in his flight: should he go north into Canada and try to make a new life there, or stay for a while in this Shangri-la?

He looked into Canada and southward into the United States, and then he turned back. He had once told a friend that he had never considered himself truly an American after his sixteenth birthday. But on this afternoon in April, as he looked into Canada, he decided that he was not yet ready to leave the United States.

As he sat at his desk in the Federal Courthouse in Los Angeles, Larry Homenick was pondering a hunch. He was imagining Chris going to a small town in the heart of America, assuming a new name, getting a job and trying to lose himself forever. For a time, that hunch proved right.

On his hike south from Canada, Chris stopped at a tavern, and somebody he met there told him that a job might be available at a tree nursery near Bonners Ferry. It didn't pay much, he said, but the work was steady. The next day, Chris found the tree farm and applied for the job. The couple who owned the business liked the young man who introduced himself as Jim Namcheck so much that

241

they hired him on the spot as a laborer for $3.25 an hour. A few days later, he rented a tiny cabin near the nursery for $15 a month and settled in with his new job, his new name and his new life.

The couple were immediately highly impressed by the diligence and charm of their new employee. He wasn't like the drifters and inarticulate out-of-work loggers who usually came looking for a job, then left as soon as a better-paying one turned up. Jim borrowed books about horticulture and visited them in the evenings and talked about forestry and said he'd like to go into the business himself someday.

Less than a week after Jim Namcheck went to work for the couple, they began talking about promoting him to a management position. Chris, however, gave up the job after holding it only a month. Gloria White had returned to Idaho, and before long he moved into her home beneath the soaring peak of Katka Mountain.

5

LATER ON, THE NEWSPAPERS WOULD COMPARE Gloria White to "Ma Barker," and some of her friends said that she secretly enjoyed it. But Gloria claimed that most of the stories about her were untrue, including the ones that likened her to Alice Barker, the middle-aged mother who had commanded a family of bank robbers during the Depression until most of them got killed off in shoot-outs with the police. Indeed, if comparisons to *anybody* were to be made, she would have been more comfortable with Belle Starr or any other illustrious female from the Old West than Ma Barker. In many ways, she was a woman who belonged more to the nineteenth century than to the twentieth.

Gloria Ann White was born in 1940 in Bend, Oregon. Her mother abandoned her when she was an infant, and she seldom saw her father—"an old redneck cowboy," she called him. At three, she was deposited with grandparents who already had a large brood of children and had little time for her. At fourteen, she quit school, left home and began supporting herself with a job in a lumber mill. In the rural logging country around Klamath Falls where she lived, young women matured early. Deprived of affection at home, she turned to men, and they responded eagerly to her stunning good looks, which were highlighted by soft blue eyes and long auburn hair. She was married at fourteen and pregnant at fifteen, but the marriage ended quickly. That was followed a year later by another marriage, and that ended quickly too. At nineteen she moved in with her second husband's brother, who was ten years older than she and who vacillated between trying to make an honest living and dealing in drugs and counterfeit money. They were married several years later, and by and large it was a happy marriage that lasted six years, until he died in a steep fall from a bridge on which he was working. According to some of the stories that were told later, Gloria's husband was high on LSD and flung himself from the bridge in an attempt to prove that he could fly. Whatever the reason for his death, he was Gloria's last husband. After that, there were a succession of lovers, but she told friends that she had decided never to marry again.

Gloria White had had little security during her childhood and hungered for the stability of owning her own land. In Oregon, before her husband died, she bought thirty-five acres in the woods not far from the sea. Later, looking for an even more remote setting in which to live, she bought four acres near Bonners Ferry and built her home overlooking the Kootenai River. Even then she wasn't through. During a hike up the side of Katka Mountain, she discovered a glistening lake surrounded by a primitive valley, and standing on the brow of a hill overlooking the vista, she had a dream. She bought twenty acres fronting on the lake and an option for one hundred additional acres. She told friends that she was going to build a lakeside resort there and call it "Robber's Roost" in honor of all the bandits who had hidden out in Boundary County during its long history.

When Gloria smiled in the sunlight, a diamond set in gold sparkled in her mouth. A friend had given her the two-hundred-year-old skull of a Flathead Indian whose mouth contained a gold molar, and a diamond was set in the gold. She never discovered how the tooth had gotten there, or why. But she decided that it was a shame to leave it there, and one day she put the skull under her arm and took "Elmer" to a dentist and asked him to fit the tooth in a bridge for her. After that, whenever she opened her mouth very wide her diamond-studded tooth flashed brightly.

With the income from her husband's insurance settlement, her own hands and the help of friends and her children (there were six of them, fathered by various husbands and lovers), she built two homes—the big log house on Katka Mountain in Idaho and a second one near Newport, Oregon. Whatever else anybody said about Gloria, she lived life on her own terms. She spurned electricity, indoor plumbing and most other conveniences of the twentieth century, with the exception of her pickup truck. She cut her own wood, raised vegetables and livestock on her property and shot deer and elk for the table. Gloria refused to send her children to school, claiming she could teach them to read and write just as well at home.

Gloria White shunned most of the Idaho and Oregon townspeople and their conventions—"Mainstreeters," she called them derisively—while gathering around her a conglomeration of castaway children and teenagers, hippies from the '60s, out-of-work loggers, ex-convicts, felons on the run, men with funny nicknames like "Fat Jack," "Dirty Dan" and "Big George" and other people of a stripe that Chief Inspector Thomas C. Kupferer, Jr., of the U.S. Marshals Service would probably have referred to collectively as "scumbags and dirtbags." Over the years, friends said, hundreds of people showed up at her doorstep asking for help. No one could remember her ever turning anyone down, and if anyone commented on it, she would talk about her bumpy childhood and say, "I know what it's like to need love."

Among the people who came to her for help was Cameron Johnson, who arrived in Bonners Ferry one day in the early 1970s. He was on the run, and a friend they had in common had asked Gloria to take him in. A romance blossomed—but Johnson, as usual, had trouble sharing his life with only one woman. For a while he lived alternately with Gloria and Estelle, the woman who later became his wife. She lived about ninety miles south of Bonners Ferry in Spokane, Washington. Gloria White, however, was not a person who could share her men, and a few weeks after the romance she packed up his belongings and took him and them to Spokane and told Estelle, "Here he is; you can have my half."

For the children who lived with Gloria on Katka Mountain, life was idyllic—not quite according to Mark Twain, but perhaps as he might have imagined life might become for children in a distant century. If some of them had trouble reading and writing, they had a self-reliance lacking in most kids of the same age who went to school. They swam in the rivers and streams, hunted and fished and rode motorcycles through the woods. They lived off the land and had no real rules to live by; if a truck or other piece of property belonging to someone else showed up on the mountain, as occasionally happened, their punishment was not severe. The children were usually introduced to sex when they were very young and encouraged to do whatever they wanted to do without shame or adult supervision, for there was also a great deal of casual sexual activity among the adults who lived there. Abortions could be handled casually on the hill. There were parties that seemed to go on permanently, and when the children finished their chores they were sometimes given a marijuana joint as a reward.

Over the years, there were many rumors about the goings-on at Gloria's home: rumors that people had seen her shooting automatic weapons in the hills; about her packing a tiny pistol strapped to her leg; even rumors that she was helping to smuggle drugs and illegal weapons across the border into Canada. Policemen claimed that sometimes they tracked fugitives to her property but then the fugitives were swallowed up by the land. In time, some cops began referring to her place on Katka Mountain as the "Hole in the Wall," because it reminded them of the hideout to which Butch Cassidy and the Sundance Kid had disappeared between train hold-ups and bank robberies.

The vast majority of the two thousand or so people who lived in and around Bonners Ferry were hardworking, honest and law-abiding. But a few possessed an attitude reminiscent of that found in certain parts of the rural Southwest during the 1930s: a sense, rooted in frustration, poverty and despair, that poor people had been wronged by a corrupt and distant power structure dominated by people of wealth, and that the only way to right the injustice and balance the scales was to take money that rightfully, they felt, belonged to them. Banks—whose cash was insured by the Federal Government—were regarded as the most convenient source of these reparations, and among some of these people robbing banks was a just and thoroughly acceptable way of righting wrongs.

According to some rumors that had circulated about her, Gloria

White not only had operated a hideout for criminals at her rural homes but was the leader of a gang of bandits who periodically left the hills to rob banks on the flatlands and shared their loot with her in exchange for hiding them out. By the spring of 1980, however, no one had ever proved anything in this regard. In 1979, Gloria had been charged by federal authorities with applying theatrical makeup to disguise four men who had robbed a Eugene, Oregon, bank in 1976; the group included George Larchmont, a career bank robber who for years had been one of the most-wanted fugitives in the Pacific Northwest. The charge against Gloria was eventually dismissed, and the mystery about what was going on up at her place persisted.

Sister Jean-Marie Bartunek, the principal of St. John Fisher, the parochial school in California that Christopher John Boyce attended, had called him "every teacher's dream"—a bright, curious, compassionate, hardworking, idealistic and sweet youth who seemed capable of achieving success at whatever he set his mind to. She was not alone. As the FBI agents learned who investigated him after his arrest for espionage, and the deputy U.S. marshals who pursued him after his escape, virtually every adult with whom Chris Boyce had come in contact as a child and teenager remembered him in much the same way as Sister Jean-Marie.

There is no way of knowing when the onetime altar boy they knew began to lose his innocence. There were some who said that he had lost, in a recurrent stupor induced by marijuana and cocaine, whatever innocence he had before he ever walked into the Black Vault at the TRW plant and was exposed to the secret CIA machinations that he claimed had so repelled him that he decided to betray his country. They said that he was already so cynical about American values, so spoiled and so bored, so amoral and so rebellious against the conservative politics and discipline of his father that it took only the slightest nudge to make him a traitor. These were the people who compared Boyce and Andrew Daulton Lee to Loeb and Leopold, the two bored young rich kids from Chicago who had murdered a child during the 1920s in pursuit of an adventure.

Whatever forces shaped Boyce after his conviction for espionage can only be guessed at: the brutality of prison life and the mentors he found during his three years behind bars as Federal Bureau of Prisons Inmate #19437-148; the effects of loneliness and desperation while he was on the run, the haunting fear of capture and being returned to prison; even, perversely, possibly the effect on his ego of having become a celebrity antihero who received letters from admiring young women comparing him to James Dean.

His family would say that the boy they knew had been first transformed by an irresponsible employer who had given a twenty-one-year-old college drop-out a $140-a-week job in a secret world of international skullduggery that was beyond his maturity to cope with—and later by a merciless criminal-justice system that had thrust an idealistic twenty-four-year-old with no previous criminal record into prisons populated by killers, bullies and sexual deviates and offered him no hope of getting out until he was an old man.

Whatever the reasons, Christopher John Boyce was in many ways not the same young man in the spring of 1980 that he had been in the springtime of his adolescence when a Roman Catholic nun had envisaged so bright a future for him.

If he had stuck with his first plan, to go to Canada and write a book deploring what he regarded as the inhumanity of the prisons; if he had stayed on the course that he chose when he arrived in Idaho and worked at a modest job at a tree farm, Christopher Boyce might have disappeared forever.

He might have been promoted, gotten married and fathered a child. As Jim Namcheck, he might have blended permanently into the landscape of one of the wildest and most scenic corners of America, the kind of wilderness in which, as a child and teenager, he had found his greatest joy.

But he did not.

6

THE TELLER DIDN'T BELIEVE HIM, AND SO HE SAID
it again:

"Give me all your money, or I'll blow your head off."

She laughed, which made him laugh, but then he showed her a
large pistol inside his jacket and insisted, "I have to get serious.
This *is* a robbery. I have to get out of here."

The woman pushed a pile of bills across the counter to the
bearded man in a baseball cap, and the former Soviet spy, polite as
usual, said, "Thank you."

On June 5, 1980, as they approached the six-month anniversary
of the escape, Larry Homenick and the other deputy marshals in
Los Angeles who were pursuing Christopher Boyce were evaluat-
ing a tip that a convict in a Missouri state prison with a curious
nickname, "Captain Midnight," might have helped him escape to
Mexico. On the same date, at a bank in a suburb of Spokane,
Washington, the career of Christopher Boyce, bank robber, began.

He returned to Spokane six days later and robbed another bank.
An automatic surveillance camera captured a photograph of the
bandit in a baseball cap. But the FBI agents who investigated the
holdup were unable to identify the man in the photos from the
watch list they maintained of bank robbers operating in the region,
and none of them compared the photograph of the bearded bandit

with the face of Christopher Boyce that looked out from Wanted posters across the country.

In May and early June, Christopher Boyce had made several purchases: a mule named ''Burlap'' that he bought from a family in Bonners Ferry and renamed ''Kelleher'' in honor of the judge who had sentenced him to forty years in prison; a well-traveled 1962 Dodge with giant tail fins that he called the ''Mud Shark'' because that was what it reminded him of after it had been driven on a muddy road; and, from a neighbor on Katka Mountain, a .357 magnum revolver. In mid-June, Gloria White, after arriving from her home in Oregon, checked out *The Falcon and the Snowman* from the Bonners Ferry library, and Cameron and Estelle Johnson arrived from California for a visit.

Cameron and Chris jogged through the forest near Gloria's home, nostalgically remembering the times they had run together inside the fences topped with razor wire at Lompoc. Cameron asked Chris when he was going to move on to Canada, and Chris said that he was thinking of putting down roots in Boundary County, at least for a while.

Four days later, one of Gloria's eldest sons arrived on the mountain with his girlfriend. Also with them was a daughter he had fathered while living with a different girl. He had lost custody of the child to her mother in a dispute in Oregon, but he had snatched the baby from her and had brought her to hide out in Idaho. The child's mother, suspecting as much, notified Oregon authorities, who in turn notified the Boundary County Sheriff's Department that the baby might be at the home of Gloria White.

Arriving early in the morning, a half-dozen deputies surrounded the big log house. As they approached the home they stepped over hundreds of small green plants scattered on the ground outside. They interviewed everybody in the house, including a man named Jim Namcheck who had a birth certificate to prove that he was not Gloria's son, but they didn't find the missing child or her father. They were hiding out on the slopes of Katka Mountain, at the site set aside for ''Robber's Roost.''

The deputies left and everybody relaxed. The raiding party had not only missed an escaped spy, they had ignored hundreds of potted marijuana seedlings that were resting on the ground all over Gloria's yard.

The next day, because of a hawk, the Falcon was almost caught again. One sheriff's deputy in the raiding party had spotted what he thought were the wings of a red-tailed hawk mounted as an ornament above the front door of Gloria's house. Since it was unlawful to kill such birds, he reported his findings to the Idaho Fish and Game Department, and the next day a warden arrived with a search warrant. He looked up at the wings and decided he couldn't be sure that they had belonged to a hawk, and after talking with most of the people in the house, he left.

Two raids in two days was unsettling. Christopher Boyce decided it was time to move into the mountain range behind Gloria's home. He loaded onto his mule his sleeping bag, his tent, a dictionary, a copy of *Roget's Thesaurus, The Federalist Papers,* accounts of the Lewis and Clark expedition, dozens of other books from the Bonners Ferry library and materials with which to write a book and hiked several miles into the wilderness. Finally, he decided to make camp beside a bed of quartz tailings near the shaft of an abandoned silver mine on 3,900-foot-high Two Tail Peak, and he began to write about his experiences, his thoughts on the world, the prison system and the obscenities of life as he saw them. He also trundled up the hill on his mule the marijuana plants missed during the two raids.

Towering trees and mountains surrounded him, and the Paradise Valley and the Kootenai River stretched before him. It was a place of extraordinary beauty, and for a time Boyce thought about staying there forever.

Many months later, he regretted that he had not.

The people who lived in the isolated cabins hidden among the trees on Katka Mountain soon noticed the newcomer on their hill. He returned their waves and blended into the forest. Border Patrol and Forest Service agents making their rounds of the wilderness got to know and like the stranger. When they chanced upon his camp he offered them coffee, made small talk and said that he was thinking of trying to reopen the old mine nearby. They encouraged him and talked about the bears and wolves and elk with whom he shared the mountain and then left to finish their patrols. The sight of the bearded man leading his heavily laden mule up the mountain reminded some of the people he met on Katka Mountain of the images of prospectors they had seen in movies about the Old West. Before long they had coined two nicknames for him, "Jackass Jim" and "Jim the Mule Man."

No one noticed, or seemed to care, that he was hauling a great deal of water up the mountain on his mule. The water was to irrigate the marijuana plants that he had dug into the ground not far from the old mine.

One morning early in July, after coming down from his mountaintop, Chris was in the yard outside Gloria's home and hunched over a piece of leather for the mule's rigging when he heard a car drive up the hill. As usual, his .357 magnum was resting in his shoulder holster; his muscles tensed, and he waited for it to stop.

Two men got out of a ten-year-old Pontiac and walked toward him. They were brothers who had moved to Idaho from Michigan five years earlier with their father, who had had high hopes of striking it rich in gold or silver but had left Boundary County when he didn't find the treasure he sought. The brothers liked the fresh air and frontier atmosphere and had decided to stay on and see if they could make it as miners or lumberjacks.

Brian Hill was twenty-four, unshaven and with long brown hair. He was husky and moved with a self-confidence that some people might interpret as cockiness. His brother was nineteen and blond. Tom Hill was almost as tall as his brother, but weighed about fifty pounds less. Both looked unkempt. They had the weathered look of outdoorsmen and were dressed in soiled Levi's, leather vests and sandals; it was the kind of uniform a lot of the people wore who hung out at Gloria's place.

They hadn't known much in life except poverty. Since moving to Boundary County the brothers had found occasional work as loggers or in the sawmills. When things were up in the lumber business, they could earn $9 or $10 an hour. But such times had become rare. They had discovered that demand for lumber was capricious, dependent upon interest rates for mortgages far from

Bonners Ferry, inflation, the size of the federal deficit and a lot of other factors they did not understand. When things were slow in the forests, as they were in the summer of 1980, the brothers tried to survive by working at odd jobs. In exchange for meals and a few dollars, they had helped Gloria White put the roof on her house. Now they were almost broke again, and the outlook for work was grim; they had driven to Katka Mountain in hope of borrowing money from her.

Chris introduced himself as Jim Namcheck and said that he was a friend of Gloria's who lived in a tent on the mountain. Gloria was in town, he said, but she would be back soon. He offered them a beer, and while they waited they became friends. The brothers tired of waiting after an hour and left. When they returned a few days later, Namcheck was gone—living up on the hill, Gloria explained. They said they had heard in town that someone living at Gloria's had a cheap old car for sale—a 1962 Dodge with big fins—and asked if she knew anything about it.

"You don't want that car," Gloria said. "It's been used in some bank robberies down in Spokane."

Like other people who were part of the constantly changing cast on Katka Mountain, the Hill brothers had heard Gloria talk cryptically about bank robberies. But they didn't ask questions. They enjoyed coming to Gloria's place, where there was always a party going on or one was being planned. It was a place where everyone had a good time. It was a place, Brian Hill would say, where it seemed that every day was Sunday.

At Gloria's there was an unwritten rule: Don't ask questions of strangers. The brothers made a point of following the rule when it came to Jim Namcheck. They sensed that Gloria and the other people living in the house didn't want to admit that he was there.

Several weeks after their first meeting, Brian recalled later, when he complained again to Gloria about how difficult it was to find a job, she suggested that he could make a few dollars by renting his Pontiac to Jim Namcheck. Before long, Brian had some money in his jeans again. He rented his car to Jim for a day or two and pocketed $200.

As the summer passed, the Hill brothers spent more and more

time with their new friend. He began to come down from the mountain more often and to go drinking with them at one of the bars on Main Street in Bonners Ferry. Their favorite was the Mint Club, the unofficial social club of many of the people who lived on or near Katka Mountain. It was a dark, narrow place with a bar, a few tables for dining and a pool table in the rear; in a town with a high rate of unemployment, the Mint was usually crowded with regulars, no matter what time of day it was. Sometimes, especially on weekends, when there was a band which drew a lot of girls, they walked across the street to Mr. C's. The good looks, sense of humor and appealing shyness of the stranger were quickly noted by the girls of Bonners Ferry. Unlike a lot of the young men who hung out at the local bars, he wore clean clothes and treated them with a gentleness they did not often see among the men who tried to outdrink each other until they fell off their stools. To some of the women there was an incongruity about Jim Namcheck's presence in Bonners Ferry that added a touch of mystery to him and increased his appeal.

On July 23, 1980, a telephone call was made from Mexico City to the National Security Agency in Maryland from a man who called himself Christopher Boyce. As the NSA, the CIA and the U.S. Marshals Service went to work to identify the caller and determine whether the call was legitimate, the real Christopher Boyce was riding in a pickup truck on a back road in Idaho.

"What would you say if I told you my name wasn't Jim?"

"Well, hey, I really don't care what your name is," Brian Hill said. "I take you for what you are."

They had all had a lot of drinks at Mr. C's.

"My real name is Chris."

The brothers said they didn't care, and they meant it. If he had a secret, that was his business. They would continue calling him "Jim."

The conversation ended.

A couple of nights later, after dinner and drinks, Brian Hill and Christopher Boyce were driving back to Bonners Ferry from

Sandpoint, a resort town about thirty miles south of Bonners Ferry on the shore of Lake Pend Oreille, Idaho's largest lake.

"What kind of name is Namcheck?" Brian asked. "You don't look Polish. Is it Russian, or what?"

"Neither. I'm Irish."

It was silent in the car. A rush of egotism welled up in Chris: "I said the other night that my name was Chris. My real name is Christopher John Boyce. Does it mean anything to you."

"No," Brian said. "Why?"

"There was a lot of publicity about it three years ago; about spying," Chris said, disappointed. "There was a book written about me."

"Doesn't mean a thing to me."

They drove back to Gloria's house.

If the ordinary parties at Gloria White's log house were legendary, they were miserly compared with those that began to occur after Jim Namcheck disappeared for a day or two and returned with a small vinyl bag stuffed with money. He bought cases of foreign beer and elk and beef steaks, and sometimes the parties lasted for days.

A few days after the trip to Sandpoint when he had blurted out his secret, there was another party at Gloria's. Chris and Brian drank beer and smoked pot.

Brian hadn't seemed very curious after Chris had made his confession, and it seemed to bother Chris. Apparently deciding to convince Brian that he was not just another hanger-on at Gloria's, he disappeared for a few moments and returned with a hardbound copy of *The Falcon and the Snowman* that was now officially listed as overdue at the Bonners Ferry library.

He opened the book and pointed to a picture of himself being led up the stairs of a courthouse by FBI agents. Brian agreed that he bore a resemblance to the person in the photograph, and leafed through the rest of the picture section of the book, which had more photographs of Chris. But then he put the book down.

Chris urged him to read it, and Brian said he would do it later. He was more concerned about finding a job than with reading a book.

The marijuana plants had budded on Katka Mountain, and everyone at Gloria's house waited eagerly for the harvest to begin.

Chris showed Brian a clipping from the *Spokane Spokesman Review*. The article reported that Spokane had experienced an unexplained epidemic of bank robberies. Already there had been five robberies during 1980, compared with four during all of 1979, while the number of holdups elsewhere in the state had declined. Bank security officials had expressed their concern over the sudden outbreak of robberies and had appealed to the public to submit anonymously any information they had about the robbers. A special $1,000 reward had been posted in a security project called "Rat on a Rat." Bank officials quoted in the article were distressed by the situation. "This is no Robin Hood, Jesse James type of thing," one security man was quoted as saying.

Brian reported later to his brother Tom that Namcheck, after showing him the article, told him that he had pulled off all five of the robberies reported in the paper and that he was working with Gloria White, who was giving him pointers; disguising him with theatrical makeup, wigs and beards; and sharing in the loot. Only the day before, Chris said, he had visited a branch of the Old National Bank in Spokane and walked away a few minutes later with $5,700. As if to prove it, he led Brian to a chicken coop behind Gloria's house and pulled out a plastic bag stuffed with cash. Later, to demonstrate that it was *real* money, he took $2,800 out of the bag and used it to buy a sports car, a 1976 Triumph, in Bonners Ferry.

"They just give you the money when you ask for it," he said.

Brian had begun to take Boyce seriously.

Chris told him that he was on the run from a forty-year prison sentence and that he was robbing banks to survive. Friends in prison, he said, had told him how to get away with it. He had to have money to survive, and robbing banks was the easiest way to do it. "If you're careful, you've got nothing to worry about," he said.

Hill was skeptical.

"What if you have to shoot someone? That's murder—the death penalty."

"I'm not going to kill anyone," Boyce said sarcastically.

In prison, he said, he had been instructed to pick a bank or savings-and-loan association in a small town or else a small suburban branch at the edge of a town, one too small to have a security guard and located where it would be easy to make a fast escape out of town. Use an older, dependable car that blends easily into traffic, but don't use the same car more than two or three times. Pick one teller and demand all the large bills. Get in and get out as fast as you can. So far, he said, his buddies in prison had been right, but there was one more thing he needed: a dependable getaway driver who had guts and could be counted on not to run away and desert him while he was in the bank—which was what had happened to some of the bank robbers he had met in prison.

Chris offered Brian the job.

"I need a driver; I'll go in the bank and get the money and split it with you."

Brian was broke and had no prospects of finding a job. Jim Namcheck made the proposition sound like an adventure. He agreed to become his driver.

The car was parked on an isolated logging road off a back road leading from Bonners Ferry to Spokane. The two young men tried to remain motionless as Gloria White, giggling, finished applying makeup to the faces of Christopher Boyce and Brian Hill.

She had sprayed a silver coating on Brian's hair and, with a toothbrush, coated his mustache with the same material; then she gave Chris's hair a salt-and-pepper look with silver and black makeup. He had shaved off his own beard, but Gloria had applied an imitation one. With his string tie and Smoky the Bear hat, Brian said, he looked like a colonel in the Confederate Army. They said good-bye near a forest of tall cedars, and Gloria drove her pickup truck back to Bonners Ferry.

On the outskirts of Spokane, Boyce and Hill stopped to buy gas at a self-service station. The attendant, a pretty brunette, watched the car drive up and studied the curious-looking men in the front seat. As Brian paid for the gas, she smiled and said, "What is this, Halloween?"

"We're in a play," Chris said quickly.

As they drove away, Chris looked back; he thought he saw the young woman look at their license plate and write something on a piece of paper.

Brian made a U-turn and headed back for Bonners Ferry.

257

7

ON THE MORNING OF SEPTEMBER 3, 1980, LESS
than a month after Brian Hill's aborted introduction to bank robbery, he parked his Pontiac in an alley on the outskirts of Spokane
and raised the hood. He got out and leaned over the fender into the
engine and pretended to be investigating a malfunctioning carburetor. At the same moment, Christopher Boyce entered the Pacific
National Bank nearby wearing what Brian called his "Fidel Castro
disguise." Most of Boyce's face was hidden by an actor's dark
beard, a hunting cap was pulled over his forehead almost to his
eyebrows and his eyes looked out through plastic safety glasses as
thick as bottle glass.

Two minutes later, he sprinted out of the bank and rounded a
corner into the alley where Hill was still trying to look perplexed
over his carburetor. He dived into the back seat holding his hat,
which was full of money. Lying on the floor, he began counting it
and moaned, "There's only nine hundred bucks!"

It was an embarrassment for the ex-spy who had boasted of the
riches so easily to be taken from banks. They drove 160 miles into
Montana and the following day, in Missoula, robbed the Southside
Branch of the Western Federal Savings and Loan Company of
$4,382.

Twelve days later, they took a leisurely three-hour drive from
Bonners Ferry to Lewiston, Idaho, cased several banks and then
258

selected a branch of the Bank of Idaho, where, for a minute or two of labor and risk, Boyce was handed almost $5,000.

On the way home, when Brian Hill brought up the unthinkable—"What would you do if you were cornered and had to use the gun?"—Boyce insisted repeatedly that he would not shoot anyone but himself.

"Either they'll kill me or I'll kill myself." He said that he wasn't going back to prison. "I'll die in the parking lot."

In Hawaii during the final weeks of summer in 1980, Chris's childhood friend Mike Adams was still under surveillance by deputy marshals on the island of Kauai. In Washington, the Senate Intelligence Committee had completed another inquiry into the whereabouts of Christopher Boyce and had let the Justice Department know that it was deeply troubled by its failure to find him. In Los Angeles, the psychiatrist called Dr. Joe had begun work on the psychological profile of Boyce for members of the Marshals Service task force that was about to convene in the city, and Larry Homenick, his desk covered with leads placing Boyce in South Africa, Mexico, Nicaragua, Ireland and the Soviet Union, began his frustrating round of interviews with the silver-tongued Brent Pope.

In Sandpoint, Idaho, Chris sat in a restaurant and studied the faces of the other customers, wondering who they were, what they did, what threat they posed to him, and he tried to finish his meal. Like Homenick, he was now unconsciously exploring every face that he saw on the street, in a restaurant, in a supermarket.

From his seat near the rear of the small café he noticed a group of people come through the door. One voice was louder than the others. It was coming from a tall man with dark hair who looked vaguely familiar. Then he recognized the face, and his blood froze.

Like a preacher working an assemblage for souls, the man spent a moment with each employee and customer before marching on. He was moving toward Chris. Indeed, he aimed himself directly at Chris, with his hand outstretched.

"Hi. I'm Frank Church. I sure would appreciate your vote."

It was the chairman of the Senate Intelligence Committee, Senator Frank Church, to whom Chris had once written a plea for help in getting out of solitary confinement; whose committee had investigated the Boyce-Lee case and Boyce's subsequent escape. Church's liberal politics in Washington had gotten him in trouble at home, and in the late summer of 1980 he was waging an uphill battle for reelection.

Chris smiled at Frank Church and mumbled something about not living in Idaho and went back to his meal.

Christopher Boyce's secret was now known by almost all the people who hovered around Gloria White, and even some of the casual drinkers at the Mint Club. Indeed, once he had made his decision to place his trust in these new acquaintances, Boyce often volunteered his secret, claiming that he had become a spy to protest the arms race and the march of the world's superpowers toward a cataclysmic nuclear war. If his polemics about the CIA and the lessons Boyce claimed to have learned from history—especially that man had never developed a weapon that he did not use in warfare— bewildered some of the loggers and drifters, it seemed not to matter. These were people who had their own grievances against government, and it didn't take much to convince them that Washington was probably as wrongheaded about the way it confronted the threat of a nuclear holocaust as it was about everything else. Many simply did not believe Namcheck/Boyce's tales of high adventure inside the Soviet Embassy in Mexico City. But even if his polemics and tales of adventure were ignored, he had become a popular regular at the bar as the summer of 1980 drew to a close.

Christopher Boyce still had a gift for making people like him. The same shyness, self-depreciating humor and interest in others that had charmed Larry Homenick made many of the women he met at the Mint or Mr. C's want to take him home. Many did. Of all the women who pursued him, he favored one of Gloria's daughters, a girl barely into her teens who, like her mother at the same age, had attained maturity beyond her years. They spent nights together on Chris's mountain, listening to the rustle of bears and elk in the forest and talking about their future together. Lee Rogers, the logger who had first picked him up on a rainy afternoon in Bonners Ferry, had heard the rumors about his past, and urged him to stop robbing banks. He told Chris that he should take Gloria's pubescent daughter up to Katka Mountain, build a cabin for the two of them and live there forever, where it was unlikely anyone would find them. But Chris demurred. He said that if he was ever going to live free he would have to leave America, and in time that was what he would do. He robbed banks, he said, to survive for now and to raise money for the future and the next phase of his flight. Occasionally he hinted that there was another reason: *he enjoyed the thrill of it.*

At the Mint, some of the regulars had noticed the new riches of Jim the Mule Man and his buddy the Kahlúa Kid, and were starting to ask questions about this suddenly acquired wealth. It started the night Brian bought the house a round of drinks with a one-hundred-dollar bill, pocketed the change and then bought another round with another hundred-dollar bill. Stories about international intrigue and prison escapes could be ignored. But in a logging town whose economy was terribly depressed, where almost a third of the labor force was out of work, two hundred-dollar bills could not.

People were asking too many questions, Chris told Brian, and it was time to move on. Even when Brian told Chris he was getting too paranoid, Chris insisted. In late September, at the same time Chuck Kupferer and Larry Homenick were setting up the task force to find him in Los Angeles, he moved to Montana.

As a hideout, Chris chose one of the most spectacular corners of America, a raw, mountainous wilderness near the town of Bigfork, Montana, a few miles south of Glacier National Park and 120 miles southeast of Bonners Ferry. Gloria White had told them that it was a perfect place to go when things got hot. It was even more isolated than Boundary County. They rented two cabins beside Swan Lake—one for Chris, and a larger one for Brian and Tom Hill and a third brother, Fred, who had joined them from the East.

It was in Montana, the Hill brothers said, that Chris revealed his intention to become a spy again.

8

"YOU COULD MAKE TWENTY-FIVE THOUSAND A month," Chris told Brian and Tom Hill as they looked out at Swan Lake.

The two brothers stared at him as if he were crazy.

"Doing what?"

"Join the Army." Chris smiled.

"What do you mean?"

"Get into the Army, get a security clearance and get documents; I can sell them to the Russians, the Chinese, the Cubans."

Chris had first dreamed of implementing his scheme when he had been behind bars at the Metropolitan Correctional Center in San Diego. He remembered how eager the Russians had been to buy *anything*. When Daulton's KGB control agents had put him under more and more pressure to obtain CIA documents from the Black Vault at TRW (and each month proved their willingness to pay for them with stacks of hundred-dollar bills), Chris had begun to randomly photograph everything in sight. He snapped photos with his Minox camera of what seemed to him to be routine TRW reports and manuals and sent them to Mexico City with Daulton. And the Russians had paid handsomely for them. To raise the market price of some of the CIA telex messages he processed in the vault, he had typed "Flash Top Secret" on them, and the Russians had been delighted. Once he had even sent with Daulton to Mexico a roll of photographs of nude women that he had copied from *Penthouse* magazine. The Russians had paid for that, too.

Toward the end of the twenty months that Christopher Boyce and Daulton Lee spent as Soviet agents, there were increasing complaints from their KGB controllers about the mediocre quality of some of the information they were buying. At one point the exasperated agents shoved Daulton out of a slow-moving limousine onto the streets of Mexico City to show their displeasure with his repeated visits to the Soviet Embassy carrying documents they called *basura*—garbage.

But Christopher Boyce was not troubled by memories of that event. He had decided in San Diego that he would outsmart the KGB, convinced that if the operation was carefully orchestrated, the Russians would buy *any* document that originated in a secret American defense facility—or seemed to.

As he lay on his bunk in his prison cell at the Metropolitan Correctional Center, Chris had thought out the scheme he would put into practice if he ever got out: he would organize a ring that would counterfeit American military secrets and sell them to intelligence agencies around the world. "Have you any idea how easy it would be to covertly influence governments, in a private capacity, by fabricating one's own 'secret' documents and distributing them among the intelligence communities?" he once asked a friend at the San Diego prison. "I will admit that it would be very dangerous, but still simple. I could easily drive hundreds of professionals to nonviolent distraction."

To carry out the plan, he needed a legitimate source of classified information, bait to get the Russians on the hook and establish the *bona fides* of his sources. After that, using the same format as the legitimate documents, he would begin to manufacture his own.

Now, in Bigfork, Montana, he outlined his plan:

Tom Hill, who was nineteen, would enlist in the Army and apply for training at a school for communications clerks or a similar specialty, then request assignment to a job with access to classified information and the ciphers used to encode and decode messages. Some people might find it naive of Boyce to think he could take a poorly educated youth from the backwoods of Idaho and use him to penetrate a high-security operation. But when the Hill brothers said as much, he said that it wasn't necessary for Tom to find his way into a supersensitive job, although that would help. It really didn't matter where he worked. No matter what job he got in the Army, he would come into contact with documents that the Russians or Chinese would pay for. They needed a cover from which to begin the distribution of secrets.

Boyce showed them a photograph in *The Falcon and the Snow-man* of the Minox-B—a camera smaller than a pack of cigarettes—that he and Daulton Lee had used to photograph documents for the Russians. "I'll get you one of these," he said. He said he would teach him how to use it to photograph the documents and not get caught.

Eventually, he said, Soviet agents would give them lessons in "trade-craft," the techniques for avoiding detection, how to fool lie-detector tests and transmit clandestine information. Tom's job would be to photograph the documents, then give the microfilm to Brian, who would give it to Boyce or deliver it to another agent whom he would recruit. They could all easily earn $25,000 a month.

Tom Hill said that he didn't want to join the Army. He might end up in the infantry. He was happy the way he was. Boyce tried to persuade him:

"If you enlist, I'll give you the TR-6," he said.

Tom liked the sports car. He had never owned a car, or much of anything else beyond his own clothes. He said that he would think it over.

During the next month, while the manhunt for Chris was being intensified in Southern California with the formation of a special task force by the U.S. Marshals Service, he and Brian Hill robbed a bank in Missoula, Montana, and another in Idaho Falls, Idaho. After the robbery in Idaho Falls, Brian decided to use some of his share of the robberies for a three-week trip back to his hometown in Michigan. After he left, Chris persuaded the third Hill brother, Fred, who was twenty-one, to drive his getaway car. On October 21, 1980, they robbed the Eastside Bank in Great Falls, Montana, of $4,000.

* * *

"How ya doin'?"

There was silence.

"Chris?"

"Man, is it good to hear your voice."

The author of *The Falcon and the Snowman* didn't ask where he was calling from, and Christopher Boyce didn't volunteer the information.

"Your mom and dad will be glad to know you're still alive. They thought you were dead."

"Tell 'em I love 'em."

He was at a pay phone in Montana two days after the robbery in Great Falls. He had been drinking, and as usual when he drank heavily, he had become homesick and depressed, and now he was doing what he had always promised himself he wouldn't do.

"How are you surviving? Do you have money?"

"Yeah. I'm fine." There was a pause. *"I've got friends. . . ."*

A few hours later, at a hastily called meeting of the task force in Los Angeles, the psychiatrist called Dr. Joe said, "Well, I guess the theory that Chris fell in a crevasse was wrong."

After the robbery in Great Falls, Boyce tried to persuade Fred Hill to join the Army and become a spy. But like his brother Tom, he said he didn't want to.

On October 28, 1980, Inspector Roger Archiga of the Marshals Service wrote a report suggesting that a pattern was developing in the investigation which pointed to Boyce's having fled to the Pacific Northwest and to Canada or the Soviet Union. Two days later, a plastic surgeon at UCLA told other members of the task force that Christopher Boyce could probably have obtained a new face in Mexico for $2,000 or so.

At the same moment the surgeon was drawing a sketch of how he might look after cosmetic surgery, Christopher Boyce was in his Triumph driving from Montana to Idaho en route to Gloria White's annual Halloween party and thinking about a completely different look from the one the physician had imagined. Beside him in the sports car was what he called his "Basic Bank Robbery Kit"—a vi-nyl overnight case containing enough theatrical makeup to outfit a modest-sized summer-stock troupe and his .357 magnum. The next day he put on a dress, padded his belly and stuffed its bodice with a pair of grapefruit. He wrapped a red kerchief around his head and blackened his face and went to Gloria's party as Aunt Jemima.

After the party, he drove back to Bigfork, where Brian Hill was waiting unhappily. Fred Hill had admitted to his older brother that he had driven the getaway car for Chris in Great Falls and had told him about his efforts to recruit him as a spy. As the oldest of the brothers, Brian considered himself the leader of the clan. He liked to make the decisions about the family. He told Chris that he didn't want Fred involved in robbing banks and decreed that neither Fred nor Tom Hill would join the Army and become an espionage agent. It was one thing for him to help Chris rob banks; it was another for his brothers to take the risks that had sent Chris to prison in the first place. Brian also said that he was thinking about not driving for Chris anymore. He was worried about getting caught. But Chris, as usual, was persuasive: not only did he talk Brian out of quitting; he convinced him that he should go into the bank on their next job.

Chris was sitting in the driver's seat of the Triumph a few days later in Lewiston, Idaho, when Brian Hill stuck a 9mm automatic pistol into his waistband. He got out of the car and walked into the same branch of the Bank of Idaho that Chris had robbed two months earlier. Once he got inside, however, he was overcome by fear; he was so frightened that he knew if he didn't leave immedi-ately he would begin vomiting violently. He turned around and jumped into the car and lied that the bank had hired a guard since Chris had robbed it in September.

A week later, on December 2, in the middle of a snowstorm, Brian went through with his promise, and he didn't get sick.

Chris and Brian had arrived in Missoula, Montana, the night be-fore and rented a room in a motel near town popular with long-haul over-the-road truckers. In the motel room the next morning, Chris shaved some of the hair from Brian's forehead to simulate a receding hairline, stuffed cotton into his mouth and nose to alter the shape of his face and put a pair of "granny" glasses on him. He no longer looked like Brian Hill.

Brian's first robbery went perfectly until he was outside of the Southside Branch of the Western Federal Savings and Loan Company in Missoula, which Chris had robbed in September.

Carrying more than $5,000, he backed out of the savings office and jumped into the Triumph. As Chris drove away, Brian looked back, and through a gray sky flecked with snow flurries, he saw the branch manager run outside and get into a Toyota. It pulled out of a parking lot and started following the sports car.

Gloria had told him Chris was not a good driver, and Brian Hill discovered she was right.

Snowflakes were coming down in a heavy, wind-blown white curtain that all but swallowed up the car. Chris accelerated the little roadster, but its wheels slid wildly on the ice-caked roadway. In the mirror he saw, through the snowflakes, the manager's car gaining on them.

The tires of the Triumph finally found some traction on the slick pavement. Chris pressed the accelerator to the floor, and the little sports car lurched forward, gained speed and headed south from Missoula on U.S. 93 toward the rugged Lolo Pass, route of the Lewis and Clark expedition. Brian hurriedly tried to sponge off his makeup as he looked out the rear of the car. A few miles outside the city, he turned to Chris and said he couldn't see the Toyota anymore. But it was snowing so hard, and the horizon was so dark, that they couldn't be sure, and Chris drove faster.

He rounded a bend and discovered that the road ahead of them was clogged with cars stalled by the snow. He pressed his foot hard on the brake pedal, but the Triumph hurtled faster toward the other cars, missed a curve and plunged off the highway and through a fence. The car was wrecked, but they weren't hurt. The road ahead seemed impassable. They had no choice but to hitchhike back to Missoula.

A middle-aged man dropped them at the edge of the city. As they got out of his car, a policeman in a passing car glanced at them, but didn't seem interested and drove on. They bought a newspaper and found a classified ad for a Ford van being offered for sale across town for $800. Within an hour, they were on their way out of Missoula. They never went back for the Triumph.

The van was on its last legs. The engine seemed to have been drained of energy, and its steel shell was red with rust, but it would have to do. Brian Hill said later that he had never seen Chris as tense as he was on the trip back to Swan Lake. When they got to Bigfork, George Larchmont, the bank robber whom Gloria White had been accused of helping in 1976, was waiting. He had appeared at Gloria's cabin seeking a place to hide out from the police and FBI, but she'd decided he was too hot for Boundary County and had brought him to Montana. Chris insisted that they all had to leave Bigfork as quickly as they could. It wouldn't be hard for the FBI to make a connection between the bank robbery and the abandoned Triumph, which was registered in Brian's name in Idaho; after that, it might be easy to trace the Triumph back to the four men who had lived in the cabins on Swan Lake.

In Los Angeles, Chief Inspector Kupferer had decided to close down the task force during the first week of December. He told a reporter that he was sure they would catch Boyce eventually; every fugitive, he said, must have a support system of relatives or friends to survive on the run for long, and in the end, this system was often his greatest point of vulnerability. "Sooner or later," Kupferer told the reporter, "every fugitive makes a fatal mistake, and Christopher Boyce will too, someday."

Boyce had now survived for almost a year as Jim Namcheck. The escape from Missoula had been close, but not fatal. As the van traveled through the rugged peaks of the Bitterroot Mountains toward Idaho, he wondered where to go next.

Four hours after leaving Swan Lake, the van, a rusted Minnesota plate dangling by a wire from its rear bumper, lumbered into the outskirts of Sandpoint, the resort town thirty miles south of Bonners Ferry. George Larchmont, at the wheel, looked in the rearview mirror and saw a police car close behind him. Then he realized that he had just sailed through a stoplight.

The red light atop the police car was flashing.

Chris and Brian and Tom Hill grabbed for their pistols. Larchmont told them to take it easy.

"May I see your driver's license, please?" the policeman asked. He told Larchmont that he had gone through a stoplight.

Larchmont dug out his wallet and handed the policeman a driver's license issued to Mike Mann. It had expired, the policeman said. He asked to see what documents Larchmont had that proved he owned the van. Larchmont showed him the Minnesota registration slip that had been given to Chris by the former owner of the van in Missoula. The policeman said that it too was not in proper order and ordered them to follow him to the police station.

At the station, no records could be found of outstanding arrest warrants for Mike Mann. Larchmont paid a $35 fine for running a stoplight, and they were allowed to leave.

As they drove north toward Bonners Ferry, Chris decided that it was time to leave Idaho and to bury Jim Namcheck.

He had also begun thinking about traveling to the Soviet Union.

9

ON AN INTERSTATE HIGHWAY BETWEEN THE Idaho Panhandle and the Olympic Peninsula of Washington, Jim Namcheck became Sean Hennessey. After the close calls in Missoula and Sandpoint, it was time not only to move on, but to become somebody else. The name of Sean Hennessey, a martyr in Ireland's battle for independence, appealed to him.

The Olympic Peninsula is at the northwestern tip of Washington and except for Alaska is the most northwesterly point in the United States. Bounded on the west by the Pacific Ocean, on the north by the Strait of Juan de Fuca and on the east by Puget Sound, it is a spectacular conjunction of sea, mountains and forest, as remote, in many ways, as the Idaho Panhandle. Like much of Idaho, it is largely rural and economically reliant upon the lumber industry. But it is blessed with a long, rugged coast that shelters hundreds of fishing boats which mine the Pacific and inland waters for salmon, oysters, Dungeness crab and an abundance of other seafood. It is also one of the few areas of the country where one of the rarest of falcons, the peregrine, still flourishes. To Christopher Boyce, the Olympic Peninsula seemed, like northern Idaho, a perfect place to hide before he made his next move.

Along with George Larchmont and Tom and Brian Hill, he went into hiding three weeks before Christmas 1980 in a cabin on the Quinault Indian Reservation owned by a friend of Larchmont's. A few days later, the friend told them to leave because they were

270

"too hot." They rented their own cabin in the nearby hamlet of Moclips and decided to lie low. Fearful that the FBI might make a connection between the robbery in Missoula, the van and the traffic stop in Sandpoint, Chris sold it to an Indian who lived on the reservation. Financed by the Missoula robbery, they settled down to let things cool off. After a few days, Tom said that he was bored and left for South Dakota to visit an old girlfriend, and Larchmont went his own way.

As Christmas approached, Chris thought often of his family. He was nearing a decision that he did not want to make; one that, once made, meant he probably would never see them again. Two days before Christmas, he chanced a call to his favorite cousin in Los Angeles, but it lifted his melancholy only briefly.

On Christmas Eve, while a detail of undercover U.S. marshals watched the Boyce home in Palos Verdes, Chris drank a lot of beer and thought a lot about his family and wished that he had not given in to that first whim that had sent Daulton knocking on the door of the Soviet Embassy in Mexico City and started him on the toboggan ride that had carried him to where he was now. But when he thought again of his disgust for the system against which he had rebelled, he decided again that he had been right; to think otherwise would have been to admit that everything he had been through was for nothing.

A few days before Christmas, Brian Hill had announced that he was not going to rob any more banks. He had gotten in deeper than he expected. If they didn't stop, they would both go to prison.

Chris had heard it before. When Brian had told him the same thing a few months earlier, he had changed his mind by giving him a second-hand pickup truck. "I bought it for you; let's use it," he had said, and they had robbed a bank using the truck to make their getaway.

Brian insisted that he was determined to quit and try a legitimate job. "It's up to you," Chris said.

He said that he had to continue robbing banks because he couldn't take the chance of getting a legitimate job.

"Bullshit," Brian said. "You do it because you get a kick out of it."

Brian looked for a job. But the Olympic Peninsula, like the Idaho Panhandle, already had more unemployed people than it could handle, and he couldn't find one.

On the afternoon of January 11, he drove Chris to Tacoma, the state's second-largest city, in an eighteen-year-old four-door Chrysler that Chris had bought to replace the van. They checked into a small motel, and in the morning Brian helped Chris put on his favorite artificial beard, tinted his face with orange grease paint and dropped him off in an alley next to the Puget Sound National Bank branch at Nineteenth and Union streets. Chris was wearing his favorite blue-and-white baseball cap. Inside the bank, he opened his windbreaker and showed a teller his .357 magnum in its shoulder holster. A few minutes later, he returned to the car with $1,692 and dived into the back seat, and Brian drove away, looking straight ahead even as they passed a Tacoma policeman on a motorcycle four blocks from the bank.

"This is it," Brian said. "My last one."

On January 21, 1981, Don North, the television journalist, arrived in Larry Homenick's office in Los Angeles with news of his television exposé that would place Christopher Boyce in Central America. United Press International sent a story around the world reporting that Boyce was operating a cocaine ring in Palos Verdes. On the Olympic Peninsula, Boyce celebrated the first anniversary of his escape with several German beers. Two days earlier, the *Seattle Times,* the largest regional newspaper circulated on the Olympic Peninsula, published an article taking note of the anniversary under the headline:

FUGITIVE SPY GIVES AGENTS THE SLIP,
BUT 'HE'LL MAKE MISTAKE,' ONE SAYS

A picture of Chris looked out from the newspaper.

"For a year now," the article began, "Christopher Boyce has frustrated the federal agents who have hunted him. Forgotten are the optimistic predictions of the agents who said last year that they would capture Boyce, a spy known as 'The Falcon,' within days of his escape from the federal prison at Lompoc, Calif. . . ." The story quoted federal prosecutors as saying that the materials Boyce sold to Soviet agents "were among the most damaging compromises of intelligence in United States history" and recounted the long search for him and the failed effort to find him by a special task force of federal marshals in Los Angeles.

If any of the new friends that Chris was making on the Peninsula saw the photograph, they did not report it to the authorities.

In their cabin at Moclips, Brian noticed that Chris was spending a great deal of time studying maps of the Olympic Peninsula and other parts of Washington State and a world atlas. He never wrote anything on the maps. He said that he did not want to leave any clues.

One evening in January, Brian saw him hunched over a map of Alaska, concentrating on its northern rim and the Bering Strait. When he asked him about it, Chris said that he was thinking about making a trip to the Far North. But first, he said, he had to find a boat for the trip.

10

AT 8 A.M. ON MARCH 1, 1981, INSPECTORS DUKE Smith, Bob Dighera and Tony Perez of the U.S. Marshals Service left San José, Costa Rica, and began the long flight home after their frustrating mission to find Christopher Boyce in the Central American jungle

On the Olympic Peninsula, Brian Hill, using the name of Alex Cooper, an alias, complete with a birth certificate, which he had purchased for $150 in a bar, rented a small house trailer in Bear Creek, a logging community about thirty miles north of Moclips, the village on the Quinault Indian Reservation where he and Boyce had hidden for almost two months.

A few days after Brian rented the trailer, the landlord noticed a second young man moving in, and he decided that they must be homosexuals. But a few days after that, he noticed that Alex Cooper wasn't around very often. The reason was that Brian had moved into the apartment of a girlfriend he had met in Moclips. When she was offered a job in Alaska a few weeks later, Brian told Chris that he was going with her to see if he could find work there.

There wasn't much to Bear Creek: just a few rustic cabins buried in the forest, some mobile homes and the Bear Creek Tavern, a small bar with a big parking lot on U.S. Route 101. The rugged peaks of Olympic National Park looked down on one side, and on the other, the Strait of Juan de Fuca offered a rippled blue-water bridge to Canada.

The loggers and fishermen who hung out at the tavern were impressed by the stranger who showed up there in the winter of 1981. It wasn't only because he ordered imported beer instead of the local favorite, Rainier; he dressed more neatly and looked cleaner than the regulars. The strongest language he normally used was "hell" or "damn," and sometimes he blushed when a dirty story was told. His favorite topic of discussion wasn't the housing recession and how it was causing lumber prices to go to hell, or the other favorite local gripe—the hard effects of federal policies that gave Indian fishermen valuable concessions in the salmon grounds that reduced the catch for others. He could talk knowledgeably about such things, but instead he talked mostly about the U.S. Government's tampering with foreign governments and about the threat of nuclear war. It was curious talk for the folks of Bear Creek, but the likable newcomer had a way of expressing his views that drew nods of agreement.

Like the residents of Boundary County, the residents of Bear Creek tended not to ask questions of newcomers. Many, maybe most of them, had migrated to the Olympic Peninsula to escape something . . . creditors, a minor brush with the law, a troubled marriage, alimony payments, a dead-end job. If Sean Hennessey wasn't inclined to talk about his past, that wasn't unusual. A lot of the people he met at the tavern didn't want to talk about theirs either. They didn't ask questions, but they noticed things. A few people noticed that for someone who didn't have a job, he had a lot of money, and a few suspected that he was a fugitive from upper-middle-class suburbia hiding out from parents or a wife. He dropped a few hints that it was a wife he was hiding from, and that seemed to satisfy his friends at the bar. He wasn't the only one. When Hennessey said that he was looking for a commercial salmon-fishing boat to buy, some of the fishermen who showed up at the tavern every afternoon for a few beers looked at his soft hands and clean-cut looks and decided that he was probably a city kid with illusions. But he made sure they realized that he was serious, and they promised to keep an eye out for a good boat.

Not long after Brian Hill left for Alaska, his brother Tom returned from South Dakota, moved into the trailer with Chris and joined him in a search for a boat. When the landlord saw the youngest of the Hill brothers at the trailer, he decided that he'd been right in the first place that Sean Hennessey was a homosexual.

They found what they were looking for a few days later at the Boat Haven Marina in Port Angeles. With about seven thousand residents, Port Angeles was the largest town on the Peninsula, its principal commercial center, a staging area for tourists bound for Olympic National Park and a terminal for ferries to Canada, less than twenty miles away across the Strait.

The *Rose-M* was a twenty-nine-foot-long double-ended salmon trawler that had seen more than fifty years of duty in and around the Strait and looked it. Its blue-and-white paint was chipped and peeling, rust was caked on much of the hardware and its engine needed overhauling; but the fisherman who owned the *Rose-M* said that it would take only a little work and a few dollars to bring it into first-rate condition. The price: $6,500.

"Think she'd make it to Alaska?"

"Sure," he said.

Many salmon fishermen in Washington went north for the Alaskan salmon run, and he figured that was why Hennessey had asked.

But if Chris was going to go into the salmon-fishing business, he needed more than a boat. He needed someone with a commercial fishing license; and he found him at the Bear Creek Tavern.

Charles "Buck" Meredith was thirty-two years old, stood six feet, three inches tall, weighed 230 pounds and had a full beard that covered most of his face like a wild evergreen bush. Like many people who lived on the Peninsula, he and his wife, Betty, were hard-workers who because of chronically depressed economic conditions in the area had to live from hand to mouth, dreaming of a break that might someday make a difference in their lives. Buck's dream was to own a boat instead of working on someone else's.

He had admired the *Rose-M*, knew it was for sale and thought $6,500 was a fair price. But he couldn't afford to buy it. When the newcomer at the Bear Creek Tavern offered him a chance to become his partner and split the profits from the boat 50-50, he jumped at the offer.

A few days later, Chris dug into his Basic Bank Robbery Kit, pulled out $3,000 and made a down payment on the *Rose-M*. He told the owner that he would be back in a few days with the balance; but he needed only one day.

"Bremerton was good to me," Chris told Tom Hill as he entered the trailer the next day. He opened his bag and dropped a green mound of currency on the bed. Tom saw that he was delighted with himself. He had tried an experiment in Bremerton and it had worked. Instead of robbing a single teller at the Olympic Savings and Loan Association, his usual *modus operandi,* he had ordered the customers to lie down on the floor and then told all three tellers to bring him their large bills. He had returned from Bremerton with more than $6,800. The next day, he paid off the balance of $3,500 that he still owed on the boat, and its legal title was transferred to Tom Hill. It was March 6, 1981; and in Tysons Corner, Virginia, the U.S. Marshals Service had just elevated the investigation of Frank Burton Riley, whose movements had been traced to South Africa, to the highest priority status in the agency.

Chris and Tom moved out of the trailer and onto the *Rose-M* a few days later and began to get it ready for the coming salmon-fishing season—and a trip. Over the next few weeks, Boyce was not the first fledgling mariner to discover that fixing up a boat can at times seem like dropping currency into the deep. Making the *Rose-M* seaworthy cost substantially more than the fisherman who sold it to him had predicted. When the bills mounted and he needed more money, Chris obtained it in the usual way. Following his practice of not using the same car more than twice, he sold the Chrysler, bought a 1967 Chevrolet station wagon for $500 and on March 18, 1981, strolled into the Lincoln Mutual Savings Bank in Everett, Washington, wearing a seaman's dark watch cap, a Navy pea coat, glasses and a false mustache and beard. He drew his gun and shouted, "This is a robbery. You have ten seconds."

One teller was so frightened by the gun that she couldn't move.

He waved the gun in her direction and barked, "That means you too. Get to your cash drawer. I want hundreds and fifties."

The woman complied. As the tellers gathered up the money, Chris paced back and forth in front of them, his gun held high.

"I want all of it or I'm going to use this," he said.

They emptied their cash drawers, put the money on the counter and stood back. He stuffed the currency into his pockets.

"Okay," said the onetime altar boy who professed to be a pacifist, as he backed out a rear door. "Nobody move or I'll blow your heads off."

Less than two minutes after entering the bank, Chris left with $4,160.

Restoring the *Rose-M* was not only expensive, it was hard work. Fifteen days after the robbery in Everett, Chris suggested to Tom that they take time off for a brief visit to Bonners Ferry. It had been four months since the robbery in December in Missoula, the accident with the Triumph and the quick flight across Idaho to Washington. It was possible that Gloria was being watched because of her connection to George Larchmont, but Chris decided to take the risk anyway. Besides Gloria he wanted to see her daughter. He arrived with gifts for everyone, including an expensive trail-riding motorcycle for one of Gloria's sons, and as in the old days, he bought them all steaks and imported beer. The following day, April 3, he drove alone from Bonners Ferry to Spokane to visit one of the first banks that he had ever robbed.

When they saw his gun, the tellers at the Old National Bank branch gave him $5,320.

Outside, striding quickly to his car, Chris started to rip off his false beard and false mustache and jump into his station wagon. A dog waiting outside a coin laundry for its mistress raced toward him, barking wildly.

Startled, Chris dropped some of the money he was stuffing into his pockets. Meanwhile, the sight of her dog attacking a stranger had embarrassed the owner, and she had run out from the laundry to apologize. When she saw Chris bent over picking up his money, she called off the dog, knelt down and, apologizing, tried to help pick it up. Chris pulled his gun and told her to "disappear," which she did, and he drove back to Gloria's house on Katka Mountain as fast as discretion allowed, worried that the woman might be able to identify him.

The reunion on Katka Mountain was pleasant for everyone. After partying at Gloria's, the group got into cars and drove across the border into Canada to a resort renowned for its mud baths, and Chris picked up the tab. On the return trip, they stopped for drinks in a small town near the border and visited the Good Grief Tavern, whose ceiling was covered with dollar bills bearing the signatures of hundreds of previous patrons; they all autographed a bill and tacked it up. Gloria, her children and other friends signed their names. Tom Hill, who, like Brian, usually ordered Kahlúa, signed *"The Kahlua Kid,"* and Chris wrote *"Jim and His Mule."*

Chris had now used the Chevrolet station wagon for two robberies. He gave it to an acquaintance from the Mint and bought a 1962 Ford for the trip back to the Olympic Peninsula.

Within a few weeks, the boat would be ready, and when the weather was right, Tom Hill and the *Rose-M* would deliver him to the Soviet Union.

11

On a damp, misty afternoon in April, over the throbbing of the *Rose-M*'s diesel engine, Christopher Boyce told Tom Hill that it was time he got out of the country. He had been studying a pair of peregrine falcons on the gray horizon through his binoculars.

He had never told anyone before, he continued, that when he met with a KGB agent in the basement of the Soviet Embassy in Mexico City three months before his arrest, he had been offered Soviet citizenship and a military commission in gratitude for his services to the U.S.S.R. and in recognition of services he would perform in the future.

Now he was going to claim them.

He was doing what he had often done with the youngest Hill brother, portraying himself as an international soldier of fortune who took no sides. Hill, as usual, was impressed and decided that he was deadly serious about going to Russia. This was the story of the conversation that he later related to his brother:

Chris said that he felt no allegiance to Russia but owed none to America either—he was revolted by the senseless nuclear war games of both countries—and he was determined to get to the Soviet Union and play his own role in the games again.

The reason he had bought the boat was to travel to the Soviet Union, and he wanted Tom to go part of the way with him. The adventure, he said, should give both of them the time of their lives.

Chris talked emotionally about his family and how he missed them and how it was obvious that he would never see them again. He said he had no regrets, no remorse over what he had done. The things he had learned about his government since his arrest had convinced him more than ever that it was a caricature of the principles upon which America had been founded. He had become a spy almost on impulse, he said. He had never dreamed of the events that would be set in motion by the impulse. Once it had begun, he couldn't extricate himself; it was as if he were tumbling down a cliff, plunging toward disaster and helpless to save himself, and before he knew it he had been sentenced to prison for forty years. Robbing banks had allowed him to survive, he said, but it couldn't last forever. He had to get out of the country.

During their first weeks as Soviet spies, he said, Daulton Lee had told KGB agents in Mexico City that his friend was willing to provide American intelligence secrets to the Soviet Union because he was a socialist committed to Soviet ideals. It had been a lie, but the Russians had believed it. When, almost two years later, Boris Grishin of the KGB had finally met this most precious source in the basement of the embassy in Mexico City and offered him Soviet citizenship and a commission, he was surprised that Chris turned them down. Boyce had no qualms, however, about taking more of the Soviets' money. He agreed to return to college at the KGB's expense to prepare for a job in the State Department or in the CIA and later resume his role as a spy. He had been arrested a few days after returning to college and never got to carry out the plan, but he had no doubt that the Russians would still want him.

Now, he said, he was going to go to the Soviet Union, collect his commission and citizenship, and have some fun.

Where else could he go? If he stayed in the United States he knew he would be caught eventually; that meant forty years in prison at least, probably more because he'd get extra time for the escape. In Russia he would be welcomed as a hero. Russia offered other, more interesting possibilities too. Who knew what fun he could have as a Soviet agent undermining its intelligence system—and America's?

"If nothing else," he would say later, "it's a chance to see the other side of the mountain."

"How are you going to do it? Where are you going to go?" Tom Hill had asked.

Chris explained that he had considered several possible routes to Russia, including making a trip to Cuba or Costa Rica and presenting himself to Soviet officials, or going to the Soviet Embassy in Ottawa. But the risk of getting caught if he did was too high. He brought out a large navigational chart and pointed to the Bering Strait, the neck of water that separates the northwestern tip of Alaska from the eastern tip of Siberia, and explained the plan he had chosen.

The Soviet Union and the United States were neighbors at the Bering Strait, separated by less than fifty miles. Between them, the final remnants of a land bridge that had once connected Asia with North America, were two small islands. The more easterly, called Little Diomede, was under U.S. control and populated by a few Eskimos. But three miles west of it was Russian territory. Chris pointed to a speck on the chart that read "BIG DIOMEDE."

"There's a Russian military garrison there," he said.

Chris said that he planned to sail the *Rose-M* from Port Angeles more than two thousand miles north through the Gulf of Alaska, past the Aleutian Islands, to Big Diomede, and present himself to the senior Soviet military representative. It was his expectation that he would be flown to Moscow, honored as an agent who had performed valuable services for the Soviet Union and given his Soviet citizenship and a commission, and then, after his features were changed by plastic surgery, he would return to the United States as a Soviet agent.

Because of winter ice, it was impossible to navigate the Bering Sea until late in May, and the narrow Bering Strait itself usually wasn't passable until the end of June. They would have to do it then. All Tom had to do was drop Chris a few miles from Big Diomede in a raft, and Chris would finish the trip to the island alone. Tom could return home with the *Rose-M* and it would be his. He could sell it or use it for fishing; it didn't make any difference to Chris.

First, he said, they would have to go to work and get the *Rose-M* ready for the trip.

The man known as Jim Namcheck in Boundary County and Sean Hennessey on the Olympic Peninsula was, by the spring of 1981, a man of several other identities too. A friend of George Larchmont's sold him a birth certificate in the name of Anthony Edward Lester, the deceased son of a harbor pilot from Portland, Oregon, and Chris used the name to obtain a Washington State driver's license. He also visited cemeteries to look for the tombstones of men who had been born, as he had, in the early 1950s and then requested copies of their birth certificates from the county records offices. That was how he became, when he wanted to, Bobby Cable.

After Buck Meredith overheard someone call his fishing partner "Tony Lester," Chris said sheepishly that he used the alias because he was trying to hide out from an ex-wife and her demands for alimony payments. Not only did this explain why he was using an alias, it answered some of the questions Buck and Betty Meredith had had about the attractive young man who had arrived in Bear Creek with plans to start a new life as a fisherman. They had grown fond of Chris and had invited him to live with them while he got the boat ready for the salmon season. Still, Buck didn't think much of him as a fisherman. He didn't like the smell of rotting fish, and he got seasick a lot. In his heart, Meredith decided, Sean probably didn't really want to become a fisherman.

Tom Hill didn't know what to make of Chris's plan to go to Russia.

As high adventure, it appealed to him—his friend made it sound exciting—but he was getting tired of working on the boat without getting paid for it. He began to complain that Chris was exploiting him as free labor. On April 27, Chris left him working and returned the next day with almost $9,000 from the Northwestern Commercial Bank in Bellingham, Washington. The next morning they went to Port Angeles and Chris bought him a $3,200 Japanese-made motorcycle to keep him happy.

The next day, Tom left for Bonners Ferry on the motorcycle while Chris and Buck moved the *Rose-M* to Lapush, an Indian fishing village on the Pacific coast of the Peninsula.

During the late spring and early summer of 1981, as members of the U.S. Marshals Service twice followed Frank Burton Riley to San Francisco and kept him under surveillance in New Jersey, the object of their search, Christopher John Boyce, shifted often between his life as Jim Namcheck in Idaho and his other life as Sean Hennessey/Tony Lester 350 miles away in Washington. He traveled frequently between the two areas, robbing banks every few weeks for living expenses and to raise money for the final phase of his flight.

In the middle of the summer of 1981, he made a new decision about his future, but told none of his friends about it.

III

The salmon is close

1

DAVE NEFF DOES NOT LOOK LIKE A MAN WHO IS likely to get an ulcer. He is tall and has curly blond hair, the build of an athlete and a relaxed self-assurance that suggests he is in control. The son of a Denver industrial-supplies salesman, he followed a course during the 1960s similar to that of many other deputy U.S. marshals. He married not long after graduating from high school, served in the Coast Guard during the Vietnam War, returned home to become the first member of his family to attend college and then gravitated to a career in law enforcement because it promised excitement and stability. Influenced by an older brother who was a deputy sheriff, he joined the Arapaho County Sheriff's Department near Denver and a year later was recruited by the Marshals Service.

Like many of his generation of deputy federal marshals, Neff soon grew bored with the routine assignments referred to as "Shag those prisoners, serve that process," and he managed to maneuver an assignment to the small Denver squad that served federal arrest warrants. He didn't have much chance to chase major-league criminals, but he learned that a check forger wanted for violating his probation could at times be as elusive as a bank robber and sometimes just as dangerous.

Like Chuck Kupferer, Larry Homenick, Bob Dighera and many of the other younger deputies, Dave Neff found so much satisfaction in chasing fugitives that he might have done it for nothing. He was disadvantaged, however, by having a talent for administration

287

that kept getting him promoted to management jobs. His dream was an assignment that would take him back onto the street, but he had been typecast. In 1976 he was sent to the Marshals Service office in Jacksonville, Florida, as operations supervisor, with orders to sharpen up the unit. Before long, several of the local deputies began an organized campaign of resistance and vowed to see to it that the Yankee didn't stay long. But they misjudged the competitive drive of the émigré from Denver. *They* were the ones who left. The victory left him with an ulcer. Friends said that Neff took his job too seriously, but he said that he couldn't change.

Neff complained regularly to Tysons Corner that he wanted to get out from behind his desk and back onto the street, but two years after he had gone to Jacksonville, he was transferred back to Denver for another administrative job.

When Larry Homenick, rushing to New York to interrogate Frank Riley, asked Neff, in the last week of July 1981, to meet an unknown informant who claimed to know something about Christopher John Boyce, he had jumped at the chance to join the manhunt.

The informant didn't know that the Marshals Service was in charge of the case and had called the Denver office of the FBI to report that he had information about Christopher Boyce. The Bureau had notified the Marshals Service, and the matter had been referred to Larry Homenick, who asked his friend Dave Neff to check it out.

Now, one day later, Neff was on the phone to Chuck Kupferer in Tysons Corner trying to convince him he had a major break in the case, and Kupferer was *bored*.

"Yeah, what've you got?" the chief inspector asked after Neff said that he was excited about an informant he had just met.

Kupferer's voice was leaden with indifference. He had just returned from New Jersey after the arrest of Riley. He hadn't slept in more than seventy-two hours; he was exhausted. He was beginning to have doubts about the ex-mercenary he had called "platinum" so many times that it was now embarrassing. Kupferer had looked for Christopher Boyce in South Africa, Costa Rica, Mexico and Australia, not to mention most of the fifty states. He and the people who worked for him had interviewed scores of "informants" who claimed they could lead the way to Boyce. He was tired of loonies, and he doubted Dave Neff had found Boyce.

Neff ventured, "The guy I have claims he knows where Boyce is now and where he's been for the past year and a half. According to him, he's living somewhere near Seattle."

"Sure."

Neff could hear two voices, both grunting negatives. Besides Kupferer, his speakerphone was amplifying a gruff, unfriendly voice that belonged to Bob Dighera, whom Neff had never met and who was as exhausted and discouraged as Kupferer.

"Let me give you some questions to ask him," Dighera said brusquely. "Ask him if Boyce still has a tattoo of a spider on his right arm. Ask him if he still smokes Camels. Ask him how he's supporting himself. . . ."

Kupferer and Dighera fired out more questions until Neff had a list of almost fifty.

Neff, who knew nothing about Riley or Babette Bekker, or the long list of other leads and false leads, and the searches and investigations that had exhausted and frustrated Kupferer and Dighera for so long, decided that now he knew how suspects feel when they are being interrogated. Given their mood, Neff decided it was prudent to hang up. He said he would call Kupferer and Dighera back in an hour. Disappointed and angry, he called the informant, still convinced that the man knew what he was talking about.

When Neff had first seen the informant walk out of a restaurant at the corner of Federal and Alameda streets in Denver, he had almost lost interest on the spot. The man looked like a hippie not a day over fifteen. His hair hung almost to his shoulders, and he wore several strands of beads around a bare neck, sandals, dirty jeans and a ragged leather vest over his bare chest. Another sleaze, Neff thought.

The young man had asked Neff coldly whether he would receive a reward if he helped him find Christopher Boyce. Just as coldly, Neff had replied that the Justice Department granted rewards for help in finding important fugitives, and that if he provided information which helped find Boyce, he would undoubtedly qualify for one.

The young man then identified himself as Tom Hill and said that he wanted to talk.

Neff had interviewed Hill for almost an hour in his car outside the restaurant following their meeting at 2 P.M. on July 31, 1981. Almost two hours later, following his disappointing phone conversation with Kupferer and Dighera, he telephoned Hill at the number he had given him and read their questions, which he had scrawled on a pad.

When he began to read off Hill's answers to Kupferer and Dighera, Neff could almost feel their blood pressure rise in tandem over the telephone line.

"He laughed when I asked him about the tattoo; he said Boyce doesn't have any tattoos."

"What kind of cigarettes does he smoke?"

"Marlboro Lights . . . and he says he likes dark beer."

Virtually all Hill's answers were consistent with what the investigators had learned about Boyce during the nineteen months they had been searching for him.

"Does he say how Boyce is supporting himself?" Dighera asked.

"He says he's robbed a bunch of banks in the Northwest."

As quickly as it had surfaced, their interest evaporated.

"Yeah," Dighera said.

"The psychiatrist said Boyce wouldn't go into violent crime," Kupferer explained to Neff. "It doesn't sound like our guy."

Kupferer sensed, however, that his investigator in Denver was not satisfied.

"Dave, how do you feel about this guy?"

"Chuck, I think we've got something here. In fact, I believe him so much that I've made reservations to Seattle for Hill and myself on the first plane out of here."

"When does it leave?"

"Seven o'clock. Should I go?"

"Let me think it over."

Ten minutes later, Kupferer called back. "Okay, go. Take another deputy with you and call ahead to Seattle to arrange for some-one to meet you.''

It was five o'clock on a Friday afternoon, and the operations center of the Denver office of the Marshals Service was almost empty. Neff called his wife and asked her to meet him at the airport with some fresh clothes, a razor and a toothbrush. He found Deputy Bill Greenaway having a beer in a bar near the office and told him they were going to Seattle in two hours. At seven o'clock, Neff, Greenaway and Tom Hill were on a United Airlines jet.

At the Seattle-Tacoma Airport, they were met by Deputy Jim Maji, a quiet, slender man with a small mustache and a stoic de-meanor. If he had been an actor, he might have been typecast as the man from Scotland Yard in an Agatha Christie play.

By the time the three of them checked in at the Hilton Hotel in downtown Seattle, it was midnight. Because of the possibility that Christopher Boyce was robbing banks, an FBI agent had been as-signed to the investigation, and he was waiting for them at the hotel.

They talked until dawn. Three times, Tom Hill repeated the same story:

During the summer of 1980, almost a year before, while the Marshals Service was focusing its search for Boyce in Southern California, Hill said that he had met a man in his late twenties who called himself "Jim Namcheck" at the home of a woman named Gloria White in a remote part of Idaho. Gloria White, Hill claimed, was involved with Namcheck in robbing banks, calling the shots and splitting the money with him.

"Did he tell you his real name?"

"Not at first; he was just 'Jim.' Everybody called him Jim. But a few weeks later he just sort of volunteered that Jim wasn't his real name, it was Chris.''

Sometimes, he went on, he used other names, including "Tony Lester'' and "Sean Hennessey.''

"Did he ever tell you he was an escaped spy?''

"Yeah, he bragged about it. I really wasn't impressed—I had never heard about him before—and he was sort of disappointed. A couple of days later he showed me a book about himself and I saw some pictures of him in it.''

"What's this place in Idaho like?"

"Gloria has a big old log cabin and has a lot of sleazy people living with her. A lot of people go there to hide out."

By the time the first rays of the summer sun were glistening on the waters of Puget Sound, and the lights along the harbor were going out, Tom Hill had told them almost everything he knew about Jim Namcheck—except that his brothers had helped Namcheck rob banks.

They had talked all night, but Tom could not answer the most pressing question of the federal agents: where was Boyce?

"I haven't seen him in almost a month."

Hill speculated that he might be living on his boat on the Olympic Peninsula, or at the home of a fisherman named Buck Meredith, where he sometimes spent the night.

"What was he using the boat for?"

"We did some salmon fishing, but he really bought it to go to Russia."

"Where?"

"He's planning to go up to the Bering Strait to an island owned by the Russians, Big Diomede. He was going to go to Moscow from there."

"Do you think he's already gone?"

"Possibly. July is when weather's the best up there."

The following morning, Robert Christman, the chief deputy in the Seattle district of the Marshals Service, telephoned Chuck Kupferer and told him that he had interviewed Hill. He believed his story and predicted that Hill would lead them to Boyce.

Kupferer hung up, took out one of his business cards, dated it, made a note about Christman's remarks and wrote, *"Join the club"* on it. He planned to mail it to him later, after this informant's story, like all the others, had turned to dust.

Then Kupferer got on the phone and began deploying additional manpower to Seattle. As he did, he turned to one of his assistants and said, "If this guy isn't Christopher Boyce, he's probably the unluckiest bank robber in history."

* * *

In New York, as July drew to a close, Larry Homenick was beginning his frustrating interrogation of Frank Riley. In Pretoria, Duke Smith was packing his bag and winding up his futile investigation in South Africa with farewells to the people who had helped him. He gave Babette Bekker $20 to buy a bottle of whiskey and accepted a spear that had been crafted by Zulu tribesmen from his friends in the South African Police, Special Branch. He said goodbye to friends he had made at the American Embassy. In a brief encounter with a member of the CIA, he was told that Christopher Boyce's name had come up recently at a gathering of CIA officials.

"The consensus was that Boyce is behind the curtain," the man from the CIA said.

2

THE INSTRUCTOR HAD NEVER SEEN A STUDENT IN such a rush to learn how to fly. When he appeared in his office on July 30, he had declared that he wanted to earn his pilot's license in one month or less, and that if necessary, he would be at the airport for a lesson every day.

He was an eager learner—not a natural aviator, the instructor decided, but more than capable, and he made up for most of his deficiencies with hard work. He obviously spent a lot of time when he wasn't at the airport at his books, studying meteorology, navigation and other fundamentals. He paid cash, never missed a lesson and was at the airport promptly at eight o'clock every morning. If his new student, Tony Lester, kept it up, the instructor decided, he probably would get his pilot's ticket within a month, although he wondered why he was in such a hurry.

The first contingent of U.S. marshals and FBI agents arrived in Port Angeles on the afternoon of August 1, a Saturday, in a big yellow van owned by Tom Russell, a Seattle-based deputy marshal. Fitted out with a large bed, wall-to-wall carpeting and a wet bar, it was an ideal undercover vehicle in a community where most people seemed to drive pickup trucks and vans.

From Port Angeles they headed south through tall stands of timber to the west coast of the Peninsula, where Tom Hill said Boyce might be living on his boat, the *Rose-M,* if he hadn't already left for Russia.

They found the boat in Lapush, a fishing village on the Quillayute Indian Reservation. The Quillayute River forms a natural estuary there, providing shelter for boats in what is otherwise mostly a stretch of rocky coast bordered on one side by rich forests that plunge into the sea and on the other by the ocean and scenic offshore islands that bristle with fir, spruce and pine.

The *Rose-M* was tied up near a salmon cannery rolling gently in a light breeze. From a distance there was no sign of Boyce. Dave Neff and Deputy Jack Tait approached it from one side, Inspector Roger Archiga and Tom Russell from the other. The trawler was empty.

Neff, his hand on his gun, was the first to jump aboard, and the first thing he noticed was that the boat smelled of spoiled fish. There were indications that it had been lived on—dishes, bedding, tins of food—but no sign of Boyce or any evidence that the boat or the gear aboard it belonged to him.

The agents, who were dressed in old dungarees and plaid shirts they hoped would help them blend into the Olympic Peninsula landscape, walked away from the empty boat toward the van. A dented twenty-year-old Chevrolet pickup truck bounced past and came to a stop near the cannery.

"Hi," Neff said to the driver, an elderly Indian from the reservation. "Do you happen to know where we can find the owner of this boat?"

The man paused, as if he didn't know whether he should talk to the strangers.

"We came down here to do some sport fishing and thought we might be able to charter it for a few days," Neff reassured him. "She looks like just what we're looking for."

"That's Sean's boat, but I don't think he's been around for a while," the Indian said. "I heard he was over in Montana."

Then he glanced at a car that had just pulled into the marina and was parking nearby. "You can probably find out from that guy over there where the owner is," the Indian said. "He works the boat for him."

A big, bearded man in his early thirties with a beer can in one hand got out of the car and walked toward the *Rose-M* with a smile on his face that suggested the beer was probably not his first of the day.

Neff, alarmed that Boyce might hear from his friends that strangers had been inquiring about him, acted casual.

"Hi," he said. "My friends and I are here looking to do some fishing, and we heard this boat might be available for a charter for a few days."

"Maybe," Buck Meredith said congenially, slurring his words. The owner of the boat, he said, was out of town, and he didn't know when he would be back. But he said he suspected that he'd probably like to make some extra money with a charter.

The deputies thanked him and said they'd come back later.

Finding the boat where Tom Hill had predicted it would be invigorated the agents, and it began to strengthen their confidence in Hill. The boat's discovery in Lapush even began to stifle the skepticism in Chuck Kupferer's office 2,800 miles away in Tysons Corner. Before long, a sense of excitement began to grip the agency, sparked by a growing but unspoken consensus that at last, they might be getting close.

After sleeping overnight in the van, the strike force of FBI agents and deputy U.S. marshals rented rooms at a motel in Forks, a nearby logging town located in the shadow of the soaring Olympic Mountains. After telling the motel clerk that they were engineers and surveyors for the Standard Oil Company, they discovered that their cover story was more than successful: within hours, rumors were racing across the recession-ravaged peninsula that large deposits of crude oil had been discovered off the coast and that hundreds of new jobs would soon be generated by an oil boom.

Under guard in the Seattle hotel room, Tom Hill telephoned the Meredith home in Beaver at Jim Maji's request and inquired if his friend Sean had been around lately.

"We haven't seen him for quite a while," Betty Meredith said. "But I'll tell him you're looking for him. We owe him his share from the boat, and I suppose he'll be by pretty soon to pick it up.'' Sooner or later, Hill said as he hung up, Boyce would go to the boat or to Meredith's home.

Tysons Corner decided to place both the boat and the home under tight surveillance.

Buck Meredith liked Tom Russell, and it provided the manhunters with an extraordinary break. After visiting the marina the first time, the Seattle deputy had returned and gotten a job with a fish buyer. He made friends with Meredith, claiming to be an out-of-work long-haul trucker dodging an ex-wife, and henceforth, when Meredith went trawling for salmon each morning, Russell was there, bidding him good-bye, and when he returned each afternoon on the *Rose-M,* Russell was waiting there for him. At night, Russell slept on the beach, waiting for Boyce.

Keeping a watch on Meredith's home was more difficult. Indeed, it became an investigative nightmare.

The small frame house was nearly hidden behind thick brush and shrouded by trees in a logging community where local people noticed strangers quickly. There weren't any tall buildings or natural vantage points nearby from which they could maintain a surveillance. Boyce could slip in and out through two entrances, both hard to see from the street. An FBI-owned Winnebago motor home was parked at the edge of the road near the house. Several deputies and FBI agents moved in and pretended to be campers.

The joint operation of FBI agents and deputy marshals was a tense marriage of convenience, and before long it was a rocky one. Some of the men and women from the Bureau earned $10,000 a year more than the deputies. This didn't help matters, since they were all doing the same work. Some agents and deputies were compatible, but for others ordinary interservice rivalries were soon magnified by boredom, the stress of trying to blend into a clannish logging community and the nervous frustration of having little to do but wait for Boyce to appear. Arguments began to flare frequently over strategy, the rival camps began to blame each other for mistakes that might blow their cover and by the fourth day of the operation, many members of the joint task force were not speaking to each other.

To obtain a truce, senior officials of the agencies in Seattle decreed that the operation should be reorganized into two-member teams, each made up of a deputy marshal and an FBI agent. If there was to be competition in this effort to catch Boyce, it was to be between the teams, not the agencies.

3

LARRY HOMENICK WAS STILL MENTALLY RETRACING his bizarre experience with Frank Burton Riley when the Amtrak train from New York City pulled into Union Station in Washington. Unaware of what the tip to Dave Neff had produced, he was met by Woody Smith, a member of the original Boyce task force, who had driven in from Tysons Corner to meet him. Smith saw the depression on Homenick's face as he walked off the train and immediately sought to cheer him up. "Don't worry about Riley," he said. "Wait till you see what we've got on Boyce!"

When they arrived at Tysons Corner, Homenick saw why Smith was excited. The first thing he saw was large photographic blowups of handwriting samples that had been sent from Seattle via a facsimile machine. Smith said that the photos had been made of receipts issued by a paint store in Port Angeles, Washington, where the informant, Tom Hill, had said that Boyce had purchased supplies for a boat and signed Hill's name on the receipts.

He didn't have to be a handwriting expert, Homenick decided, to notice that there were striking similarities between the way that several letters were formed in the signature of "Tom Hill" on two receipts from the paint store and Christopher Boyce's handwriting.

Next, Smith showed him photographs taken by automatic surveillance cameras in several banks in the Northwest that had been robbed over the preceding year. In each photo, a young man with a beard and wearing glasses held a large revolver. The robber looked slightly different in each photo, but Homenick conceded that there was at least a small resemblance to Chris in all of them.

One picture showed a bearded bandit brandishing a .357 magnum that looked almost as big as he was. When Homenick saw the gun and thought of the seemingly gentle prisoner he had once known, his reaction was to deny that it was Chris. A few minutes later, his doubts began to subside.

"Look at this, Larry," Carole Shaffer, one of Kupferer's senior deputies, said. She put an old newspaper photograph of Boyce in front of him on a desk. It was from the *Seattle Times*.

She had penciled a beard and eyeglasses over the photo. With the changes, Chris looked almost exactly like the man in one of the bank photographs.

Kupferer told Homenick to fly back to Los Angeles and get some rest from his bout with Frank Riley, but to keep his bag packed because he might have to leave in a hurry for Seattle.

In Los Angeles, Homenick visited "Dr. Joe," the psychiatrist who had been so close to the investigation, and showed him copies of the bank-robbery photographs and the handwriting samples. "The FBI says he's a suspect in sixteen bank robberies," Homenick said.

"It looks like him," the psychiatrist admitted as he studied the pictures and then turned to the handwriting specimens. "But bank robberies don't fit; this may be our guy, Larry, but he also may be just another bank robber."

While Homenick was meeting with Dr. Joe, Tom Hill, in the Seattle hotel room where he was under guard, was dreaming how he would spend his reward.

Chris had told him that he was an important spy, an international adventurer, and the rushed trip with Neff to Seattle, the all-night interrogation and the constant phone calls between the hotel room and Washington, D.C., had confirmed it. At a minimum, he decided, his reward would be $150,000, and it would probably be more than that.

Tom had been fascinated by the stories of espionage and intrigue, but he was tired of Chris's incessant talk about the arms race and nuclear weapons and Australia and the CIA. He was tired of his ego. He was tired of having himself and his brothers used by Chris. Now that he was away from him, he no longer believed the stories Chris had told them trying to justify his decision to spy against his own country.

Besides everything else, Chris had reneged on a loan. In June, he had asked Tom for $100 for a few days until he could rob another bank, and Tom had sold one of Brian's rifles to get the money for him. But when Tom asked him to repay the loan a few weeks later, Chris had refused, claiming he had bought him the motorcycle and had already shared more money from the bank holdups than Tom deserved. Tom had mulled over the offense for several weeks. Then he had driven the motorcycle to Denver, where his parents had moved from Michigan, and told them about the man he had first known as Jim Namcheck. His parents had urged him to call the FBI. There should be a big reward for someone like Boyce. Now he was looking forward to spending the money, and he decided that he wouldn't be surprised if the reward came to $250,000.

In Tyson Corner, Kupferer was growing worried that Boyce had slipped out of his grasp. The undercover teams in Beaver and Lapush had maintained around-the-clock surveillance on the house and boat for almost two weeks. They had absolutely nothing to show for it. No one had seen Boyce, and it was possible that he had left the country. The option Kupferer faced was obvious: send a team to Idaho and look for Boyce at Gloria White's home. But that posed a risk. Hill had said dozens of her friends lived in cabins on the mountain near her home. If anyone spotted strangers in the woods, Boyce might be tipped off and race for the border, a few miles away. The discovery of the boat and the handwriting samples supported Hill's contention that Boyce was living on the Olympic Peninsula. But time was catching up with them there. The task force couldn't maintain its cover in Buck Meredith's neighborhood much longer. Children were asking the deputies why they kept the Winnebago parked on the street instead of going to a campground. Even the press was inquiring about them. Using a truck borrowed from the Clallam County Public Works Department, several agents had dressed as construction workers and spent eight hours a day in front of Meredith's home pretending to repair the street. After driving by this crew several days, the editor of a local newspaper had become puzzled over why they were lingering so long at one spot and had told county officials that she was planning to publish an exposé about a waste of county funds. The truck and the crew were removed.

Kupferer decided that it was time to open a new front in the manhunt. He called Robert Christman, the chief deputy in Seattle, and they agreed to send a plane over Katka Mountain, with Tom Hill as guide, and photograph Gloria White's house and the wilderness near it, including the mountains where Hill said Boyce had made his camp. The reconnaissance photographs would be used if it became necessary to conduct a raid on Katka Mountain. Christman ordered Dave Neff from Beaver to Seattle to interview Hill. Neff had developed the closest relationship with Hill among the deputies and was told to find out what Hill knew about Boyce's hiding places in Idaho.

Jim Maji, who was already working the case in Seattle, asked the U.S. Coast Guard for a report on the registry of the *Rose-M* and was informed that it had been sold on March 31, 1981, to Anthony Edward Lester, who had given an address in Beaver, Washington—the same post-office box number listed for Buck Meredith. "Tony Lester" was one of the aliases that Tom Hill said Boyce used.

Maji sent a request to the Washington State Department of Licensing inquiring whether anyone named Anthony Edward Lester had ever applied for a driver's license in the state.

To prolong the use of the Winnebago near Buck Meredith's house, deputies had jacked it up and told the neighborhood children that the axle was broken and they were waiting for spare parts to arrive. But even that explanation had begun to draw curious glances from the children, who were now on a first-name relationship with some of the federal agents. It was decided that the motor home had finally outlived its usefulness.

As it lumbered out of the neighborhood, a handsome couple

moved into a house almost directly across the street from the Meredith residence. The woman who rented the house, Sue Palmieri, did not tell the owner that she was a deputy U.S. marshal or that the man posing as her boyfriend, Dave Hill, was an FBI agent. Deputy Tom Russell introduced Hill to Buck and Betty Meredith as his brother-in-law. Soon the Merediths, Russell, Palmieri and Dave Hill were spending evenings together, drinking beer and enjoying each other's company at the Bear Creek Tavern or one of the dockside watering holes near the marina.

In Seattle, Jim Maji, Dave Neff and FBI agents were troubled by the discovery of inconsistencies in Tom Hill's descriptions of the bank robberies pulled off by Christopher Boyce. Moreover, it appeared that his brother Brian might know about his cooperation with federal agents. Two deputies guarding him overheard Hill, in a conversation with his mother in Denver, say angrily, "What did you tell him for?"

From the beginning, he had insisted that Boyce robbed the banks alone and had driven the getaway car himself. But as they pressed him for details of the holdups, he slipped twice and referred to "they." Under harder questioning, he admitted he had lied. Brian, he said, had been the wheel man in several robberies, and Brian had even robbed one bank himself. And from what he could tell from the conversation with his mother, Brian knew that he had turned in Boyce.

Then, speaking rapidly, trying to regain the ground he had lost, Tom Hill said that a reward was only one reason he had turned in Boyce. "He was using my brother. He was a bad influence on him."

He had decided, he said, that the only way to keep his brother out of jail was to see to it that Boyce went back to prison. And he refused, he said, to say anything more until it was guaranteed that his brother would not be prosecuted. "I want sort of a trade," he said.

"If Brian knows, will he tip off Boyce?"

"I don't know."

The federal agents said they couldn't make any promises, but would do their best to help Brian if Tom helped them find Christopher Boyce. "Our main interest is in finding Boyce," Neff said. "Where do we look?"

In a couple of days, Tom said, a wedding was scheduled near Bonners Ferry. "Jim didn't get along with the people who are getting married, but he might show up." Brian, whom he hadn't seen for weeks, was likely to be there, he said, and if Brian was there, Boyce might be with him.

Overlooking Chuck Kupferer's desk in Tysons Corner was a huge world map. For more than a year and a half he had placed white strips on it marking the places where he had sent deputies to look for Christopher Boyce. He was tired of waiting for the strike force on the Olympic Peninsula to give him anything but discouraging news. He decided, with Howard Safir's consent, to set up a second strike force and lead it himself.

Before leaving Tysons Corner, he did some quick research on Boundary County, Idaho, and discovered that he would be reliving part of the history of the U.S. Marshals Service. Deputy marshals had been going after fugitives in the wilderness of northern Idaho for more than a century. Now it would be his turn.

4

EACH MORNING WHEN THE FLIGHT SCHOOL opened at eight o'clock, Tony Lester was waiting, and he was usually there when it closed eight hours later. He came six days a week—every day except Sunday, when the school was closed. At his rate of progress, the instructor said, he should solo in a few days.

This pleased his student, who asked a lot of questions about flying in polar regions. The instructor was curious and asked him why he was interested in polar aviation. Tony Lester replied vaguely that he was thinking about making a trip into Alaska.

On August 13, 1981, fourteen days after he had met Tom Hill outside the restaurant in Denver and flown with him to Seattle, Dave Neff pulled up to Spokane International Airport in a jeep borrowed from a federal motor pool in Seattle. It had been so hot during his drive across the flatlands of eastern Washington that heat from the engine firewall had melted the heel of one shoe. Neff was waiting at the airport when Kupferer, Dighera and Maji arrived an hour later on a Northwest Airlines flight from Seattle. They bought a cooler, filled it with beer and ice to help them cope with the heat that was broiling Spokane and headed east. Neff was almost as large as Dighera, and with the contentious phone calls about Tom Hill in the background of their relationship, they eyed each other silently like a couple of moody elephants in the tiny jeep. But after half an hour and a couple of beers they started to share ideas on how to find Boyce. Outside Coeur d'Alene, Idaho, the jeep pulled up to a sign with arrows pointing right to the Idaho city of Moscow and left to Sandpoint and Canada. They turned left, toward Canada and Boundary County.

In the Los Angeles Federal Courthouse, Larry Homenick walked a few steps from his desk and waited for the facsimile machine to roll.

The day before, Maji had learned that a driver's license had been issued July 21, 1981, in Forks, Washington, to Anthony Edward Lester and that he had been photographed when he had applied for the license. A copy of the license, with Lester's photograph, was being transmitted to Homenick, the only deputy who knew Boyce, to verify that Lester and Christopher Boyce were the same person.

The drum began to move, and as it rotated faster and faster, shadows appeared. Homenick saw a forehead, eyes, a face. Before the drum had stopped spinning, he knew it was Chris.

When would he be called to join the others? Finding Chris had been on *his* shoulders for almost nineteen months. The responsibility had turned a dream into a nightmare; he deserved to be there at the end.

Duke Smith, who had flown to Washington from South Africa and taken over some of Kupferer's duties, told Homenick to keep his bag packed. But the phone didn't ring.

While Homenick waited in Los Angeles on the afternoon of August 14, Kupferer, Dighera, Neff and Maji were out in the wilderness of northern Idaho. The night before, they had established a command post at the Travelers Inn Motel in Sandpoint, a resort town on Lake Pend Oreille. They had rented backpacks and fishing gear for their cover—insurance executives on a fishing trip.

On the morning of August 14, they had driven the thirty miles to Bonners Ferry, looked it over quickly, decided not to approach Gloria White's cabin yet and continued north across the Kootenai River toward Canada, looking for Smith Falls, where the wedding was to take place the following day. They found a world as primitive as it was beautiful, with mountain peaks thousands of feet high, shimmering lakes and rivers, and deep gorges rimmed by virgin forests. The serenity and menace reminded Dighera of the Costa Rican jungle where they had looked for Boyce six months earlier. They followed dirt roads and byways into the wilderness, strayed into Canada across a boundary not even marked by a sign but finally found Smith Falls. It was a site, they thought, worthy of a wedding.

Against a stunning mountain backdrop, Smith Falls thundered down a rocky cliff, turned into a whirlpool and then, underneath a glistening veil of white spray, re-formed into a placid river and meandered toward Canada. The wedding vows were to be exchanged on a bridge over the falls. Kupferer, Dighera, Neff and Maji chose the positions where each would be in the morning. On the way back to Sandpoint, they agreed to have Tom Hill brought to Idaho. They were going to need a guide.

Shortly before eight o'clock the next morning, three hours before the wedding was to start, Kupferer, Dighera and Neff were fishing the Smith River, hoping for better luck hooking Boyce than they were having with their fishing tackle. Maji was on a rise where he could see the falls. Two miles north of the falls near the Canadian border, a tracker from the U.S. Border Patrol was waiting in a truck whose four-wheel drive would allow him to chase Boyce into the mountains if he made a break for it.

After an hour or so, an old man hiked past Kupferer toward the bridge. The chief inspector, looking preoccupied, studied him out of the corner of his eye. He was about seventy-five years old and he looked as if he possessed all the world's wisdom about fishing; he also had a glistening string of thirty or so salmon.

"Morning," the man said cheerily, and Kupferer looked up, smiled and returned the greeting.

"It's a little late to do any good fishing," the man said. "Any luck?"

"Not yet. My friends and I just got here a little while ago."

"Little late to get anything, but here, try this." He reached into his pack. "They're bitin' on these."

He presented Kupferer with a mysterious handful of bait—

clammy organisms about the size of a thimble with a hard shell like a snail.

Kupferer had to struggle to attach one of the hard shells to his line. Finally, he managed to cast it into the river. But as soon as he bent his wrist, the bait flew off, arced gracefully through the air and plunked decisively into the fast-moving stream. He tried again and got another piece of the bait as far as the water, but then it too fell off. Kupferer examined the remaining examples of the mysterious organism and squeezed one of them. To his surprise, a fat pink worm popped out.

He put it on the hook, cast it into the river and in less than thirty seconds felt a firm tug on his line. In less than a minute Kupferer had pulled out a huge silver salmon and was waving it at Dighera and Neff, who were having no luck at all.

Nor did they have any luck hooking Boyce. The wedding took place on schedule, with about sixty guests, but Christopher Boyce was not among them. One member of the wedding party, however, attracted their interest. The best man was a blond man in his twenties who had a shaggy beard and was wearing black pants and a black silk shirt. Neff, who was nearest the bridge, saw the man staring nervously down at him. Neff looked away, but when he turned his head back a few moments later, the man's eyes were still fixed on him. Neff decided that he must be Brian Hill.

After the wedding ceremony, the four deputy marshals twice drove slowly past the community hall where the newlywed couple were being honored at a reception. It looked like a convention of hippies, Neff thought. There seemed to be lots of drinking, eating and dancing going on; but none of the guests looked like Boyce.

Forest Service rangers, whom Kupferer had taken into his confidence, along with Border Patrol officers in Boundary County, remembered seeing a lone man with a mule camped out near an abandoned mine. The following morning, a caravan of four-wheel-drive Forest Service trucks climbed up Two Tail Mountain to the old mine. It was the spot where Tom Hill said Christopher Boyce sometimes lived. The agents found traces of an old camp, a long-abandoned cabin, fresh bear tracks and the tracks of an elk, but no recent human tracks.

The same day, Dave Neff and Jim Maji stood on a table at the Good Grief Tavern in Addie, Idaho, five miles south of the Canadian border and twenty-two miles north of Bonners Ferry, looking up at a panorama of dollar bills. There may have been hundreds of American and Canadian bills tacked to the ceiling of the tavern. They were searching for a single one. They saw it on a beam midway through the tavern, just as Tom Hill had said they would. It was dated *4-81*. Scrawled around the face of George Washington were nine signatures . . . including *Gloria White, The Kahlua Kid* and *Jim and His Mule*.

With Bob Dighera sitting beside him, a Forest Service ranger drove a fire truck slowly up Katka Mountain on the road leading to Gloria White's place. They paused at each cabin, knocking at the door, telling the occupants that there had been a report of a fire in the area and asking whether anyone had seen any smoke.

"Haven't seen any smoke," one man replied. "But I hope you find a fire. We can use the work."

Finally, they knocked at Gloria's house, but no one was there.

By nightfall, Kupferer was feeling as he'd felt much of the time during the past nineteen months: defeated and frustrated. He looked out at the huge wilderness that spilled into Canada. It could swallow Boyce so easily, he thought. Worse, Boyce might not even be there.

Things were going no better on the Olympic Peninsula. Deputy Sue Palmieri, FBI Agent Dave Hill and Hill's "brother-in-law," Deputy Tom Russell, were welcomed each night, along with the other regulars, at the Bear Creek Tavern. But after almost three weeks of surveillance, none of them had a clue as to where Christopher Boyce was.

Moreover, their cover might be unraveling. On the afternoon of August 16, at about the same time that Neff and Maji were craning their necks to find a dollar bill at the Good Grief Tavern in Idaho, two of Buck Meredith's small children had spotted a telescope pointed at their home from the living room of the house rented by Dave Hill and Sue Palmieri. After they told their mother that people were looking at them from across the street, Betty Meredith decided that she had had *enough*. For almost three weeks strangers had been coming and going in the neighborhood. Now people were spying on her family. She crossed the street and knocked on the door and asked about the telescope. Dave Hill gamely tried to assure her that no one had been spying on her, and she left. But that didn't solve the problem. An hour later, the agent who kept the log made a note that the Meredith children had approached the house rented by the Federal Government and thrown rocks at it.

Two hours later, Deputy Michael O'Brien, who was coordinating the search for Boyce in the Beaver area, together with a U.S. border patrolman and a sergeant from the Clallam County Sheriff's Department, knocked on the door of the Meredith house. After pledging Betty Meredith to secrecy, they identified themselves as law-enforcement officers and disclosed that they were investigating a ring of drug runners who were smuggling marijuana from Canada into the United States. Pointing to a small parking lot near her home, they said that it was the practice of the smugglers to park a certain car there as a signal to confederates that a shipment of marijuana was imminent. That was why there was a telescope in the house across the street, O'Brien said. The people living in the house, he said, had agreed to let the detectives use their home for surveillance but had not told Mrs. Meredith about it because they too had agreed to preserve the detectives' secret.

When Buck Meredith came home that evening, his wife said that she was relieved: "Thank God. I thought it had something to do with us."

Buck took a beer from the refrigerator and all but forgot about it. He said that he was eager to tell Sean that Tom Russell was interested in buying the *Rose-M*. He was also going to tell him about all the people who had been asking about him lately in Beaver and the marina.

"He should have called last week. I wonder what happened to him," Betty Meredith said.

5

CHUCK KUPFERER HATED WAITING FOR A FUGITIVE to make the next move. By nature, he hated any kind of inaction, but most of all, he hated to give a fugitive the right to control an investigation. But that was what they were doing by waiting for Boyce to show himself.

By the time the next day that Tom Hill, guarded by two deputies from Seattle, arrived in Sandpoint, the resort town thirty miles south of Bonners Ferry where Kupferer had established the command post for the search, he had a plan to break the impasse.

He gave Hill the ignition keys for a maroon Chevrolet Malibu with Colorado plates that the deputies had rented and told him to use it to look for Boyce in Bonners Ferry, and if he didn't find him to ask Gloria White and other people in town if they had seen him recently. A new car on Katka Mountain, Hill said, would make him as conspicuous as if he were wearing a tailor-made suit. Kupferer's response was "Tell people you had to rent it because your motorcycle broke down in Denver."

Neff and Dighera, he said, would go to the U.S. Border Patrol station in Bonners Ferry and wait for Hill to report on his progress. "Check in there at least once every four hours," he said.

Dighera and Neff needn't have gone to the Border Patrol station. After Hill left for the half-hour drive to Bonners Ferry, they didn't hear from him again for more than twenty-four hours. When he finally showed up at the motel the next day, Kupferer was furious.

311

"Where in hell have you been?" he demanded.

"I couldn't find him." Hill said that he had spent almost all th[e] time waiting at Gloria's house hoping that Boyce would show up; when he hadn't, he had gone to the Mint Club and Mr. C's, but n[o] one had seen him there either.

Dave Neff was skeptical. While Kupferer grilled Tom, h[e] checked the odometer of the Malibu. The car had traveled abou[t] sixty miles farther than Hill said he had.

In a whisper, Neff told Kupferer that he suspected Hill had vis[-] ited his brother, who was staying with the newly married couple [a]t Smith Falls.

"Did you go see your brother?" Neff asked.

"No," Tom said. He looked uncomfortable.

"Your brother knows about us, doesn't he?" Neff demanded. "You said you wouldn't, but you told him about us."

"No, I didn't."

Tom Hill held his ground for almost ten minutes, then yielded. "I had to let him know what was going down; he's my brother."

"Did you tell him *everything?*"

"Yeah."

"What'd he say?"

"He wasn't very happy, but there was nothing he could do abou[t] it. But he said he doesn't want to get involved in it."

"He *is* involved," Kupferer said sharply.

Now he had something else to worry about: the possibility th[at] Brian Hill would tip off Boyce.

"Do you think he'll tell Boyce?"

"No, but he doesn't like cops, and he thinks I'm going to g[et] him in trouble over the bank robberies."

"Look, I know you want to protect your brother; it's only natu[-] ral," Kupferer said. "I don't blame you. I might do the sam[e] thing. But he *is* involved; he's facing bank robbery, harboring [a] spy, weapons charges and a lot of other shit. And the only way h[e] can do himself any good is to cooperate. We can't promise any[-] thing, but he might be smart to talk to us."

From the moment they had spotted Brian Hill at the wedding[,] Kupferer had weighed the possibility of putting a tail on him in th[e] hope that he would lead them unwittingly to Boyce. Now that option was gone. He decided to take another gamble, and if he lost it, he told Neff and Dighera, the whole investigation might blow up in their faces. He ordered Neff and Tom Hill to bring Brian back to the Travelers Inn Motel at Sandpoint.

They approached a wooded area a few miles from Smith Falls. A dirt road ascended a hill and disappeared in a forest of pine trees. Neff got out of the car, Tom Hill gunned the engine and the Chevrolet sped up the hill, bound for the cabin in the woods where the newlyweds lived.

Neff sat down on a slab of granite at the foot of the hill. After forty-five minutes had passed and the car hadn't returned, he decided that the brothers might have fled on another road out of the woods, possibly alerted Boyce and then headed for Canada. But a few minutes later he saw a rust-colored cloud of dust at the top of the hill and then the Malibu. It pulled up beside him. Tom was at the wheel, and Brian was looking straight ahead. He recognized him from the wedding.

Neff sensed that they were at a turning point, that the words he chose now were important.

"Brian," he said, "I don't care what you've done in the past. We're not interested in that. All we're interested in is capturing Christopher John Boyce. We want your help.

"I can promise you this: whatever you tell me about other things will be kept in the strictest of confidence, and I won't screw you; I won't burn you. And if the heat starts coming down on you . . . the pressure . . . and we don't meet our promises to you, then I'll make sure that you and Tom get away and I'll cover for you."

Brian swiveled around in the front seat, his eyes as cold as two pieces of dark ice, and looked at Neff.

He studied him for a moment. "Okay," he said. "You've got it."

They bought a six-pack of beer at a liquor store, opened three cans and drove to Sandpoint—where Chuck Kupferer was not as gentle as Neff.

If he was going to find Boyce, Kupferer decided, he had to squeeze Brian Hill. The older brother was the key to the investigation now. He was the smarter and the stronger of the brothers. He had robbed banks with Boyce and had spent more time with him than Tom had. But he had to be squeezed carefully or they would lose him.

"Let's clear the room," Kupferer ordered in the voice he used at the start of an interrogation to establish who was in charge of things.

Everybody left the motel room except Kupferer and Brian Hill. They sat down in chairs a few feet apart and Kupferer said, "Let me tell you something, Brian: You're up to your ass in alligators. You've got bank robbery, harboring an escaped spy, all kinds of other charges facing you. You're looking at twenty years at least. Tell me one thing: was anybody killed in the robberies?"

"No."

"Was anybody injured?"

"No."

"Okay—if that's accurate, I'll get all the assistance for you that I can if you cooperate with us and help us find Boyce."

If he didn't cooperate, Kupferer added, he'd do everything in his power to see that Brian went to prison for assisting the escape of a fugitive Soviet spy and for robbing banks.

"Believe me, my only concern is arresting Boyce. I'm not interested in bank robberies. I can't make any promises, but I'll try. You've got my word. If that's okay, let's talk."

"I just want to get out of it."

And then Brian Hill described, from the beginning, his life with Christopher John Boyce.

"We haven't been getting along lately."

"What made you change your mind about him?"

"It was the way he treated us."

"What do you mean?"

"It was like he was using us, which I didn't realize at first."

"Where do you think he is right now?"

"If he wasn't at the boat or at Buck's he'd probably be living in Port Angeles."

Port Angeles was the small town that served as the commercial heart of the Olympic Peninsula. It was almost forty miles from

314

where Buck Meredith's house was staked out in Beaver. The search teams had driven through Port Angeles many times but never conducted a search for Boyce there.

At almost precisely the same moment that Brian Hill, alone with Kupferer in the motel room in Sandpoint, Idaho, suggested that Boyce was in Port Angeles, Buck Meredith and his wife, Betty, were entering their favorite bar, the Bear Creek Tavern, 350 miles away in Beaver. They were sitting down to have a few beers with two new friends, Sue Palmieri and Tom Russell, when the bartender spotted them and said, "Hey, Buck. I saw Sean, your partner in crime, this afternoon coming out of the Tradewell store in Port Angeles."

Sue and Tom finished their beer with the Merediths, drank another and excused themselves. Then they radioed the command post from Russell's yellow van:

"We have information the salmon is close. We're coming in."

By dawn the next morning, the motel rooms in Sandpoint occupied by Kupferer, Dighera, Neff, Maji and the Hill brothers were empty. The search had shifted from Idaho back into Washington.

6

A SEMITRANSPARENT GRAY MIST WAS CLINGING TO the mountains beneath the fluffy cumulus clouds that almost always obscured the highest peaks of the Olympics, and from the air the sight was so overwhelming that it was distracting. Below him, pleasure boats and fishing vessels carved their signatures briefly into the sea, as if a company of artists were painting scrolls on a rippled sheet of blue slate.

Three days earlier, his flight instructor had taken a large sheet of butcher paper, written a few words on it with a felt-tipped marker and tacked it high on a wall of the flight school:

8-16-81
1ST SOLO
TONY LESTER
CONGRATULATIONS

Now, Christopher Boyce banked to the right over the Strait, dipping the wing of the light plane as he had been taught to do. He straightened out, completed the procedural turn to line up with the runway and prepared to lower the flaps. He aimed the nose at the foot of the runway, eased off slightly on the power, started to feel the cushion of air between the concrete runway and the wings, and prepared for touchdown. As he descended, the nose rose slightly, and he corrected for it. It continued to rise, and he adjusted the

316

flaps again. But it was too much; he had overcorrected, and the little plane dropped toward the runway.

It hit hard and bounced up about twenty feet, then came down hard again; it bounced a third time, then established a footing on the runway and rolled down the concrete.

Too bad, he thought: it had been a perfect landing until then. Embarrassing, but not fatal. He still had time.

In Los Angeles, Larry Homenick was still waiting for his summons to the Northwest, not realizing that it would not come. Chuck Kupferer had decided that because Boyce knew Homenick so well, it would be dangerous to have him join the undercover operation. They couldn't take the chance of losing Boyce now if he were to recognize Homenick.

As Homenick waited, he pondered why, contrary to what everybody had predicted about him, Chris had turned to common crime. How would he have reacted if an off-duty cop had wandered into one of his bank robberies and the cop had drawn on him, tried to stop him? Would he have shot to kill? Despite a lingering measure of affection for what he had once been, Homenick decided that Chris probably would have murdered the cop rather than go back to prison. He had seen the prisons that Chris had been locked away in, and he had seen prisons change other men. Some of the inmates he had interviewed after the escape had told him that Chris hadn't belonged there, that prison had changed him, made him harder, taught him a way of life he had never seen in Palos Verdes.

Homenick remembered the intensity of Chris's contempt for the CIA, and what he thought of a country that had allowed its moral principles to be corrupted. Chris had called himself a political dissident. But how could that explain his decision to become a modern Billy the Kid and rob sixteen banks and wave a .357 magnum in the face of frightened tellers? He recalled that Chris had lured Daulton Lee into their plot to sell secrets to the Soviet Union. Now it appeared that he might have manipulated his accomplices in the bank robberies. He wondered how many other people he had manipulated, how many people he had used. Homenick wondered how well he really knew Chris. He thought of a book he had once read about the Old West. A frontier outlaw named Henry Starr had said, "It isn't only the lure of money that takes a man into outlawry. There's the thrill of dashing into a town after an all-night ride, guns blazing, and cowing it for half an hour. . . . The boys who had gone into the bank come running out with a grain sack bulging with loot. It's time to leave . . ." and the sheer excitement of getting away with it made the juices flow. Homenick recalled something he had read about Harold "Kim" Philby, the Soviet double agent who, like Chris, had come from a privileged stratum of a Western democracy, betrayed his country and claimed that he had done it for ideological reasons. The British writer Malcolm Muggeridge, who knew Philby well, had said he doubted that ideological motivations in fact ran very deep in the Soviet spy. "Far stronger in him than anything of this kind," he had written, "was his romantic veneration for buccaneers and buccaneering, whatever the ideological basis, if any, might be. Boozers, womanizers, violence in all its manifestations, recklessness, however directed, he found irresistible." Homenick thought of Muggeridge's remark, and he thought of the day he had sat across from Chris and his friend had said, "Larry, I guess I'm a pirate at heart. I'm an adventurer."

And then it came to Homenick: he must have betrayed his country for *excitement*.

Homenick continued to think about Chris, his bag beside his desk, packed and ready to go.

Chris was also planning a trip.

7

HUNGRY AFTER A DAY OF FLYING, HE THOUGHT about dinner and then about calling Buck to ask him how the fishing was going and to let him know that he was going to sign over the boat to him, now that he wouldn't need it. Taking the *Rose-M* north had seemed sound when he had bought it. Now, five months later, he agreed with the fishermen who had told him that the passage to the Bering Strait was too much for the old boat—it could make it to Alaska easily enough via the inland passage, but not through the rough open sea to the Strait—and he had made other plans.

Chris decided there was no hurry, that he would call Buck and give him the news in a few days.

He locked the door of the small apartment in Port Angeles where he had lived for almost a month and, on the evening of August 19, started the engine of a black-and-gold 1969 Oldsmobile, one of the big old gas-guzzlers that had been a glut on the used-car market since the start of the gasoline crunch but which suited his needs because it was cheap and not flashy and could be quickly replaced.

For dinner, he chose the Red Lion Inn on Lincoln Street in Port Angeles, one of his favorites when he was in a mood for something more substantial than a hamburger. He washed his meal down with a beer while he studied his flight lessons. As he left the dining room, he noticed three tall men with beards and backpacks, checking into the inn. Their clothes were scruffy and they looked tired, like a lot of the people who came to the Peninsula to work in the forest or to climb the Olympics.

Then Chris left the inn and went out into a cold and misty night, paying no more attention to them.

Bob Dighera, Dave Neff and Chuck Kupferer leaned over the desk, signed the registration cards and picked up their backpacks. After a shower and a brief rest, they agreed to meet for a strategy session.

They had not noticed the dark-haired young man in the lobby.

After a nap, they hit the bars in Port Angeles to search for Boyce, but they didn't see anyone who looked like him.

As usual, it was raining on the Olympic Peninsula. The tires of the Oldsmobile hissed on the wet pavement as it passed through a feathery corridor of tall cedar trees not far from the ocean. The driver did not notice the police car until its red light went on.

The policeman cited him for speeding, but did not check with his dispatcher to learn if any warrants were outstanding for the driver. Had he checked, he would have learned that the driver, Anthony Edward Lester, was an escaped spy.

By the morning of Thursday, August 20, twenty-one days after Dave Neff had met Tom Hill outside the restaurant in Denver, almost two dozen deputy marshals and FBI agents were on the Olympic Peninsula intent on tightening a circle around Christopher Boyce, although they still did not have conclusive evidence that he was there. Eight of the agents were in Port Angeles, organized into four teams each made up of an FBI agent and a deputy marshal. According to protocol, strategy for the manhunt was established by senior officials of the local district of the Marshals Service in Seattle. To minimize the risk of scaring Boyce away, they had decided that it was prudent to put the city under a low-key, restrained surveillance rather than launch a full-scale search—a decision that was to cause problems later.

Port Angeles had been divided into quadrants on a grid system. Each undercover team was assigned to check streets, bars, restaurants and stores in one of the quadrants but instructed not to ask any questions about Boyce. Any break in the security, Seattle officials had said, might make the Falcon fly.

* * *

Brian Hill had arrived at Buck Meredith's home on the evening of August 19 riding a big Harley-Davidson motorcycle rented for him by the Marshals Service. Buck remembered that Sean hadn't been getting along with Brian or his brother Tom, but wasn't surprised by the visit. He said he hadn't heard from Sean for several weeks, but that a lot of people seemed to want to talk to him. If he saw him, he told Brian, he should tell Sean about all the people who had been asking about him.

One by one, Chris deposited the coins into a pay telephone. He needed almost $3 for the call from Port Angeles to Beverly Hills, California. The most-wanted man in America was calling the 20th Century–Fox film studios because he was curious to learn, before he left, about the status of filming *The Falcon and the Snowman*.

The woman who answered in the Fox production office didn't recognize the name that he invented to introduce himself, and thinking he might be another applicant for a part in the movie, she declined to let him speak to the producer.

Port Angeles reminded Bob Dighera of Redondo Beach, the coastal town in Southern California where he had wasted so much time during the preceding nineteen months trying to forge a connection between Boyce and the drug trade. There was the identical mixture of salt and fish in the damp air, the same kind of run-down look along parts of the waterfront, the same kind of narrow streets where teenage boys cruised in their cars looking for girls.

Driving through the town in an FBI car, a beer in his hand and half a smoked salmon on the seat, he turned to the FBI agent beside him, one of the few he liked, and said, "Imagine what J. Edgar Hoover would be doing in his grave right now if he could see a marshal driving an FBI car."

The man from the Bureau, who also had a beer in hand, laughed and said he wondered too. In Washington, a senior official of the Justice Department mentioned discreetly to an official of the Central Intelligence Agency that the Marshals Service appeared to be closing in on Christopher John Boyce in the Pacific Northwest.

321

"Did he really do much harm?" the man from the Justice Department asked.

The CIA man said that he couldn't go into the specifics, because they were classified, but he said, "What he did was a national calamity."

Christopher Boyce and Andrew Daulton Lee, he said, probably didn't know themselves what information they had transmitted to the Russians, because they seemed to have photographed everything in sight in the communications vault where Boyce worked.

But among other things, he said, they had provided the Russians with detailed operational information about a covert intelligence system that the United States was secretly using to monitor Soviet missile tests and collect other intelligence data. After the Russians learned about it they had revamped their telemetry system, making it much more difficult for the United States to gather certain kinds of data about Soviet weapons.

Nothing, he said, was more important to the survival of the United States than being able to collect accurate and up-to-date information about the evolution of Soviet ballistic missiles, if for no other reason than to verify compliance with a strategic-arms-limitation agreement. What Boyce and Lee had done, he explained, was impair America's ability to do that and thus maintain the climate of mistrust that prolonged the arms race.

In Los Angeles, Larry Homenick borrowed an atlas and located Port Angeles and Bonners Ferry. He had been furious when he discovered that Kupferer had decided not to include him in the operation. Now, a day later, after a lecture from Tony Perez about being a good soldier, he was still angry at Kupferer, but he was beginning to concede that it might have been the best decision. He didn't want to lose Chris now either. Bob Dighera had telephoned to express his sympathy and promised to call him if anything happened in Port Angeles.

August 20 passed without a sign of Christopher Boyce in Port Angeles, Beaver or the marina at Lapush.

Deputy U.S. marshals and FBI agents spent the evening drinking in virtually every watering hole in Port Angeles, along with the Bear Creek Tavern. But the most memorable event of the night was the discovery that Chuck Kupferer's partner, FBI agent Jane Turner, could shoot pool better than just about any male in Port Angeles.

The passive surveillance ordered by Seattle was beginning to grate on the nerves of Dighera and Neff, who, after their frigid initial confrontation on the telephone, had become good friends. Waiting didn't suit the metabolism of either man. At a stormy strategy session that night they implored Seattle to loosen the reins.

"Let's stop sitting back; let's reach out. Let's talk to people," Dighera demanded.

"If we do, we'll blow it," the senior man from Seattle said, and the meeting ended acrimoniously.

In the morning, however, under prodding by Kupferer, who didn't like the conservative approach to the search any more than Dighera and Neff, he consented to allow the investigators to show a photograph of Boyce discreetly at selected motels and stores—but only after it was decided in each case that the risk was small and the agents in the field had conferred first with the Seattle officials, who had set up a command post in a room at the Red Lion Inn.

Bob Dighera was first to come up with anything promising.

He showed Boyce's photograph to clerks in four or five motels without eliciting any sign of recognition, then visited the rental office of a rundown apartment complex at the edge of downtown Port Angeles. Wearing shabby clothes and carrying his backpack, which only added to his normally threatening stature, Dighera told a clerk that he was down on his luck and wanted a free bed for the night. The clerk turned him down, but not before Dighera spotted a registration card that showed Room 16 was rented to someone whose handwriting was very similar to Christopher Boyce's. He decided it was too risky to ask the clerk for the name of the tenant in Room 16 and left.

From the motel, he walked to a small supermarket nearby. It was the Tradewell store where the bartender of the Bear Creek Tavern had told Buck Meredith he had seen Boyce a few days before. He asked to speak to the manager, who turned out to be a friendly middle-aged man who Dighera decided could be trusted. He showed him his badge and a photograph of Boyce and asked if he had ever been in the store.

The manager studied the photograph carefully. "He looks a little familiar. Why don't you ask the clerks?"

He led Dighera to a storeroom in the rear of the store and said he would send the clerks, one by one, to be interviewed.

Dighera had only a short wait. The first clerk who came into the storeroom said, "Sure, he comes in all the time; he buys a lot of dark beer and cigarettes."

Dighera had shown mug shots to thousands of people since he had come home from Vietnam to become a deputy U.S. marshal. He knew when someone really recognized a face looking out from a photograph. The clerk had not hesitated a moment. There wasn't any doubt in her voice. He knew they were close.

"What kind of cigarettes does he buy?"

"Marlboro Lights."

"Do you have any idea where he lives!"

"Not for sure, but I think I've seen him head down the block toward those little apartments over there."

Dighera looked in the direction of her finger. She was pointing to the apartment complex he had just come from.

8

WHEN HAD HE FIRST FELT THE URGE TO FLY?

Was it the first time he had climbed a tree and looked down from a limb and felt at once a sense of freedom and a sense of danger? Or was it when, as an infant, he had approached a bird, and as he had reached out to touch it, it had bent its wings and fluttered away from him?

Was it when Daulton had tied a rope to his waist and lowered him down a cliff and a hawk had looked out at him from its eyrie and then hurtled past him defiantly? Or was it when Nurd or Pips or one of his other falcons had leaped off his wrist and corkscrewed into the sky until he could no longer see it, broad wings giving it a freedom no man had ever had?

He had looked into the eyes of his birds and envied them. He had wondered what it was like to lift away from the earth on a whim, unfettered by gravity, free of rules or restraints; free to fly, if he chose to, across the world.

Now he knew. Alone, with his hands and feet on the controls, he was rising over the mountains, over the ocean, as his birds had done, and he felt proud and wanted to tell his mother and father and his friends at home, "Look, I can fly." But he couldn't, and it made him sad. He was certain now that he would never see them again, and it made him even more depressed.

He pulled back on the throttle, landed smoothly and taxied back to the Pearson Flight School at Fairchild International Airport in Port Angeles. Seventeen miles away, across the Strait of Juan de Fuca, was Victoria, Canada, and beyond that Alaska.

Tomorrow morning he was scheduled to take a lesson in cross-country, long-distance flying, and very soon after that he would be gone.

After the clerk at the Tradewell store identified Boyce as a regular customer, the combined task force—the marshals, who wanted Boyce for escaping from a federal prison, and the FBI agents, who wanted him for bank robbery—decided that it was time to close in. If the clerk was right, Boyce was probably living in the shabby row of apartments that Dighera had visited or somewhere else within walking distance of the market. The boredom and frustration of the past weeks were suddenly replaced by an urgency that ignited the morale of the manhunters.

On a map of the city tacked to a wall of the motel-room command post, Kupferer drew a circle almost a mile in diameter. The store was in the center.

"Let's move in tight here," he said, pointing to the area encircled by the line he had drawn. The Seattle representatives concurred, but insisted that it was still essential that they move with caution and not break their cover except if there was no other option.

By noon Friday, the net was in place.

Inside the store, wearing a borrowed clerk's smock, FBI Agent Jane Turner was sweeping the floor.

On a rise across the street from the supermarket, Kupferer was parked near a Kentucky Fried Chicken store and looking down at the front door of the Tradewell.

Dave Neff and Deputy Jack Cluff parked their car on a slope above the apartment complex where they could see Apartment 16.

Bob Dighera and FBI Agent Richard Collier were on a bluff parked near an automated car wash, watching the supermarket through binoculars.

Other deputies and FBI agents were on foot or waiting in cars near the edge of the circle drawn by Kupferer.

Jane Turner had her gun beneath the smock. If Boyce appeared, her plan was to approach him from behind, stick the barrel into his ear and threaten to kill him if he moved.

Once the teams were in place, the momentum slowed, and it was time to wait again.

In the car he shared with Dighera, Agent Dick Collier tried to make the time pass by reading a newspaper column on biorhythms. According to the article, he said Friday, August 21, was a day on which everything was supposed to go wrong for Dighera.

"You bastard," Dighera said. "You had to tell me about it, didn't you?"

Dighera had not seen his wife, Betty, for more than a month because of Boyce. A few hours earlier, he had telephoned her and said he missed her and was getting discouraged. "I'm about ready," he'd said, "to throw it in and come home tonight."

"Stay up there," she had said. "You've put too much time in on him to give up now."

Betty Dighera said she was so confident that he would find Boyce soon that she had booked a plane reservation for him to San Diego in the morning.

He had told her he wasn't nearly as optimistic.

At four o'clock, the tedium was broken. A dark-haired man in his twenties approached the front of the supermarket, paused and then continued walking past it. From a distance he looked to be about the same age as Boyce.

"There's a subject coming up First Street who could be C.J.," a tense voice, using the code chosen for references to Boyce, boomed over the radio circuit being used for the surveillance.

"Somebody eyeball him," Kupferer said.

One of the backup teams stationed at the periphery of the mile-wide circle drove slowly down the length of First Street. The two men in the front seat tried to look straight ahead while they studied the man on the sidewalk.

Abruptly, the man turned his head toward their car and began waving his arms wildly. Then he smiled and stared at them.

"He looks a little like C.J.," one agent said. "But he doesn't fit the profile of our guy. He's waving at us. Maybe he's retarded."

Then they saw him waving at all the cars on First Street.

"It isn't him," the agent said, and they returned to their station at a street corner to wait.

Friday was payday for many people in Port Angeles, and the supermarket was busy as customers stocked up for the weekend. As the afternoon passed, the streets grew more crowded with cars and pickup trucks of local people. The first wave of weekend tourists arrived to visit Olympic National Park or take the ferry across the Strait to British Columbia.

Darkness was falling over the town and there was still no sign of Christopher Boyce. Some of the people staked out near the Tradewell supermarket turned to each other and said that once again they had chosen the wrong time and wrong place to look for him.

Because of the excitement earlier in the day gettting ready for the stakeout, Kupferer hadn't eaten much lunch. Now his car was filling up with the aroma of fried chicken, and he wanted to make a quick trip to the Colonel Sanders kiosk—but he couldn't risk it, because Boyce might walk into the market and ask for cigarettes or dark beer and his partner would need help in a hurry.

A block away, Bob Dighera sat in the FBI's Mercury bored and impatient. He radioed the command post at the motel to say that he thought the supermarket and the apartment were covered by enough people and asked for permission to make a laundry run. Everybody was running out of clean clothes, and he said it was a good time to drop some clothing off at a laundry. Permission was granted.

It was true that the Mercury was filled with dirty laundry. But Dighera wasn't planning a laundry run. He had decided that he couldn't sit in the car doing nothing any longer. If they didn't reach out for Boyce, they were going to lose him.

For an hour, he and his partner cautiously showed photos of Boyce to bartenders and motel clerks in Port Angeles. No one recognized him.

328

By seven o'clock, Kupferer's optimism was fading. The streets were empty of cars, and there weren't many people left on the sidewalks. The Friday-afternoon rush was over, and they had missed him. He decided to stick it out until nine o'clock and then review the situation.

Meanwhile, he wished someone would bring him some fried chicken.

9

IT WAS GETTING DARK RAPIDLY.

Across the Strait, a few lights could be seen flickering in British Columbia. A mist was rising, and inside the cars, it was damp and cold.

As Dighera and Collier drove through the streets looking for Boyce, Dighera remembered a sheet of yellow paper in his pocket. It was a list of places that Tom Hill said Boyce had visited when they had been together in Port Angeles. He found it under his wallet, jammed into the bottom of his back pocket.

There were eight places on the list: a health spa where Hill said they had exercised; a Safeway store; a couple of hardware stores where they had bought materials when they were repairing the *Rose-M* and four restaurants—Aggie's, Hagwood's, the Pit Stop and Andy's Outback.

Without conferring with the command post for approval, Dighera and Collier decided to ask some questions.

At the spa, a young woman studied the photograph for perhaps thirty seconds and then looked inquisitively at Dighera.

"Why are you looking for him?"

"It's a police matter."

He noticed that the girl seemed stunned and then was almost in tears. It was only later that he learned she had had a crush on Christopher Boyce.

330

"Can I help you?" a man asked, as the girl stepped back. Dighera showed him the photograph.

"Yeah. He came in here a couple of months ago. Nice guy. He bought a lot of vitamins. He seemed to have a thing about vitamins. I haven't seen him for a while, though."

They drove past the hardware stores, which were closed, then two of the restaurants on the list, Aggie's and the Pit Stop. Both were crowded, but they couldn't see anyone who looked like Boyce.

Across from the Tradewell store, Chuck Kupferer was thinking about having a meal and calling a strategy session to decide their next move. It was almost eight thirty.

Bob Dighera, meanwhile, returned from his rounds and made himself popular with the chilled agents in the other stakeout cars by giving them chunks of smoked salmon and beer while agitating for them to join him in a rebellion against Seattle.

They had been waiting more than eight hours. They were useless in their cars, he said. If Boyce was in Port Angeles, this wasn't how to find him. They had to reach out.

"God damn it, let's do *something*," he told Neff.

Neff, like Dighera, felt a sense of failure after three weeks of eighteen-hour days and he also wanted action.

"Okay, let's do it," he said. "Let's stop this bullshit and run this like a normal fugitive investigation," Neff said.

"Okay," Dighera said.

Neff said that he was going to look for the Port Angeles fisherman who had sold Boyce the *Rose-M* and ask him if he had any idea where he might be living.

Dighera and Collier said they were going to return to the knoll near the car wash for a quick look at the streets and then start asking more questions.

As he drove away, Dighera decided on an impulse to drive down First Street for another pass of the Pit Stop.

The Pit Stop was part of a vanishing element in America's pop cultural heritage, a drive-in restaurant. It was laid out in the shape of a T. The main restaurant was at the rear of the lot, parallel with the street. Extending from the center of the building almost to the

331

street was a tall, perpendicular canopy. Along each side of it were parking spaces where drivers were served by carhops, although at the Pit Stop they really didn't *hop* in the traditional sense, but *rolled*—on roller skates.

A half-hour earlier, when Dighera had passed it the first time, the Pit Stop's parking area beneath the canopy had been crowded with cars. Now all the cars were gone except for one, a black-and-gold Oldsmobile, in which there was a lone man.

"Let's check it out," he told Collier, and they turned into the drive-in. As they pulled into a space near the Oldsmobile, it occurred to Dighera that the FBI's Mercury smelled strongly of smoked salmon and dirty laundry.

"If it's Boyce, I hope I can recognize him," Collier said.

"When you see those blue eyes, you'll know it's him."

The Mercury came to a stop under the canopy, and the driver of the other car looked over at them with a friendly expression of acknowledgment.

Dighera nodded his head in response. Inside his chest, his heart was pounding.

"It's him," he whispered.

Collier was also looking at the other car. His expression told Dighera that he recognized Boyce too.

No carhops had rolled out of the restaurant to serve them.

Dighera seized on that as an excuse to leave.

"The service is lousy in this place," he said out the window, and backed out slowly.

Christopher Boyce looked up from a book he was reading and smiled again, as if to acknowledge their departure, then returned to his book and took another bite of his hamburger.

"To all units," Dighera said over the radio. His voice was relaxed. "We have a subject here. We are nine-tenths sure he is our man."

Chuck Kupferer asked him where he was, and Dighera replied that he and Collier were in an alley behind the Pit Stop restaurant.

Orchestrating a finale that had been on his mind for nineteen months, Chief Inspector Thomas C. Kupferer, Jr., summoned the players together quickly. The cars converged on the drive-in

There were no screeching tires; they pulled up quietly in the alley and on the street, far enough away so that they could not be seen by the lone customer at the Pit Stop, but near enough to stop him if he fled.

Dave Neff ran up to Dighera in the alley.

"It's him," Dighera said.

"You take that side, and I'll get him from the other side," Neff said. Together, they ran to the Oldsmobile.

Christopher Boyce was absorbed in a book about flying when he looked up and saw their guns.

"U.S. marshals. You're under arrest," Dighera said. His long arm extended across the width of the front seat of the Oldsmobile holding a 9mm automatic, and it was trained on Chris's right ear.

"Drop the hamburger," said Dave Neff, whose gun was pointed through the open window at Chris's left ear.

As they pulled him out of the car, the half-eaten hamburger and the book on flying fell to the floor of the Oldsmobile.

No one had announced the policy, and it wasn't written anywhere, but by tradition, the man who found Boyce had the right to make the formal arrest. Bob Dighera pulled out his handcuffs and clamped them around one arm. Then Neff cuffed the other wrist.

By now, all the agents were out of their cars with guns drawn, and the carhop was outside the building wondering what was happening.

Kupferer stood in front of the Oldsmobile, watching Dighera and Neff put the handcuffs on the man he pursued for a year and a half. He waited a moment and then walked over to him and said, "Hi, Chris."

"It's been a long time since anybody called me that," Boyce answered.

"Who are you guys, anyway?" he asked Neff and Dighera as they led him up the stairs to the command post at the Red Lion Inn.

"Are you CIA?" he asked, unable to understand why he was being escorted to a motel instead of a jail.

"No," they both said at once, "U.S. marshals."

* * *

333

It was after midnight in Virginia when Howard Safir got the telephone call from Kupferer:

"The Falcon is back in his cage. It's over."

A Coast Guard helicopter was on its way to take Chris to Seattle, and already several deputies had gone out to buy champagne for a party that would last all night.

"There's one call I've gotta make," Bob Dighera told Neff. He was dialing the home of Larry Homenick, who he felt had been wronged by not being allowed to be present at the finish.

"It's over, Larry. We got him."

Homenick was close to tears. So was Karen, standing beside him.

"Whose handcuffs are on him, Bob? Are they yours?"

"No, Larry; they're yours."

Then Bob Dighera called Betty and said that he would be on the flight she had booked for him in the morning.

EPILOGUE

On September 15, 1981, at Tysons Corner, Virginia, Larry Homenick was presented the Distinguished Service Award of the U.S. Marshals Service, the agency's highest honor, for his leadership in the search for Christopher John Boyce. At the same ceremony, Thomas C. Kupferer, Jr.; Robert E. Dighera; G. Wayne "Duke" Smith; David R. Neff; Patricia Susan Palmieri; Thomas B. Russell; Glennwood L. "Woody" Smith; Robert M. Brown and Robert W. Christman were presented Special Achievement awards by William E. Hall, the director of the Service, who congratulated all of them for helping to remove "an albatross from around the neck of the Marshals Service."

Attorney General William French Smith; William J. Casey, the director of the Central Intelligence Agency, and other senior members of the Reagan Administration and members of Congress sent congratulatory letters. The crisis regarding the future of the Marshals Service was over, and in the months that followed, its budget and manpower were increased and the Administration strongly endorsed the agency's resumption of its old frontier heritage as federal manhunters.

Thomas Hill, the friend of Christopher Boyce's who had turned him in, was given a reward of $15,000 by the Justice Department, not the $250,000 he had expected. He spent it within a few months.

Brian Hill also applied for a reward, but his application was rejected. In return for his testimony against Christopher Boyce and Gloria White, the Justice Department agreed not to prosecute him for joining Boyce in the robbery of six banks. He got a job at an Idaho sawmill, married, fathered a child and told friends that he intended to go straight.

Fred Hill, the third member of the family, also agreed to testify against Christopher Boyce and Gloria White, and in return, the Justice Department did not prosecute him for driving the getaway car during the robbery at Great Falls, Montana.

No charges were brought against Tommy Lynch, the ex-mercenary who had led the manhunt on its futile detour into the jungles of Central America, and in time the Marshals Service lost track of him.

Frank Burton Riley, the ex-mercenary who had staged the elaborate and frustrating ruse that diverted the manhunt to South Africa and San Francisco, was convicted of illegal possession of a firearm and sentenced to four years in a federal prison. The judge who sentenced him called Riley mentally "sick" and a danger to society. On the eve of his return to prison, Frank Riley married Vickie, the prostitute he had met in San Francisco.

Andrew Daulton Lee, Christopher Boyce's childhood friend and partner in espionage, also made plans to be married, to a woman who had read about him in *The Falcon and the Snowman* and had written an unsolicited letter to him in prison offering to help him fight for a new trial. But the effort to obtain a new trial failed, and prison authorities rejected his application to marry. Lee, arguing that he had been a model prisoner, asked the U.S. Parole Board to reconsider its decision denying him a parole; but his petition was rejected, and he remained in prison, his next parole hearing scheduled for 1991.

Cameron Johnson was indicted by a federal grand jury for harboring Christopher Boyce after the escape and for conspiring with Boyce and Gloria White to rob banks. But after a federal judge ruled that the testimony of his wife, Estelle, could not be used against him because its substance was privileged as marital communication, the case against Johnson was dismissed for lack of evi dence and he was freed. Johnson told friends that he intended to go straight and settle down with one woman.

Captain Midnight—Robert Merman—remained in a Missouri prison, serving a twenty-year sentence, still preoccupied with the teachings of Jesus Christ.

On February 23, 1982, a federal judge in Los Angeles convicted Christopher John Boyce of escaping from the Lompoc Federal Penitentiary, and three years were added to his forty-year sentence for espionage.

On April 2, 1982, in a federal court in Boise, Idaho, Boyce pleaded guilty to robbing eleven banks in Idaho, Montana and eastern Washington and to illegal possession of firearms.

On April 14, 1982, a jury in Boise, after thirteen hours of deliberation, found Gloria Ann White guilty of harboring an escaped prisoner, conspiring to rob banks and two counts of bank robbery. She was sentenced to five years in prison.

On April 30, 1982, in Boise, Christopher John Boyce pleaded guilty to robbing five banks in western Washington. Federal District Judge Harold Ryan sentenced him to twenty-five years in prison for all the crimes he had committed as a fugitive. It meant that Boyce, at the age of twenty-nine, after being credited with three years that he had served before his escape, faced a total of sixty-five more years in prison.

Because of the escape and the crimes he had committed as a fugitive, prison authorities said that it would probably be twenty-five years before he was considered for a parole.

Larry Homenick and Christopher Boyce met in a Seattle prison cell on the morning after his capture. It was a friendly reunion, considering the circumstances.

"You know, Larry," Boyce said as they looked at each other through the bars of his cell, "I had a dream every night that I was going to get caught."

His onetime friend responded, "Chris, I had a dream every night that I wouldn't catch you."

Boyce autographed a copy of *The Falcon and the Snowman,* writing *"To my friend Larry . . ."*

337

In the months following his recapture, a day seldom passed when someone—a guard, a deputy marshal, a court clerk, an FBI agent—did not ask Chris Boyce to autograph a copy of *The Falcon and the Snowman.* He was a celebrity who seemed to enjoy his special status, and his sense of humor and boyish shyness seldom failed to ingratiate him with the people who guarded him.

On the Olympic Peninsula, one restaurant placed a new item on its menu: a "Spyburger," a patty of ground beef covered with Russian dressing. On Hollywood's Sunset Strip, punk-rock bands sang songs for a while about the captured former spy; one song, "Where Are You Tonight, Christopher Boyce?" was a modest, if brief, hit. In Bonners Ferry, several young women were seen wearing T-shirts marked FREE CHRISTOPHER BOYCE.

Boyce was sent to serve his time at the federal penitentiary in Leavenworth, Kansas, where he was interviewed for an Australian television program, *60 Minutes,* that was probing possible American interference in Australian affairs. He criticized the United States and recounted his story that he had become a spy because of his contempt for the CIA and American foreign policy and because of deceptions against Australia that he claimed to have seen in the Black Vault. The Australian broadcasters presented a sympathetic portrait of the spy as a man following the dictates of his conscience, and in the weeks that followed, hundreds of Australians wrote to him at Leavenworth to express their thanks and condolences. A less appreciative audience had also monitored his remarks at Leavenworth. Several hours after the interview was filmed, before his cell had been locked for the night, two inmates entered the cell, punched and knocked him down and then kicked him in the face and ribs as he lay on the floor.

Fearful that the prison gang called the Aryan Brotherhood, which had threatened him at Lompoc, had issued a contract on Boyce's life, the Federal Bureau of Prisons transferred him from Leavenworth to a high-security protective-custody unit in its most escapeproof penitentiary—a fortress near the small town of Marion, Illinois, that has often been called America's "new Alcatraz."

He was placed in solitary confinement at the center of the penitentiary, locked in a prison within a prison, where special guards were posted to protect him from assassination, his food was tested for possible poisoning, and his wrists and ankles were manacled whenever he was taken from the narrow confines of his cell, however briefly. To help make the time pass, he began work on a novel about sixteenth-century Europe.

At Marion, he was interviewed by a correspondent for the American *60 Minutes*. A few weeks later, an arrogant, defiant Christopher Boyce looked out from television sets across America and declared that he had no regrets about his decision to become a Soviet spy. His intensity and bitterness surprised many of the people who had known him in Palos Verdes, before he had become a spy. Even knowing that it would all end as it had, he said, he would do it over again, "only better."

On the same broadcast, Senator Daniel Patrick Moynihan resolved at least part of the public mystery over how high the stakes had been when Christopher John Boyce and Andrew Daulton Lee had sold American spy-satellite secrets to the Soviet Union. "With respect to the satellite systems that were compromised," Moynihan said, "they made them, temporarily at least, useless to us. Because the Soviets could block them. And the fear that that would happen, had happened, permeated the Senate and, as much as any one thing, was responsible for the failure of the SALT treaty. And if you think, as I do, that the breakdown of our arms negotiations with the Soviets is an ominous event, then nothing quite so awful has happened to our country as the escapade of these two young men."

The investigators who had pursued Boyce checked out many leads in an attempt to confirm whether, as Freddy Gray and other inmates had claimed, he had hidden a cache of secret documents in the desert or elsewhere. But they never found any documents and were unable to resolve the question of whether such documents had existed. Andrew Daulton Lee had told a prison acquaintance that a third young man had been involved with him and Boyce in the original espionage operation, and during the manhunt for Boyce investigators had uncovered leads pointing to one friend as the possible third man, but they did not find enough evidence to prosecute him.

* * *

As Boyce was being fingerprinted at the Federal Courthouse in Seattle following his arrest on the night of August 21, 1981, he glumly told a deputy marshal: "If you'd been two weeks later, I'd have been gone."

But he refused to tell anyone where he had planned to go.

The federal agents who tried to reconstruct his movements afterward said that they found maps and charts indicating that he was planning to fly to the Soviet Union, and they became convinced that this had been his plan. But Christopher Boyce refused to discuss his destination, and it remained a mystery.

In his isolation cell at Marion, Christopher John Boyce again became preoccupied with the thought of escape. He knew, he told friends, that he would never be able to escape as before from the high-security penitentiary. He had begun to dream, he told them, of another kind of escape—the only kind, he believed, that would enable him to live outside a cell. His dream was that a grateful Soviet government would claim him in exchange for a captive American agent—any agent whom the United States wanted back badly enough to allow Boyce to go to Russia.

He enrolled in a Russian-language correspondence course, studied and waited.

Overtures were made to the Reagan Administration, but they were ignored.

An emissary representing Boyce went to the Soviet Consulate in San Francisco and made a formal proposal that the Soviet Union take the initiative in arranging an exchange.

The Soviet government never replied to this appeal from Christopher John Boyce.

Acknowledgments

I am indebted to many people for help on this book—foremost of all my wife, Sandra, for her love, encouragement and patience.

It is my good fortune to be associated with some of the finest newspaper editors in the world, and while they bear absolutely no responsibility for this work, I want to thank A. M. Rosenthal, Seymour M. Topping, Arthur Gelb, James Greenfield and David R. Jones for their patience in allowing me to pursue the story, as well as for setting standards of excellence and creating the kind of atmosphere that generally reporters can only dream about.

My deep thanks to Alice Mayhew, the editor of *The Flight of the Falcon,* for sensitive and insightful improvements that she made throughout the manuscript, and to David Masello and Lynn Chalmers of Simon and Schuster, both of whom also made substantial contributions to it. My thanks also to my agent, George Diskant, a good and decent man, and Jonathan Coleman, an editor of high standards who first put me on the trail of the Falcon.

This book would not have been possible without the generous help of many members of the U.S. Marshals Service, which started within a few days after Christopher John Boyce escaped from the Lompoc penitentiary and eventually totaled hundreds of hours of interviews.

My thanks also to Gloria White and to many of the people of Boundary County, and her lawyers, former Congressmen Charles O. Porter and Thomas Mitchell, and their investigator, Paul Rosa. Finally, I thank Christopher Boyce and the members of his family.

Robert Lindsey

FREE!!
BOOKS BY MAIL
CATALOGUE